The Modern Girl's Guide to Fabulousness

Your Lifestyle Bible of Services, Places, Tips and Tricks for Modern Life
(UK edition)

Bethanie Lunn

Book Guild Publishing
Sussex, England

First published in Great Britain in 2010 by
The Book Guild Ltd
Pavilion View
19 New Road
Brighton, BN1 1UF

Printed in Great Britain by
CPI Antony Rowe

Design by Marcus Duck Design

A catalogue record for this book is available from
The British Library.

ISBN 978 1 84624 510 7

Contents

Preface

Why?

The Modern Girl's Guide to Fabulousness is a collection of the most fabulous finds and titbits from across the UK. Think of it as your pocket concierge or 'little black book'.

I wrote this guide for a number of reasons. First, I think it is about time someone cut all the cr*p out of this noisy, ad-inundated world and delivered news and tips on what really *is* great out there, giving tried and tested, unbiased, unbribed-by-money opinions. I have cut to the chase to promote *intelligent spending*, so women know what and where to spend their time and money on with confidence (now more essential than ever).

It is also part of my role as a style and beauty writer and presenter to source stories, new ventures and covetable finds. Couple this with my undeniable fascination to discover new places and meet creative people. Throw in my genuine passion to support new talent and note my in-demand opinion to industry and peers on 'where to go, what to try, who to wear' – then you have the workings of an incredibly desirable 'little black book' of contacts and sources.

So, with overspilling notebooks and filing cabinets of excellent discoveries, a bulging contacts book and a journalistic role to uncover all that's new and wonderful, I felt it my duty to share this wisdom with women everywhere.

What?

Inside, you will find a blend of entrepreneurial talent that you may have discovered here first, existing businesses that, although fully established, should be celebrated in their own right, and the weird, the wonderful and the whimsical.

The guide is laid out as an A–Z, divided into particular areas of fabulousness, from Accessories to Naughty Pleasures, from Motoring to Vintage. There is an entire section on Shopping, including online shopping, independent boutiques and sales secrets. After all, what fabulous life would be complete without shopping?

There's no 'fluff' – I address the fact that women want to know about things like extreme sports and gadgets and not just about lipgloss and shoes (although they're all wonderful, of course), truly catering for the modern woman. My **fab tips** throughout will also come in handy.

Who?

I also invite a selected number of celebrities and experts who figure on my personal list of fabulous people to offer advice on everything, including *how to look your best at every age*, from your 20s to your 60s, the different 'breeds' of *driving instructors* to beware of, and even *what beer or wine to use for every occasion* – so that's your first date, the in-laws visiting and that impressive dinner party all catered for.

How?

You can dip into the A–Z guide as a means to answer specific dilemmas or grant specific wishes. Use it as your inspiration to try new things, or read from cover to cover and decide what to try and where to go first. Before you know it, you'll be playing the expert with panache and people will start to ask what your secret is.

You will laugh (with joy), you will cry (if you can't have *everything* in this guide) and you will enjoy (your more fulfilled life), thanks to this guide.

What all the services and finds have in common in *The Modern Girl's Guide to Fabulousness* is that they're useful, they're included because of their greatness, and by knowing about them your life has already become more fabulous.

Enjoy!

Bethanie Lunn

With Thanks To…

Thanks to all the PR companies for cooperating with me so efficiently from start to finish and for being patient with my hectic schedule. And to all the small businesses for their enthusiasm and will to succeed in a competitive and challenging world. To all the businesses, brands and products featured: you truly are fabulous, or you wouldn't be featured – keep up the good work! For the new businesses that have found it tough, but are taking on the challenge and have been brave and insightful: I admire your entrepreneurial spirit and imagination – don't let the b**tards grind you down.

Thank you to *all* my friends who made personal recommendations for me to try and who always showed an interest in my ideas. From notebook stage to publication date, thank you for your belief in me.

Thank you to my darling husband, Neal, who not only puts up with my energy in creating new ideas on a daily basis, but also believes in me and gives me the strength to fulfil every single one of them. Thank you for listening to my rants about the latest lipstick, fashion boutique and spa treatment (bless you). You make me feel that I can achieve anything.

Thank you to *all* my family who have supported me. With special mention to:

Dad – your strength of character and will has always inspired me, more than you know. Mel – you have always believed in your little Sis despite, in your teenage years, not wanting to admit it! 'Love ya.' Ced – you've taught me to laugh at myself, a skill that has certainly come in handy writing this book! I look up to you so much. Anita – thank you for reading the first script! Mum – thanks for believing in me from birth, for keeping my first book, *The Green Cat*, that I wrote when I was seven years old and for instilling in me that I would be a published writer from then on. 'Give them roots when they're young, and wings when they're old' – you certainly have, and now I'm flying.

Finally, thanks to all my readers. I hope you enjoy this slice of fabulousness.

A Note On Entries

Some of the companies featured have stores nationwide or in more than one city across the UK. Where this has been indicated to me, I have marked all nationwide businesses with the character (N) next to their contact information. In addition, where there is more than one address available, I have credited the flagship store, main branch or website so you can find your nearest stockist.

I have aimed to mention companies with more than one branch where this has been brought to my attention, and I have used all the information provided to me.

It is important that you check the websites credited regularly to keep up to date with any changes in concept, closures, content and contact details – though all details have been checked and updated as close to the print date as possible.

Unless otherwise stated, all telephone numbers are based in the UK. If you are calling from overseas, please add the appropriate prefix.

There is a reason why there are no specific prices in the guide. Prices of products and services alter often and with speed. Since this guide is designed to last a lot longer than a price change, the essential fabulous information has been provided for you to check the most up-to-date prices online or by telephone should you wish.

I have chosen to print a paperback edition, as this guide is ideal to keep on your desk to refer to when in need, to carry with you on those shopping trips and to pass around to share the wisdom.

Everything in this guide has been tried and tested, the majority by me (yes, it has been a jam-packed year), or recommended to me by a trusted source who has in-depth knowledge of that product, place or service.

Thank you.

Accessories

Accessories are no longer an addition to an outfit – they are a narrative that can instantly update an old outfit or transform a dull dress into a sensation, and best of all, they rarely break the bank. From impressive champagne trunks to covetable notebooks and sassy clutches, here is my pick of some of the coolest accessories and portals to keep you inspired…

••••••••••••••••••••••••••••••••

Everyday items go glam: ZPM

••••••••••••••••••••••••••••••••

ZPM is one of the most colourful and innovative accessory labels in the UK. For over ten years, Zoe Phayre Mudge – the brains and brawn behind the collection – has been filling our homes with practical designs in the most fantastically fun, energizing and humorous prints. As Zoe says, 'Just because something is useful doesn't mean it has to look dull.' Zoe's imagination has transformed everyday items from hanging washbags and shower caps to make-up rolls and changing bags for babies, using fabrics that inject life and glamour into the potentially mundane. My black net shower cap with a red tropical flower on the side made my other half say I looked 'elegant' as he burst into the shower room. If I can look elegant in the middle of de-fuzzing my legs, then ZPM has an art.

••

• W: www.zpm.com (N)

Celebrity favourites: Angel Jackson

The sisters behind the brand wanted to create an international fashion label that produced handcrafted products in ethical working conditions while also being recognized for well-designed, stylish and glamorous items.

Sick of the 'generic, poor quality that is the high street', they wanted to design and produce collections that were both different and also benefited the lives of the people who made them – ethics that make this brand a favourite of mine.

The style of Angel Jackson accessories makes a statement, yet the high quality makes them timeless. The feather bag is the design I most covet, with a stream of coloured feathers hanging delicately from the smooth leather bag. It is mesmerizing, fun and super-stylish.

Since the first collection launched in 2005, Sienna Miller was photographed wearing one of their designs, Kirstin Dunst has one of their bags, and the brand has won various awards for its sheer fabulousness!

• W: www.angeljackson.co.uk (N)

Swaine Adeney Brigg: Luxury leather goods

Where do you keep your bottle of Bolly? If your answer is 'in a steel bucket with ice' or 'next to my bed', this just will not do. Opt for the classic Champagne Trunk by Swaine Adeney Brigg, who know luxury when it comes to leather goods. You'll find an accessory to take you from dinner party to commute in style. The leather business card holders and bespoke trunks and chests offer the height of lavishness.

• T: 020 7409 7277
• W: www.swaineadeney.co.uk

Turn unwanted old jewellery into a new design: Rachel Helen

Rachel Helen jewellery is truly unique. I usually detest brands that claim they're 'unique' but are just the same as all the many others out there, but every piece at Rachel Helen is a true one-off. The vintage range is to die for; using old, broken, unloved or neglected pieces of jewellery that Rachel Helen herself gathers from charity shops, car boot sales and online sales, making the range ethical too. Rachel also works on commissions for the vintage range, where you can give her sentimental pieces of jewellery that you wouldn't necessarily wear or are bored with. She then works with them to design something totally unique and wearable, so you can love them for another generation.

Also available is bespoke jewellery for weddings or simply to treat yourself.

• T: 077 890 70 298
• W: www.rachelhelendesigns.com

The brand to watch: La Diosa

La Diosa ('The Goddess') specializes in luxurious statement jewellery using semi-precious stones. Their handmade one-of-a-kind pieces are inspired by queens

Fab Tips

- Accessories are a fantastic way to introduce a bold trend to your outfit without screaming 'fashion victim'. Loud colours and patterns look great worn as a belt or bag and add a splash of vibrancy to an ordinarily plain outfit.
- I personally think you can layer accessories and have as much fun as you like with them. I wear up to four pearl necklaces at once in different hues to add some funked-up ladylike glam – just don't go too overboard. The look you're after is 'look at me', not 'Christmas tree'.
- Don't forget your hair. Alice bands, bows, sparkling clips, headbands and even corsages make instant hair glamourizers, turning you from drab to darling in seconds.
- Check out flea markets, car boot sales, vintage stores and charity shops for fresh accessories. You might be able to find chic vintage staples for a lot less!

See S: Shopping and V: Vintage for some great places to try.

and goddesses of the past and present, so you can expect elaborate, oversized designs that scream style, beauty and confidence – much like the two talented young women who created the brand, Natasha Faith and Semhal Zemikael, who travel the world to seek inspiration for their jewellery range.

• **Available from Harvey Nichols, London and www.Astleyclarke.com**
• **W: www.ladiosa.co.uk (N)**

Comfort in silk: Holistic Silk

Truly effective and fair made, Holistic Silk is a luxury range of aromatic silk products filled with herbs and ancient wisdom to promote wellbeing, alleviate stress and administer comfort. Inspired by the lack of practical and gorgeous beauty saviours for those with an increasingly fast-paced and stressful life, Holistic Silk founder Joanna Weakley has developed an enviable reputation for effective design and innovation. The silk slippers and eye masks will make you look and feel a hundred times more glam.

See also Y: Youthful Looks for their silk anti-ageing pillowcase.

• **Holistic Silk Ltd, 34 St John's Avenue, London NW10 4EE**
• **T: 020 7965 0075**
• **W: www.holisticsilk.com (N)**

Business style: Violet May

Violet May's mission is to bring a touch of fabulousness and luxury to everyday working life.

Claire Collins is the founder of Violet May Ltd. Perpetually frustrated by the lack of stylish business accessories aimed at women, Claire decided to branch out by designing the ultimate luxury laptop bag and laptop sleeve collection, in addition to other business essentials such as chic Blackberry purses. I'm so glad she did – I have never loved a laptop carrier more! You will find a luxurious array of styles that make sumptuous arm candy and are practical to boot.

• **Violet May HQ, Dynamis House, 6–8 Sycamore Street, London EC1Y 0SW**
• **T: 020 7253 2048**
• **W: www.violetmaylondon.com**

Accessory heaven: Accessories Online

If you love accessories, want inspiration or have the urge to get your claws on designs from across the globe, you can do that with Accessories Online. They often have the most quirky creations from Paris, Los Angeles, London and California. Saves you a bit of travelling and carbon footprint, doesn't it?

• **T: 08451 083 073**
• **W: www.accessoriesonline.co.uk**

The only place for earrings: The Earring Boutique

The Earring Boutique offers exactly what the name suggests: an online emporium of earrings for every style, occasion and desire. Most designs are made with Swarovski Crystallized Elements and there are some beautiful creations you won't be able to resist.

You can pick a design to suit your budget; delivery to the UK is within 48 hours and completely free. When your little parcel arrives, you will love the deluxe packaging. Mine takes pride of place on my dresser.

• W: www.theearringboutique.com (N)

Inspired by nature: Vinnie Day

Vinnie Day's main collections are inspired by the different countries from which she sources her semi-precious stones and components namely: Africa, India, Turkey and Spain. With her Irish roots and African upbringing, Vinnie developed an early love of nature and trees in particular, which is visible in much of her work. The jewellery is made in silver and 24 carat gold plate (vermeil) with a rich satin finish, complemented by beautiful semi-precious stones.

• 8 Hansard Mews, London W14 8BJ
• T: 020 8969 0196
• W: www.vinnieday.co.uk (N)

Eel skin chic: Heidi Mottram

Heidi Mottram produces beautiful, high-quality eel skin accessory designs. Eel skin is amazingly durable and has a combination of qualities that make it a valuable alternative to other luxury leather products. The juiciest colours are available, such as deep purple and hot pink. The longer you have it, the more gorgeous it looks – and having a glam accessory that can take the pace pleases me greatly.

• W: www.heidimottram.co.uk (N)

Hat heaven: CA4LA

Pronounced 'ca-shi-la' (derived from the word *kashira*, meaning 'head' in Japanese), this Hoxton-based London shop is dedicated to one of my favourite accessories – hats! Thirteen designers provide stand-out-from-the-crowd headwear. Stock is replenished every two to three weeks, so new bonnets are always available. Styles include cashmere and mohair beanies and inventive trilbies.

Don't be afraid to try hats. If you think they don't suit you, you'd be wrong, as there is a style to suit all face shapes and personalities. The very cool website allows you to search by brand and colour too, but the trick is confidence. Find a style that suits you and you will ultimately look very confident and subsequently feel it. CA4LA is a great place for try-on sessions – enjoy the admiring glances.

• **CA4LA, 23 Pitfield St, London N1**
• **T: 020 7490 0055**
• **W: www.ca4la.com or www.weavetoshi.co.jp**

Custom-made shoes: Hetty Rose

Hetty Rose shoes are all uniquely made to measure for individual ladies. The shoes are based on the concept of reusing and reworking vintage fabrics in a creative and sustainable way, to create stunning handmade shoes that actually fit. The Hetty Rose label is perfect for the modern woman as the shoes are ethical as well as bespoke and uniquely designed for each customer. Clients can choose their own fabric and leather and have made-to-measure shoes created to fit them individually. No more pain, just pure pleasure.

• **W: www.hettyrose.co.uk (N)**

If you love shoes, see also F: Fashion for designers and tips.

Bejewelled genius: Louis Mariette

The award-winning and in-demand Louis Mariette uses jewels to create tailored masterpieces. This amazingly fabulous designer/ milliner extraordinaire creates sensational bespoke hats, fascinators and bejewelled headpieces and accessories. The bejewelled Alice bands and tiaras, the handbag brooches and astonishing hats are

all Stunning (with a capital 'S') and certainly worthy to be top of anyone's wish list.

• **T: 020 7730 3050**
• **W: www.louismariette.com (N)**

Personalized and luxury stationery: Smythson

I just had to include 'the world's foremost purveyor of luxury stationery', Smythson, who offer a superb collection of leather-bound books to suit any purpose. The chic and fun notebooks make the perfect luxury treat with titles such as *Yummy Mummy*, *Places to Remember*, or the *Make It Happen* notebook so you can scribe in style. If you are feeling really marvellous you can have your own personalized stationery sets and 'social cards' too (like your own business cards for your private life).

• **T: 0870 521 1311**
• **W: www.smythson.com (N)**

The ultimate writing instrument: Diplomat

You may have the fab notebook, but you simply can't pull out a plastic biro at that all-important meeting or hot date number exchange! A Diplomat pen is the ultimate writing instrument for fabulous girls, made from materials and components of the highest quality such as pearl lacquer with polished chrome fittings (my preference).

Diplomat has been hand-assembling its beautiful pens at its German workshop since 1922, and has gained an international reputation for producing these sought-after scribblers. Each pen comes with a five-year guarantee, which is longer than most other pen brands.

• W: www.diplomat-pen.de (N)

My personal search for laptop carriers

Bags are such a style statement now – it is the one piece that women feel comfortable splurging on, as you really can see the quality of a bag. Handbags are now as signature as your favourite scent.

Being the ever-practical yet stylish lady that I am, I went on a hunt for a sexy laptop carrier, asking the question, 'Can fashionable and functional co-exist?'

My favourites, in addition to Violet May, include the laptop bags by **Paperchase**. From paintbox stripe designs to crazy comic-strip-style prints, their styles are a snip for bargain hunters.

• W: www.paperchase.co.uk

The **Ignes Francis Bag** has double shoulder straps, an extra body strap and interior cushioning, and the bonus of double slit pockets for your mobile phone and iPod makes it a practical and modern choice. The range of colours and materials is wide; I favour the dark grey patent design for understated elegance. In fact, Ignes Bags have a fantastic facility on their website – Ignes Elite – where you can design your own handbag! You choose the shape first, followed by the colour of the leather, fastenings and lining. Hours of fun.

• W: www.ignesbags.com

Cambridge Satchels offer satchels, 'batchels' and music cases made of leather in a range of colours from classic vintage browns, dark browns and black to vibrant yellow, purple and pillar-box red. A batchel is merely a satchel with the addition of a top handle, to make it easier to carry, and their music bags are ideal for carrying notebook laptops and documents too. The real coup for this brand is the embossing service, where you can have your initials or a personal name or message inscribed in silver, gold or 'blind' (the same colour as the satchel). I have my eye on a bright red batchel with 'Ms Fabulous' in gold, and my other half is set to buy me a purple one with 'The Missus' in silver. Who said fashion can't be practical? Sizes range from 11 inches (more like a handbag) to 15 inches (ideal for laptops).

• T: 01223 294313
• W: www.cambridgesatchel.co.uk

So what do you put in your fabulous bag? The gorgeous **Hi-Grade** W5900 leopardskin laptop almost makes IT fun with its pink and silver print!

W: www.highgrade.com

Fun and quirky jewellery: Punky Pins, Elsie Belle and Temporary Secretary

Punky Pins' purse-friendly range of kitsch and funky jewellery is made of acrylic and famed for its bright, bold and quirky designs. Loyal fans include a bevy of stylish, kooky ladies including Cheryl Cole, Peaches Geldof, Agyness Deyn, Alexa Chung and Fearne

Cotton. Guess what necklace I opted for? The one that says 'Fabulous' in hot pink, of course.

- **T: 01642 244422**
- **W: www.punkypins.co.uk**

Another of my favourites for fun, tongue-in-cheek jewellery is Elsie Belle. They design vintage-inspired pieces with an extra bit of wit thrown in – from animal charms, chunky rings and trinket-style pendant necklaces in acrylic, to genuine vintage and reproduction stamped brass. My favourites are the Scrabble piece pendants, where you choose a letter that means something to you, whether that is the initial of your name or a loved one, for instance. Elsie Belle then mount a vintage Scrabble piece in your chosen letter onto a silver- or gold-plated chain. I also adore the range of 'I ♥…' motif necklaces, with my most-wanted being the 'I ♥Tea' necklace. Quirky, gorgeous, genius.

- **W: www.elsiebelle.com**

Temporary Secretary is created by a very talented young lady, Sarah Wong, who also happens to be a fine illustrator. Her collection of jewellery includes a deliciously cute selection of necklaces and bracelets, earrings, rings and hair accessories. Every item is so endearingly sweet you could eat it (but don't try that). From tea cups on a silver chain necklace to ice cream cone earrings and cupcake charm bracelets – you will be spoilt for choice if you love a little fun in your accessories. For girly-girls and big kids alike.

- **W: www.temporary-secretary.com and www.sarah-wong.com**

Get your head candy: CandyBand

My favourite brand for head candy is CandyBand Accessories. Their beautiful headbands are carefully handcrafted using the finest materials and ornaments, offering an element of grown-up chic. They're pretty and feminine while simultaneously oozing a sense of confident attitude and individual style.

I'm a fan, and I can see the likes of Sarah Jessica-Parker and the Gossip Girl set wearing them soon. Paris Hilton has been spotted already!

- **W: www.candybandaccessories.com**

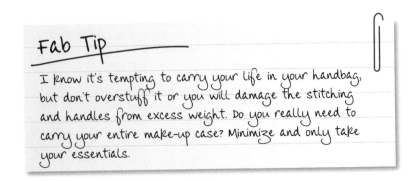

Fab Tip

I know it's tempting to carry your life in your handbag, but don't overstuff it or you will damage the stitching and handles from excess weight. Do you really need to carry your entire make-up case? Minimize and only take your essentials.

Pull in style: Trendy Trolleys

If, like me, you find yourself hauling along your groceries and impulse buys in handfuls of bags or eco-shoppers, you must get yourself a trolley!

Trendy Trolley has a great selection of funky shopping trolleys in a range of colours, patterns and finishes – from red patent to simple pebble grey – each of which has been carefully hand-picked for their unique design, quality and value. I personally love their 'Kitty' design. Made of red PVC with a cartoon kitten poking its head out of the top of the trolley, it always grabs plenty of attention and admiring glances but is also extremely lightweight.

Yes, OK, trolleys are the bags on wheels you normally see grandmas pulling around, but Trendy Trolleys shake off that image and are so fantastic, you can at last enjoy the practicality of a trolley without compromising your fashion sense. Banish those old-fashioned fears and trawl along a trolley. I'm determined to make them en trend!

• W: www.trendy-trolleys.co.uk

Brolly-tastic, keeping dry in style: Romanelli

The rain is pouring down, so you've pulled on great shoes and a classic mac, but what about your umbrella? Some of us don't see an umbrella as a fashion accessory, but in typical British weather, it's a fashion essential!

For more than 75 years, Romanelli has been creating umbrella collections of sophisticated and novel styles. There's a wide selection of specially treated fabrics and styles so you can choose a design to suit your mood. Three other favourites of mine that you must check out from the same stockist are Frank Usher (for vintage-style charm), Chantal Thomass (for her lingerie-inspired sensual designs) and Guy De Jean (for the deep frilled parasols).

• W: All available at www. umbrellaboutique.co.uk (N)
• T: +34 985 35 08 08 for Romanelli stockist enquiries

Art

Today, art comes in so many forms and you don't have to be an art aficionado to appreciate it either. Often the many formats and emerging artists can be a challenge to keep up with, so I dish up some of the most promising artists, desirable outlets and knowledgeable curators. Whether you are an investor, are starting a collection, or simply like pretty wall hangings, check these out…

Willard Wigan

Born in 1957 in Birmingham, UK, Willard Wigan began his artistic life at the tender age of five. Willard says, 'I started making houses for ants because I thought they needed somewhere to live. Then I made them shoes and hats. It was a fantasy world I escaped to where my dyslexia didn't hold me back and my teachers couldn't criticize me. And that's how my career as a micro-sculptor began.'

From that day to this, Willard's celebrated micro-sculptures have become more and more minute – each piece commonly sits within the eye of a needle or on a pin head. They're so small, they're only visible through a microscope. Indeed, some are only three times the size of a blood cell. Designs include a collection of fairytale-like characters and icons such as Marilyn Monroe and Jonny Wilkinson.

• **W: www.willard-wigan.com (N)**

Robert Ryan

Robert Ryan creates the most delightful and thought-provoking designs, mainly by the means of paper-cutting. From that original starting point he applies his emotive art to a range of methods from screen prints to textiles, ceramics and laser-cutting. Imagine scenes of fantasy shoes, loving embraces or quirky characters with humorous quotes such as, 'You can still do a lot with a small brain.'

Having collaborated with the likes of Paul Smith and Fortnum & Mason, Ryans' paper-cut artistry can sell for thousands, though there are smaller pieces and accessories, such as his laser-cut greetings cards, that make his work more accessible. Visit his London shop, Ryan Town, and start your collection fast!

• **126 Columbia Road, London E2 7RG**
• **T: 020 7613 1510**
• **W: www.ryantownshop.blogspot.com, www.etsy.com and www.misterrob.co.uk**

Stella Vine

Stella Vine is the well-known British artist who makes colourful childlike paintings, often based on contemporary figures and from her own life. Vine rose to prominence in 2004 when Charles Saatchi featured her work in his controversial *New Blood* show.

Vine appeals to an array of audiences, from serious art collectors to a new breed of young art fans. Her work has been incredibly successful at auction, and her painting *Superman* (2004) sold for over £12,000.

• **W: www.stellavine.com**

Particle Article

These quirky fairytale-like creatures created by sisters Amy Nightingale and Claire Benson are made with recycled, abandoned and reclaimed objects. Each creation is curious, clever and captivating. Encased in glass, these winged creatures are reminiscent of museum specimens from a fairytale world just waiting to escape!

Amy and Claire state, 'These highly individual and beautiful works of art provide commentary on society and women's hectic lifestyles, while adding a humorous and satirical twist. They act as protectors and preservers of common everyday objects, the value of which has diminished in our modern age.'

• **T: Amy, 07743862420**
• **T: Claire, 07787812979**
• **W: www.particlearticle.co.uk (N)**

Kate Talbot

Kate's art practice combines painting, mixed media, textiles and embroidery to create 'ironic iconic' imagery. Witty, provocative and stimulating, the range includes creations such as the Marmite jar, 'Loves me, loves me not', pouting 'Trannies' and English stereotypes – hilarious!

- T: 01264 738564
- W: www.hungdrawnquoted.co.uk

Si Scott

Si Scott's characteristic style looks like digital imagery but is actually all originally hand-drawn with good old pen and paper. You are bound to have seen his work somewhere and will recognize his style of delicate vines, swirling curves and intricate line drawings when you see it, as his client list boasts names such as MTV, Casio, Nike and Hugo Boss. His work has been received into the fine art collectors' arena, he exhibits and lectures around the world, and he has been named as an 'Artist to Invest In' by *Men's Health* editorial.

- W: www.siscottstudio.com (N)

Fabulous Masterpieces

Fabulous Masterpieces specializes in the ultimate solution to blank wall syndrome by supplying museum-quality, hand-painted reproductions of famous (and not so famous) paintings. A world away from the usual poster/ print reproductions, these luxury linen canvases are oil-painted for that authentic, textured finish, adding a touch of luxury to the home.

The style-conscious can also choose to use the Designer Art service, where an interior stylist will come round to your home and design

bespoke pieces of art specifically tailor-made to complement and enhance the style of that particular room.

- T: 020 8740 8708
- W: www.fabulousmasterpieces.co.uk

StolenSpace Gallery

I love this gallery. You can buy at the shop in London and online, choosing from such pieces as the delicate and emotional drawings of David Bray to the post-graffiti future visions of Ronzo.

- StolenSpace Gallery, Dray Walk, The Old Truman Brewery, 91 Brick Lane, London E1 6QL
- T: 020 7247 2684
- W: www.stolenspace.com

Robert Archard

UK-based designer Robert Archard works on a range of projects, but nearly everything he turns his hand to has a social, environmental or conceptual focus. From recycled tins to comically cute ceramic biscuits that are exactly the same size as the real biscuits they represent, Robert's designs are intelligent but with a sense of humour.

- W: www.beyondthevalley.com

Art Republic

Artrepublic.com is the art lover's online print and poster gallery. You will be able to discover and purchase limited edition art prints, work from today's cutting-edge artists and a vast range of open edition museum prints and poster art by world-famous artists. To see who the latest name is and to uncover new releases, the 'New Arrivals' section will keep you up to date.

• **W: www.artrepublic.com**

Jules Balchin

Art curator and one of three directors at concept store Paper Scissor Stone, Leeds, Jules is a commercial art curator, sales negotiator and womenswear buyer from London. Having cut her teeth in the commercial art world working with the UK's leading fine art publishers Eyestorm (Britart), who have published artists such as Damien Hirst, Anthony Micallef, Jamie Reid and Stanley Donwood, Jules has worked on a variety of collaborations with artists, DJs and party-makers by teaming her art network with her involvement in fashion, music and event management. Clients have included Jade Jagger, Pacha, Smirnoff, Electric Cabaret and Azuli Records.

If you want a slice of her expertise, Jules offers the Art Investors' Service. As an experienced art curator, dealer and sales negotiator, she offers a personal art finder's service. Advising on art for investment purposes, Jules will track down and negotiate for artwork on your behalf, whether that be a hard-to-come-by Damien Hirst *Valium* print, a Paul Insect piece, or a sought-after Bob Carlos Clarke photograph.

Jules says, 'I can advise and design the hanging of your artwork to complement your interiors. I also curate small collections of artwork to beautify your office walls and offer

collections for boutique hotels and other small businesses.'

• **E: jules.blankcanvas@gmail.com**
• **W: www.paper-scissor-stone.co.uk**

Museum shops

A hot tip if you can't make it to the museums or can't afford the originals is to use their online shops:

• *Designmuseumshop.com* is great for design classics.

• The V & A's *vandashop.com* is fab for iconic homeware and art deco goodies.

• *Tate.org.uk/shop* is the ultimate hit for exclusive collections.

• *Museumofchildhood.org.uk* is great for gifts, toys and comics with retro appeal.

Beauty

If you're anything like me, you feel overwhelmed with the amount of information, places and advice out there. The media is full to the brim with suggestions of where to go, how to look, how to feel – and it sends me dizzy. For the fulfilment of all fabulous women out there, I dish the dirt on some of the most effective and enjoyable beauty necessities available...

Ask a girl which one beauty product they could not live without, and a good majority would say their mascara. This make-up essential makes a huge difference to your peepers, worn alone to open up your eyes or with eye shadow to add definition. I often look a little 'unfinished' or tired without my magic wand, and from volumizing to lengthening, from thickening to eye brightening, there's a 'mazzie' for you.

I chat with one of the most successful make-up artists of today, Ariane Poole, who offers you a *Mascara Masterclass* to perfect your flutterability. Ariane has worked with an impressive list of celebrities, including **Catherine Zeta Jones, Sadie Frost, Uma Thurman, Yasmin Le Bon, Christy Turlington and Anna Friel, to name but a few. In addition to her own make-up range, Ariane works on photo shoots, private make-up lessons (also available to groups), stage work (National Wedding Show and Vitality Show, among others), and has a TV career including *GMTV* and *This Morning*.**

Mascara masterclass by Ariane Poole

How to choose your mascara

Decide what you want your lashes to look like.

- Do you need added length? Then try L'Oreal Double Extension Mascara, Dior Show Mascara and Lancôme L'Extreme Lengthening Mascara.

- Do you want more fullness? Then try Maybelline The Colossal Mascara, Prescriptives Lash Envy and Mac Plush Lash.

Fab Tip

You may love the mascara you've had in your collection for three years, but every cosmetic has a shelf life. After you open it, you're exposing it to air and can introduce bacteria to it if you use your fingers to touch it. As a general rule, moisturizers, sun creams and false tan all last six months. Foundations, lipsticks, blushers, eye shadows and bronzers last up to eighteen months and your mascara lasts three to six months. Also look out for a little symbol on the side of the product that looks like a little pot with the lid lifted off. It will have a number in it indicating how many months the product will be at its best after opening. For instance, '12M' means it will be fresh for twelve months once opened. Yep, it's not just your meat and two veg that have an expiry date!

- Do you want your mascara to enhance your eye shadow or eye colour? There are some terrific coloured mascaras around that look elegant, not garish. Try Ariane Poole Ultimate Volume Mascara in Plum, Urban Decay Big Fatty Coloured Mascara in Indigo, and Blinc in Dark Blue. These mascaras are not bright or over the top, but offer a hint of colour that can really brighten up the eyes.

How to apply the mascara

1 Always apply your mascara after eye shadow.

2 Roll your mascara tube in your hands to warm it up. Don't pump up the tube as this pushes air into the tube and causes the mascara to dry out prematurely.

3 Draw the wand from the tube and rub the excess back into the tube rather than on a tissue. It's much more cost-effective and your mascara won't clump.

4 Now look straight ahead into your mirror, tilt your head back slightly so that your eyes are looking down. Starting at the base of your top lashes, sweep the mascara from base to tip. Gradually build up the layers until you have achieved the look you desire. If you want extra impact from your lashes, apply mascara to the top of your lashes first. Allow the top lashes to dry before you do the lower lashes.

5 Apply mascara to your lower lashes by looking up and dabbing the mascara onto your lower lashes. Doing it this way will give you definition, not spider's legs.

Top tip for mascara!

If your mascara is getting a bit thick and gloopy, stand the tube in a cup of boiled water. The heat from the water will make the mascara in the tube become more fluid, making it easier to apply.

All mascaras mentioned are available at leading chemists.
• **Ariane Poole products are available online and at Errol Douglas, London, but call for your nearest stockist: 020 7235 0110**
• **W: www.arianepoole.com (N)**

How to glow

Many people compliment me on a glowing complexion (thanks, ladies!), but of course I don't wake up with radiant, flawless skin – it can take some work! I try hard to make time to exfoliate once or twice a week to slough away dead skin cells. Never scrub your face, just use gentle circular motions across your face, avoiding the delicate eye area, then rinse.

One of the best products I've ever tried is St Ives Apricot Scrub, using 100% natural ingredients. The granules are gentle to skin, but also feel coarse enough to let you know it's working.

Try to treat yourself to a face mask once a week too. You don't have to lie there with cucumber slices over your eyes; you can do the washing, watch TV or read the paper while the mask gets to work. Choose one for your skin type and follow the instructions. I have combination skin (an oily T-Zone – which is the forehead, nose and chin – and drier cheeks), so I often use two face masks for those two different skin types – a nourishing mask for my drier areas and a purifying mask for my T-Zone. You can use as many as you like according to different areas and needs.

I never fail to cleanse my skin – even after one or two Bellinis – so never fall asleep with a full face of make-up, or you'll risk clogging your pores and causing break-outs. After cleansing, my secret is combining two parts moisturizer to one part illuminator for daytime.

One of the best ever illuminators is MAC's Strobe Cream. It gives you a glow reminiscent of a goddess living on a wonderful beach somewhere far away, with a diet of fish and fruit. Well, perhaps not … but it is fan-bloomin'-tastic. My favourite highlighter for my cheekbones is Benefit High Beam – still the best. Tap sparingly with your fingers across your cheekbones and under your eyebrows to lift your face.

• **St Ives: www.stives.com (N)**
• **MAC: www.maccosmetics.co.uk (N)**
• **Benefit: www.benefitcosmetics.co.uk (N)**

Also see the Clarisonic Cleansing System for deep down cleansing.

Salons and professionals

Mobile beauty and glam pit stop: Powderpuff Girls

The Powderpuff Girls have been pampering women for years in their gorgeous pink air-hostess-meets-Agent Provocateur-girl outfits! They arrive at private events, parties or places as an exceptionally glam-looking team of specialists offering treatments such as manicures and makeovers.

The Powder Room is the latest

string to their perfectly pink bow, serving tea and biscuits in a 1950s-style setting, as The Powderpuff Girls take over. They'll expertly refresh and beautify you to ensure not a hair or lash is out of place, before sending you on your way feeling marvellous.

If you're rushing from office to party, you can even change your outfit, leave your things securely with them and they will courier them back to you the next day. If that isn't sitting up and taking notice of our busy modern lives, I don't know what is!

The boutique sells treats from the likes of Paul & Joe cosmetics, Blouse & Skirt cosmetics, Mavala Nail Care and The Powderpuff Girls' very own Shimmer Powderpuffs. They can also be hired for private parties, including hen parties, where groups of girls can gossip over a glass of bubbly while being pampered.

- 136 Columbia Road, London E2 7RG
- T: 020 7704 8009
- W: www.thepowderpuffgirls.com

Feels like my own crib...

The Crib salon is great as it combines hair and beauty under one roof (I don't understand why this concept isn't everywhere yet) and has a real home-from-home setting.

There are three gorgeously furnished rooms to choose from, you can watch a DVD while you're being preened, and choose from the drinks list, including vino, if you fancy it, as you sit back and become all goddess-like.

Once you're done, they'll ensure there's a taxi waiting outside for you so you can preserve your new barnet and avoid the (likely) rainfall.

- **The Crib, Apartment One, 176a Kings Road, SW3 4UP**
- **T: 020 7349 0666**
- **W: www.thecribclub.com**

As cool as a cucumba

A self-described 'urban pit stop', Cucumba is one of the coolest salons London has to offer, catering perfectly for the busy urbanite with its range of express treatments and top-ups. Based in the heart of Soho, you can escape the buzz and de-fuzz in your lunch hour!

At Cucumba you simply buy the time to fit your budget and then choose any therapies you desire. You can have your eyebrows preened and your chipped nail varnish corrected and still make it on time to your meeting, all without breaking the bank.

Prices start from under a tenner and treats on offer include manicures, pedicures, waxing, threading, facials,

Fab Tip

If you like the sound of a treatment in this guide, but the mentioned salon isn't near you, use Wahanda to search for one that is!
- W: www.wahanda.com

massage, make-up artistry, spray tanning and even the option of a red, pink or blue dye with your Brazilian wax.

Their Ladies' Night is also worth a mention, run once a month. Groups of friends are treated to 'unlimited drinks' and up to three treatments for only £35.00 (prices subject to change). Treatments on offer include spray tanning, waxing (any area you fancy), massage, manicures, pedicures, threading and/or facials.

- **12 Poland Street, Soho, London W1F 8QB**
- **T: 020 7734 2020**
- **W: www.cucumba.co.uk**

Femi Beauty Clinic

Femi Beauty Clinic is without doubt the best, most accomplished and forward-thinking clinic in Leicester city. With the driving force of Femi herself, it is always going to be at the forefront of its game. The Highcross Street salon offers a calm haven away from the bustling city. In your soft and fluffy towelling robe, you can sit comfortably and enjoy beauty treatments that cater for all needs, from top to toe, including the classic manicures and pedicures and more developed systems such as gel nail application, eyelash extensions and tanning treatments, as well as Decleor facials and heavenly full-body massages. It's a pleasure to be there and the therapists are knowledgeable – it's one of my fave places outside of London for getting a full beauty MOT!

- **Femi Beauty Clinic, 60 Highcross Street, Leicester LE1 4NN**
- **T: 0116 253 2393**
- **W: www.femibeautyclinic.co.uk**

Katherine Jackson

Katherine Jackson is something of a legend in the beauty world. Her experience spans over 37 years and she is often approached as an authoritative source of information in the field of natural health and beauty. A fully qualified acupuncturist (including electrical acupuncture), practitioner of Chinese medicine, shiatsu and reflexology, she combines these with cutting-edge technologies such as the Perfector and the Ultra Sonic Spatula.

Katherine's difference lies in her flexibility and determination to treat every client as an individual – after all, each of us is different, and so are our requirements. She says, 'When performing a facial, for example, I like to address the problem from the inside out using fusion therapies I've mastered over the years, so I won't just work on the face.' I've never before had a scary Hollywood wax followed by some healing.

A bikini wax is often painful, to say the least, and only aspirin and/or a shot of tequila beforehand will numb it for me! However, Katherine uses wax that she peels off directly from the skin (as opposed to strips that can break the hair and cause quick regrowth), and she applies it in very small patches which lessens the pain – all good. Her genuine nature, desire and talent to improve the way her clients look and feel is both adorable and appreciated.

I opted for acupuncture and reflexology afterwards, and Katherine sensed I'd also benefit from a shoulder massage (true). I have to tell you, this is now the only way I will have this treatment and this, Katherine insists, is

Fab Tip

When choosing a concealer, go to a make-up counter and seek their advice about matching one to your skin tone. As a general rule of thumb, you should choose a shade lighter than your skin tone to correct dark circles, one that matches your skin tone to camouflage blemishes, and a green concealer to counteract any redness. When covering under-eye dark circles, apply the concealer in dots underneath your eye, starting from your tear duct and moving out to the outer corner of your eye. Use your ring finger gently to pat in the concealer (as opposed to rubbing, which can lift it off). Your ring finger has the lightest touch and will therefore blend it in perfectly without dislodging it.

the way she normally does it.

Put yourself in the hands of this expert and you'll be glad you did.

....

• **W: www.katherinejackson.co.uk**

See also **Q: Quitting for the Nicolite treatment by Katherine Jackson,** and **T: Treatments for other treatments she offers.**

• •
Help finding a salon: Wahanda
• •

If you're searching for a spa or salon near you, or wish to find a place that offers that sought-after treatment you read about, then Wahanda is the online spa and wellness specialist with comprehensive listings of spas, salons and wellness centres that will satisfy your hunt. Doing for wellbeing what Amazon did for online retailing, Wahanda provides an intuitive and easy-to-use website where you can learn all about different treatments (everything from acupuncture, facials

and massages to pilates, botox and personal training). Look out for the generous competitions too.

....

• **Wahanda, 4th Floor, 14–18 Great Titchfield Street, London W1W 8BD**
• **T: 0800 121 4536**
• **W: www.wahanda.com**

Must-try places and experiences

• •
Make-up lessons: The Beauty Lounge
• •

If you want to look like your fave celebrity icon, or if you think that's naff and you just want to look incredible, then book a lesson with a make-up artist who works regularly for high-profile clients and celebrities including Keira Knightley, Kylie and Scarlett Johansson.

The make-up artists at cool salon The Beauty Lounge are not attached to any one brand of make-up, so the advice you receive is totally independent. Plus you take away skills that allow you to recreate the look yourself, and you leave with a recommended list of products to buy – maintaining your gorgeousness.

• **The Beauty Lounge, 1 Kingly Court, London W1B 5PW**
• **T: 020 7734 6161**
• **W: www.beautylounge.co.uk**

Banish chipped nail polish: Bio Sculpture Gel

If you are bored and irritated with having to reapply your nail varnish every day (and let's face it, chipped polish is ugly), then you must get gel overlays on your natural nails.

Bio Sculpture Gel is used at various salons nationwide and comes in various colours from clear to hot pink. You can choose a colour or have a French manicure finish that lasts.

The gel is painted on like a thick nail varnish, then is set under an ultraviolet lamp which leaves your nails strong yet flexible. The gel won't damage your nails; in fact it nourishes them, so expect to see healthy growth to boot.

• **Participating salons are nationwide, so visit the website below for your nearest one:**
• **W: www.biosculpturegel.co.uk**
• **Harvey Nichols nationwide offers the treatment at their champagne nails inc. nail bars, but call head office for your nearest store: 020 7529 2340.**
• **Look out for Shellac nails too on www.salongeek.com**

Minx nails

Minx nails is an art form loved by the likes of Lady GaGa, Beyoncé and Rhianna, amongst others.

Minx nails are pre-made vinyl nail patterns that look like and are applied like transfers. They come in an assortment of designs to suit your style, from zebra print to metallic silver. Once you have chosen your pattern, the craft begins. The designs are heated beneath a lamp to make them malleable and then smoothed onto your natural nails and cut to shape.

They need no drying time, but can be fiddly to apply, so I suggest you go to a reputable salon such as Gielly Green for the most impressive results.

They can last up to two weeks on your hands and up to six weeks on your toes. I think Minx nails are most suited to your toes as they don't come under as much daily pressure as your hands do, so they last for longer. If they start to lift or wrinkle, simply use your hairdryer to heat them up and smooth them out.

I opted for the metallic silver with a mirror-like shine – they were so dazzling I could almost see my reflection in them (now, there's an idea!), and the amount of compliments I drew in was immense.
Dare to be different…

• **Gielly Green, 42–44 George Street, London W1U 7ES**
• **T: 020 7034 3060**
• **W: www.giellygreen.co.uk**
• **Visit the Minx site for a salon near you: www.minxmynails.co.uk (N)**

The Red Carpet Treatment

The Fire & Ice medical facial is dubbed 'the Red Carpet Treatment'; so called since A-listers have it before their red carpet appearances. Fans include Halle Berry, Gwyneth Paltrow, Evangeline Lilly and yours truly!

This intensive clinical facial is a wonderful deep pore cleanser, designed to rapidly resurface the skin, reducing fine lines and wrinkles, smoothing and encouraging skin cell renewal. It is therefore most suitable if you require anti-ageing effects, or for skin that suffers from acne or has sunburn.

The facial involves a combination of two therapeutic masks using **iS Clinical** products.

First, a gentle resurfacing mask laced with cinnamon spice is applied. It gets toasty as it heats up on your skin, hence the 'Fire' term. It is clinically formulated with 18% unbuffered glycolic acid, lactic acid, citric acid, malic acid, retinol, vitamin B3 and potent antioxidants, including green tea extracts. In truth, it tingled greatly but was in no way painful and is only on your skin for a total of 3–5 minutes, all that is needed to work its magic.

Next came the 'Ice' part, a rejuvenating mask which was instantly cool and soothing. The blend of hyaluronic acid, aloe vera gel, Japanese green tea extracts, liquorice extracts, grape seed extracts and rosemary extracts make for an intensely hydrating finish. This part felt hotter on my skin than the first part, but everyone's skin is different. None of it hurt, you can just feel it really getting to work.

The entire treatment lasts around 20 minutes and my skin felt rejuvenated and firm. Surprisingly, there was little redness and just one hour later my skin returned to its natural colour, but was extraordinarily luminous. I attended a big event that evening and got many compliments on looking 'healthy' and 'glowing'. A must-try.

The skincare is also pretty darn good. There is a range of products you can use at home to continue the effects, including Youth Complex, for rapid initial hydration for 'plumping' fine lines and wrinkles, and their best-selling Active Serum. This baby reduces the appearance of fine lines, wrinkles and hyperpigmentation and is also great for acne sufferers. You will be left with smoother skin of a clearer and more radiant appearance. The products are not cheap, but when they work as effectively as this and on a long-term basis, the results – along with the huge celebrity clientele – speak for themselves, making them worth every penny.

Please note, though: iS Clinical are medical grade products and require the skills of a trained medical aesthetician. The facial costs £80–100 dependent on your skin. The product range for home use ranges from £21 to around £100.

• **Available at Harrogate Aesthetics, 13 East Parade, Harrogate, and other selected clinics nationwide**
• **W: www.isclinical.com (N)**

Fancy a girls' night in with a difference?: you need Dstress24

Dstress24 uses a fleet of therapists to

form their mobile team of hand-picked professionals who are skilled in the art of therapeutic relaxation and beauty treatments. Delivering services direct to your door, they work with clients across London to provide beauty treatments for hen parties, sleepovers or just to treat you and your gaggle of girlies before a night out.

• W: www.dstress24.ning.com

A Return to Glory

Another mobile beauty favourite of mine is A Return to Glory, where you can book the leading mobile massage, beauty and fitness specialists local to you, charged simply by the hour. So that you know who you're dealing with, the specialists' photographs, client recommendations and certificates are on the website and there's a specialist for almost every treatment you require. I was able to fit in a BeauBronze tanning treatment with therapist Zoe Clarke in between a business meeting and a glamorous restaurant visit and arrive looking great, thanks to A Return to Glory. The finish was very natural and non-sticky, so I could dress shortly after, and they made the whole booking process incredibly easy and came to my hotel room to carry out the treatment. I love the salon experience but if you're a busy modern woman like me, you will appreciate the uncomplicated approach and the rescue remedy that is mobile beauty.

You can book by phone or online, where you enter your postcode on the website to see the leading specialists

working in your area, in addition to a range of mobile services to choose from.

• T: 0845 337 4933
• W: www.returntoglory.co.uk

See B: Beauty, *How to apply false tan* for a review of BeauBronze tanner.

Saviours and must-haves

We don't all wake up looking like the goddesses we truly are: looking lovely can take some serious work! Use this section to inspire and rescue. You'll never be without your fix of gorgeousness and will always have a beauty solution at hand...

Cocoa loco for the butter: Palmer's

There are some beauty classics that will never go out of fashion and if you have tried them you will know why – because they work incomparable magic. Palmer's Cocoa Butter Formula is one of those cult classics which has stood the test of time and developed a range that is both budget and high quality. A favourite of so many women, Palmer's have created new products that contain SPF protection, have designed a Swivel Stick for targeted moisture and formulated an Olive Butter range as an alternative to the original Cocoa Butter. I have tried and tested other brands of cocoa and olive butters and *none* of them compare – so don't be tempted to stray from this particular formula, or you'll only be disappointed.

• **Available from chemists nationwide**
• **W: www.etbrowne.com (N)**

No hair Nair

Nair Exfoliating Hair Removal Cream is suitable for the legs and body with effects that last up to seven days, smoothing skin and removing unwanted hair in one go. You do it once, it takes about five minutes, and you have hair-free, smooth and soft skin and you don't have to worry about maintenance all week. It's friendlier than waxing, longer lasting than shaving and cuts so many corners in a flash. Every modern woman who wants a stunning pair of pins needs this.

• **Available from chemists nationwide**

Clarisonic skin cleansing

The creators of the raved-about Sonicare toothbrush have created Clarisonic – a soft, gentle brush that charges at the mains and that oscillates more than 300 times per second to give an intense, deep skin cleanse. The results leave your skin fresher and softer, and dry patches and ugly open pores appear reduced. Clarisonic is proven to remove six times more make-up and twice as much dirt and oil than manual cleansing, and with gorgeous fans like Courtney Cox, you'll find it hard not to become a fan yourself. I used Clarisonic for the first time following my usual manual cleansing routine and was shocked to see remaining dirt on the brush. After years of manual cleansing and feeling my routine was actually pretty darn good, I'm now a convert, since all the evidence was before me on the brush itself (*eww*), and now my skin looks even brighter. This magic wand is the future of high-tech cleansing.

• **T: 0800 988 4864**
• **W: www.clarisonic.com/uk (N)**

Beauty experts on hand at the click of a mouse: the-beauty-pages.com

This is the 'must-have' website to visit online for your weekly beauty fix, with all the latest expert tips and hottest beauty news. Like the Trip Advisor of the beauty industry, you should look here first before investing in your next beauty buy.

• **W: www.the-beauty-pages.com**

Elle Macpherson The Body

Elle Macpherson The Body is inspired by Elle's personal philosophy of 'Intuitive Beauty', offering women choices depending on how they feel, with three distinctive concepts designed to clarify women's choice in an overcrowded marketplace: Bare – citrus-scented pick-me-ups for everyday use; Glow – patchouli-scented skin enhancers to add shine, gloss and colour to your skin; and Self – lavender-scented indulgent bathing products to chill you out.

From body washes and body butter to bath soaks, dry oil and self-tans, this range has everything you need to stay looking and feeling beautiful. My favourite is the Dry Oil Shimmer Spray, which is gentle enough to use on the face, body and hair for pure nourishment.

- Available at Boots the Chemist (N)

Cult Beauty buys online

Another great beauty bible, if you need help sourcing those cult beauty buys or have read about a great product only to find that it's from a store in a country halfway around the world, is Cult Beauty. It casts its net globally to cherry-pick the best beauty and grooming products, backed by consumer trial and expert opinion, to create an indispensable site that presents what works, simply and thoroughly. Cult Beauty have created an inventory of top products (and some exclusives) using the knowledge of their panel of top hair and beauty experts, including Mary Greenwell, Sarah Chapman, Teresa Hale and Charles Worthington.

- T: 08456 529 521
- W: www.cultbeauty.co.uk

See also H: Hair for some top tips from Cult Beauty expert James Corbett.

Make-up for teeth: Pearl Drops Instant White

Pearl Drops Instant White is a beauty innovation and works as a simple paint-on white tooth veneer that dries in seconds to leave you with whiter-looking teeth. Like 'make-up' for teeth, this wonderpaste will give your smile an instant lift. It's so easy to use, with fast results – perfect on-the-go sparkle to boost your confidence (and your chances of a snog).

- From all good chemists (N)

LIP-INK to make the boys wink

LIP-INK Lip Colour is a semi-permanent lipstick that stays put so you can have luscious-looking lips minus the boring top-ups and cringe-worthy lipstick-on-the-teeth moments. The colour lasts, so you can pout for hours. This suits me perfectly, since my role as a writer and presenter requires

Fab Tip

If you're wearing LIP-INK, try to steer clear of oily foods, as I've found this is one of the only things that can budge it - and don't lick your lips, or it can go crumbly. Use the gloss top coat to keep lips moist and sparkling for full pout appeal.

me to look good, but the busy schedule the role demands means I have little time for top-ups and mirror checks. With LIP-INK, my lip colour did not fade all night. Just don't forget to take the special lip-off cleanser with you (included), so you can remove it, 'cos when I say it doesn't budge, I'm serious.

If you order a kit (mini or sampler) after looking at the online colour chart or testing on the 'look-alike models', you can try before you buy by requesting 'testers' to be sent – to ensure you get the perfect shade for you. *Mwah!*

• W: www.lip-ink.co.uk, and
www.lipink.com for video demonstrations

Barry M

The most colourful name in cosmetics, Barry M offers over 400 different shades and a vast range of quality beauty products at affordable prices. It's one of my much-loved brands, offering fun and frivolity in every shade. I adore the hot juicy lip colours and sparkle eye dust – such fun.

• W: www.barrym.com (N)

Your own signature scent: Floris

Perfumer Shelagh Foyle offers the Floris Bespoke Perfume Customization, presenting Limited Edition Fine Fragrances to signature perfumes.

Shelagh Foyle consults with customers, explaining formulations, and can add personalized components to your existing favourite fragrance if required. For those who desire the ultimate perfume experience of the full bespoke service, you will be able to have your unique perfume created and blended on request.

With the unrivalled knowledge and experience of nine generations in the fragrance business, Floris will ensure you understand the essential oils of the scent that best suits you, and small samples will be made up. Bottling and labelling will also be individual, and genuine antique bottles are available from the Floris original bottle designs. I know what's on my wish list.

• 89, Jermyn Street, London SW1Y
• T: Stockists and mail order, 0845 7023239
• W: www.florislondon.com

Fab Tip

Whenever I get a spot or irritation, my two skin saviours are very basic and very cheap but they work serious wonders – Sudocrem and Tea Tree Oil. Not very glam, but I'm never without them. Sudocrem is used for bedsores, minor burns and even nappy rash, but I use it to keep my skin clear and get rid of any spots! I rub a tiny bit in and leave it overnight to soak in completely, and then wake up to see dramatically improved results. Tea Tree Oil is also great for zapping zits, but don't apply it directly: use a cotton bud to apply gently over the offending area.

• Both available from all good chemists

Ethical beauty: Elysambre

Elysambre make-up is nine times more micronized than usual cosmetics – which, in English, means the products have an extremely fine finish that allows skin to breathe. As well as being organic, you can refill your make-up cases with the product and cut down on waste, and, unlike some eco-chic products (sorry), the packaging still manages to be very stylish and slimline. The powdery products come in engraved metallic cases which are magnetized, so that the colour 'clicks' into place. Foundation comes in squeezable tubes that fill up reusable glass bottles. Even the lippies are refillable. Ingenious.

• T: 08450 725825
• W: www.elysambre.fr (N)

Beauty Boxes

The website at *beauty-boxes.com* offers a gorgeous range of beauty cases and trolleys for the stylish woman-about-town. The perfect solution for storing eye shadows, mascaras, lipglosses, make-up brushes and all the beauty paraphernalia a woman needs – especially great for when you travel, or if you're a beauty junkie like me and you just need a chic place to store it all.

• 21 Decimus Park, Kingstanding Way, Tunbridge Wells, Kent, TN2 3GP
• T: 01892 552692
• W: www.beauty-boxes.com

Móa – natural, organic, healing skin balm

This is a true little wonder! Móa balm is 100% organic with remarkable healing properties. Móa's key ingredient, yarrow, is renowned for its nourishing, healing effect. For centuries this herb has been used to treat wounds, burns and infections and is even mild enough for babies with nappy rash.

Used by mountaineers to heal frostbite, it promotes healing and scars are visibly reduced. Dry patches and rashes are soothed, itches are reduced and skin is softened. It is even effective for soothing a variety of skin conditions soothing eczema and mild cases of psoriasis. What's not to love?

I use my marvellous pot to heal any scars or blemishes, to moisturize drier areas such as elbows, knees and lips, and even my man steals it to use post-shave. It seriously works little miracles; no bathroom cabinet should be without it.

• **Available at Harvey Nichols stores**
• **W: www.thegreenbalm.com (N)**

How to apply false tan

I'm a fan of the fake stuff. It's the safest way to get a year-round tan and today's formulas leave your skin looking and feeling smooth to the touch. The pong

★ Fab Tip ★

Apply the tanner before you go to bed and let it develop overnight for best results. The tan will wash out of your sheets easily enough.

Of course, if it's your first time or you want to treat yourself, have it luxuriously applied by a professional either at home or in a salon. **A Return to Glory** offers a mobile service, and one of my favourites is the organic label founded by QVC TV beauty presenter and celebrity spray-tan technician Abigail Oleck, who has given us **BeauBronz**. The choice for those in the know, this natural spray-tanning solution is free from alcohol and harsh chemicals, is not tested on animals at any time and contains organic and natural ingredients. If the do-gooder factor isn't enough, BeauBronz is also quick drying and long lasting, so the zombie-like walk around the house as you wait for it to dry is banished and you look radiant for days on end.

• **W: www.beaubronz.co.uk**
• **Specialists at A Return to Glory offer this treatment too: www.returntoglory.co.uk**

See also **H: Hotels** for spa treatments including St Tropez Tan.

Fab Tip

Imagine that wherever you apply the solution you will go brown, so never leave any areas untouched. Apply front and back, and stroke in circular motions to ensure the solution joins, leaving no gaps or patches. Using a tinted self-tanner will make it easier to see where you have applied it.

has improved too, so there's no excuse not to get glowing. However, there is a knack to applying it so that you don't look as if you've had a fight with a tin of Bisto.

There are many formulas out there. Wash-off and tints simply coat your skin with colour and wash off in the shower, ideal for a temporary hint of bronze. Self-tanners and wear-off formulas are those that develop on the skin over a number of hours and last for days. Every formula is different, but the basic rules of application are the same.

1 First choose your self-tanner. Don't be tempted to go for the dark shade if you're very fair and have never used a self-tanner before – it will look unnatural. Opt for a shade that resembles the colour you tan in the sun naturally.

2 The night before you apply the tan, remove dry skin using an exfoliator in order to get rid of any rough patches and uneven skin tone that the tan could cling to, thus giving you a patchy finish. Pay close attention to typically drier areas such as your elbows, knees and feet. Then moisturize head to toe.

3 The following day, start the tanning process. I find that if you apply moisturizer immediately beforehand, the tan can sometimes slide off and not 'take' as well, so doing this the night before is advised. Tanned palms are a dead giveaway, so buy special tanning gloves that are like thin rubber gloves, usually in sizes small, medium and large. They should fit tightly so you can apply the solution evenly and smoothly.

4 Add a tiny bit of moisturizer on the drier areas only – I usually include my knees, heels, toes and elbows. You want the solution to glide over these areas and they tend to be the areas that really absorb the tan – not a good look.

5 Stroke the solution over your shins and thighs, back and front, and use the residue on your palms to graze very lightly over your knees and feet, blending it with the moisturizer you previously applied. Always leave the drier bits until last. Starting with your legs is ideal, so you don't lean over having done your upper body first, risking rubbing the solution off.

6 Next apply the solution to your

stomach, stroking round to your back and not forgetting the sides of your body.

7 Apply more to your upper back, or, if you can't reach, get a friend to do it or use a special back applicator, which is like a long-handled sponge.

8 If you like a tanned behind (always good to camouflage any orange-peel skin or stretch marks!), apply to your rear too.

9 Add more moisturizer to your underarms and then stroke the tan over your arms, turn them around and apply the residue on the underside of your arms. The underside is naturally lighter in colour, so using the residue only keeps it looking natural. Graze lightly over your elbows and underarms and then continue down the sides of your body to ensure it all joins up!

10 Now apply the solution to your face. You can buy separate facial tanners, but some brands offer solutions that are suitable for both body and face. Apply moisturizer first to your eyebrows and hairline to protect from absorption. Avoid eyebrows and lips when applying. Stroke onto your cheeks and forehead, continue the strokes down over your nose and chin and join up with your neck, front and back. Don't forget your eyelids and ears – only light strokes are needed here. Stroke gently into your hairline using only the residue.

11 Take off your gloves and stroke an even solution of tanner and moisturizer over the backs of your hands. Stroke in the solution gently, rubbing the backs of your hands together, rubbing it up your fingers. Don't use your palms, just the backs of your hands. Use the backs of your fingers to apply to your wrists.

12 Finally, apply a small amount of toner to a cotton-wool pad and dab over your drier areas and round your hairline to remove any excess, and you're done! Avoid getting dressed immediately.

Breakfast

Some of my favourite smells in the world (next to Coco Chanel) are of the breakfast variety – bacon, eggs, freshly brewed coffee, freshly baked bread (dribble, dribble)... Too many of us see breakfast as a practicality, whereas it should be savoured. Remedies and diet solutions, supplements and vitamin shakes – sorry, but unless it's in aid of a healthy detox, you won't find any of that in here. It has been claimed that breakfast is the most important meal of the day. It also happens to be one of the most scrumptious – so never skip it or supplement it. Instead, go out and treat yourself to a brekkie at one of these establishments...

Selly Sausage, Birmingham

The Selly's homemade pancakes are American-style stacks with numerous topping combinations. From maple syrup to Nutella and cured bacon, this funky independent will not leave you hungry. They go for the top brands that, in my opinion, will always be the best, so expect Heinz beans and HP Sauce to complete your typical English breakfast. *Mmm!*

- **539–541 Bristol Road, Selly Oak, Birmingham**
- **T: 0121 471 4464**
- **W: www.sellysausage.co.uk**

Brompton Quarter Café, London

Set in London's trendy Knightsbridge, expect to devour modern English cuisine with a Mediterranean influence for breakfast – from the simple and light seasonal fruit salad with Greek yoghurt and honey to the delectable and substantial homemade pancakes with mascarpone and honey, or full English breakfast with organic fried eggs, bacon, sausage, Portobello mushrooms, tomato and toast. It's tempting to order more than one dish at once.

- **225 Brompton Road, Knightsbridge, London SW3 2EJ**
- **T: 020 7225 2107**
- **W: www.bromptonquartercafe.com**

Bill's Produce Store and Café, Brighton

This is predominantly a vegetarian café, but, quite uniquely, meat eaters are also really well catered for. The menu includes a host of homemade delights, from healthy choices to the more indulgent. Combined with the eating environment, you'll find fresh and organic fruit and vegetables, herbs, flowers, plants, groceries and hampers in their shop, so you can take all the deliciousness home with you.

- **Depot, 100 North Road, Brighton, East Sussex**
- **56 Cliffe High Street, Lewes, East Sussex**
- **T: Brighton, 01273 692894**
- **T: Lewes, 01273 476 918**
- **W: www.billsproducestore.co.uk**

Craigie's, Edinburgh

Famous for its jams and chutneys, Craigie's fruit farm is home to a first-rate deli-café. Take in the unforgettable views across the Firth of Forth and Pentland Hills as you bite into the delectable food, sourced from local artisan producers. A simple sausage sandwich got me going!

- **West Craigie Farm, South Queensferry, Edinburgh**
- **T: 0131 319 1048**
- **W: www.craigies.co.uk**

Aubaine, London

Aubaine's breakfast follows the formula of butter croissant, pain au chocolat, baguettes with homemade jams and country butter, and a grande crème or a mug of unctuous chocolate.

Their idea of 'continental breakfast' is far removed from the hard biscuit, thin soup and porridge that French breakfasts used to consist of (thank goodness), and I have to say that Aubaine's are one of the best. There's also a second branch on Heddon Street, London.

- **260–262 Brompton Road, London SW3 2AS**
- **T: 020 7052 0100**

If you fancy breakfast in the comfort of your own home, try these quirky options:

● ●

Rude Health

● ●

Why not be a little bit rude and a lot healthy with 'Morning Glory', one of Rude Health's sauciest porridges? Rude Health source organic, sustainably grown ingredients and their packaging is either recyclable or biodegradable. So every Rude Health breakfast will also give a boost to wildlife, hedgerows and farmers. A very delicious way to get healthy and save the planet!

• W: www.rudehealth.com
• Also available from Sainsbury's and the Co-op

● ●

Sow your oats at Muddy Cook

● ●

Online muesli mixery Muddy Cook allows you to go online and mix your perfect muesli from over 100 organic and fair trade healthy ingredients. Each pack is blended to order and can be personalized, so you can name it what you wish and add a personal message. You start with your base, a huge selection of oats or granola, and then add your choice of fruits, berries, nuts, sugar and spice toppings. Choose as many or as few ingredients as you like to blend your own creation. I'm a fan of the Chocolate Bliss base with raspberries and macadamia nuts – that's 'Muesli au Fabulousness' to you!

• W: www.muddycook.co.uk

Cocktails (and Other Beverages) C & Confectionery

Cocktails

Cocktails have come a long way since the days when Del Boy asked for a 'Baileys with cherryade' topped with bananas and paper umbrellas (yuck)! No longer seen as 'fancy girl drinks' that are a pain to make and a pain to wait for, cocktails are now *de rigueur*, don't ya know. From talented celebrities to award-winning mixologists, these recommended magical potions will tantalize your tastebuds!

. . . .

The Cointreau Teese by Dita Von Teese

. . . .

Dita Von Teese adores violets. So it's no surprise that violet adds that extra touch of soul when blended with Cointreau's orange notes in her cocktail. Dita adds, 'I love its delicate taste contrasting with its strong personality.'

Mix your own at home, or taste it perfectly made in bars around the UK, including Below Zero in London, W1, Chocolate Club in Birmingham and The Orange Rooms in Southampton.

Glass

Chilled Martini glass

Composition

- 50ml Cointreau
- 25ml fresh apple juice
- 15ml fresh lemon juice
- 10ml violet syrup (Monin, or Giffard Violette, available from *TheDrinkShop.com*)
- Garnish with a violet or purple edible flower

Method

Rub a small piece of fresh ginger around the rim of the glass. Shake all other ingredients with ice and strain into the glass.

• W: www.ditasdomain.com/cointreau

6 Inch Stiletto created by Ben Clark, Bar Manager at The Zetter

The Zetter is in my top five for cool hotel bars due to its funky and upcoming art work, laid-back vibe and exclusive cocktail list. My favourite poison here is Ben Clark's '6 Inch Stiletto', not least because of the glam name, but also because of its fiery yet fruity kick. Ideal for a girly night out.

Glass

Martini glass

Composition

- 1 tsp strawberry jam
- 2 slices of chilli
- 35ml Wyb vodka
- 10ml Cherry Heering
- 10ml Framboise
- 10ml cranberry juice

Method

Muddle the chilli and the jam. Then add all other ingredients and shake. Double-strain over a Martini glass and serve with a fresh wedge of chilli.

See also H: Hotels for more about The Zetter.

Sangria Aperitif

This Sangria Aperitif is famous throughout the Italian and French Riviera (especially in the summertime), but there is nothing stopping you enjoying it in the UK. Created by celebrity chef Maria Liberati from the best-selling book series *The Basic Art of Italian Cooking.*

Glass

Punch glasses

Composition

- 1 bottle of rosé wine
- 3 fresh pineapple slices
- 3 fresh orange slices with skin on
- 1 pear, peeled, cored, cut into cubes
- ½ cup Cointreau

- 2 bottles of sparkling water
- 5 tbsp strawberry-flavoured syrup
- 10 strawberries, hulled, cleaned, cut into slices

Method

Put all the ingredients into a crystal punch bowl – except the sliced strawberries – and stir. Refrigerate for half an hour, then serve in punch glasses with sliced strawberries and ice cubes.

© 2009, Maria Liberati

- **W: www.marialiberati.com**

Park Plaza Sherlock Holmes, London signature cocktail, Nuts & Berries

Glass

Martini glass

Composition

- 30ml Baileys Liqueur
- 25ml Chambord Liqueur
- 5ml Amaretto
- 6 fresh raspberries
- 5ml fresh cream

Method

Muddle the raspberries in the base of a shaker, add the other ingredients, shake with ice and strain.

See also H: Hotels for more on Park Plaza.

The Daiquiri by Robert 'Skippy' Jupp of Speciality Brands

'Rum, lime and sugar: the beauty of a daiquiri is in its simplicity; three small parts combine to make a much more effective whole,' says Skippy. 'A good daiquiri is all about the balance of sweet, sour and alcohol and is not unlike the balance of a good wine. Most of all, a well-made daiquiri will hinge on the quality and depth of the rum used; the different characteristics found in the young rums of the Caribbean are only emphasized and improved in a daiquiri. The daiquiri's popularity was sealed in pre-revolution Cuba, as the likes of Ernest Hemingway introduced the drink to his US market. Many variations have since followed, but remember, the key to a great drink is the ingredients used.'

Glass

Serve straight up in a Martini or Coupette glass.

Composition

- 50ml White Rum (for a truly memorable daiquiri try with Venezuela's finest – Diplomatico Reserva Blanco)
- 25ml freshly squeezed lime juice
- 20ml sugar syrup

Method

Shake all ingredients with ice and fine-strain into a chilled glass.

• Diplomatico Rum is available from Selfridges (N). See www.selfridges.com for your nearest stockist.

Personalized mixology classes at The Dorchester Hotel

If you want to impress like Tom Cruise back in the day, you won't want to miss the mixology class with Giuliano Morandin, bar manager at The Dorchester, London, for more than 30 years. Giuliano offers private or group mixology lessons (for up to five people) behind the bar of the legendary five-star hotel.

Learn to make the cocktail, mocktail or martini of your choice in just two hours and then blend your own using your favourite ingredients. After naming your masterpiece, the bar will put it on the menu for the rest of the day (unless it's disgusting…)!

• The Dorchester, Park Lane, London W1K 1QA
• T: 020 7629 8888
• W: www.thedorchester.com

Beer

Beer has never been so chic. It's not just wine or fancy cocktails that ooze sophistication. Beer has often been overlooked as a top tipple for the ladies, but with a host of flavours and strengths to choose from, it's only right that I quiz the UK's only female beer expert, Melissa Cole, to offer you top tips.

Melissa Cole is the country's leading female beer writer and broadcaster. She's been writing about beer, pubs and brewing for ten years and can often be seen getting her hands dirty at artisan breweries all

C

Cocktails & Confectionery

over the country. She also writes a popular blog called 'A Girl's Guide to Beer – Taking the Beard Out of Beer', and runs a beer-tasting business in the world-famous Borough Market called lovebeer@borough.

What follows here is Melissa's advice on different beers to suit different occasions (from impressing your guests at a dinner party to wowing your first date), and we've even put together a 'beer glossary' for you to get up to speed with all the phrases. Please see the section called 'Beer jargon debunked', read on and guzzle with glee...

Ideal dinner party beer

If you would like to impress your hosts, take a bottle of **Deus** as an aperitif. This beer is made with champagne yeast and is a truly extraordinary product with its bright sparkling nature and tones of spicy orange, banana and red apple. It is fermented and matured in Belgium, re-fermented in the bottle, and then follows the champenoise method of *remuage** and *dégorgement*** in France. Just to top it all off, it also comes in a magnum bottle with a cork seal – so it has lots of wow factor as well as tasting amazing!

• Available from www.ocado.com or www.utobeer.co.uk

Spice up your life

Why not take a proper **English India Pale Ale** to dinner and teach those shandy drinkers and lager lovers a thing or two? Traditionally high

in alcohol and heavy in its use of hops, India Pale Ale (or IPA, as it's commonly known) was the first ever beer style brewed specifically for export. Making it high in hop content and alcohol was necessary to protect the beer from spoiling on the long journey to India, which, in the days before the Suez Canal, meant sailing the length of both sides of Africa and traversing the Cape of Good Hope, which took the beer from England's temperate shores, into the tropics and across the equator not once, but twice. It was also necessary to ensure the beer was drinkable even after it had reached the heat of India.

Choose something like the all-time classic **Worthington White Shield**, which is redolent with red apple and spice smells and flavours, or perhaps you could choose the historically brewed **Meantime IPA** – a fascinating beer with a strong marzipan and herb scent followed by a rich soothing taste of orange blossom water mixed with aniseed, which comes in an impressive champagne-style bottle.

• **Available from Sainsbury's, or widely online**

If you're feeling more adventurous, perhaps go for a more extreme American version like **Great Divide's Titan IPA**, which is not for the faint-hearted with its strong but well-balanced bitter lime and grapefruit flavours. If you're feeling a little less brave, you could go for the smoother, creamier **Goose Island IPA**, which has more tropical rather than citrus fruit notes.

• **W: www.utobeer.co.uk**

Death by chocolate?

For the chocoholics amongst you, why not enjoy a chocolate beer? Choose from the British classic **Young's Double Chocolate Stout** or **Brooklyn Brewery's Black Chocolate Stout** – both do very much what they say on the bottle. Or perhaps you can reach out for something a little less obvious that still satisfies your chocolate cravings? **Fuller's London Porter** is a rich, historic brew full of chocolate and coffee notes, with a lingering finish of luscious liquorice. Or, if you're having a chocolate dessert and don't want to overdo it, try a total contrast in the form of a fruit beer – but don't reach for sickly sweet concoctions made up of exotic-sounding cheap syrups. Go for something like the truly amazing fruity, dry and refreshing **He'Brew Origin**, a pomegranate beer (which has the added bonus of being kosher), or **Cantillon Rose de Gambrinus** – once described to me by Si King from the Hairy Bikers as being like 'a Sherbet Dib Dab without the Dib'!

Girl's night out beer

Going to a bar or pub that you feel comfortable in is the first step to having a good girls' night out. Take a look around and if the ale looks good and a decent amount of people are drinking it, then why not ask for a taster of what's on tap? If the landlord or barman refuses, then leave: chances are, they don't keep good beer! Once you've found a good pub, talk to the bar staff, get a sample and see if they've got any local beers for you to try. If not, then try what other people

seem to be drinking a lot of, but if you're not too sure, the following beers are those that I consider will be a sure-fire hit for any group on a night out, and they're not just for the ladies.

Blue Moon Belgian-style wheat beer is a really refreshing beer with strong notes of orange and a slight creaminess that lets it slide down nicely. It's sometimes served with a slice of orange – refuse it, as the citric acid kills the head on your beer.

Budweiser Budvar lager – don't let the name fool you, this is the original from the Czech Republic and is a world away from its bland American wannabe cousin. It has a great balance of sweet and bitter flavours, unlike your average cold one, with a lemony zing that quenches even the strongest thirst!

Dress (and drink) to impress

First and foremost you should be drinking things because you enjoy them; but, let's face it, being a bit impressive never hurts either! But remember, girls, tipsy is cute, hammered is not. Confidence of any sort, and especially about beer, is definitely sexy, so be sure to brush up on the jargon (see below). Once you're armed with your new-found beer expertise, impress with **Sierra Nevada Pale Ale**. It's got the carbonation of a high-quality lager (not too gassy and definitely not bloating) and the depth of flavour of a good ale, without being overwhelmingly bitter – think caramelized orange with a hint of chocolate digestive … *mmm!*

Why not reach for a proper British pint of stout? No, not the smooth-flow famous stuff – seek out products like

Samuel Smith's Oatmeal Stout, or perhaps even their oak-aged **Yorkshire Stingo**, which weighs in at a hefty 8% ABV, so give it some respect.

Alternatively, why not give a **Porter** a go? Very similar to stout, less creamy but generally with more chocolate and less bitter coffee notes. **Fuller's** does an excellent version called **London Porter** (this being where the drink was invented).

If you're absolutely loaded or now very seriously into your beer, you could always indulge in a **Sam Adams Utopia** – the world's strongest beer at 27%. It will set you back at least £100, but does come in the most beautiful bottle and is designed to be sipped and savoured.

•**Sam Adams beer is sold internationally, and on www.BeersofEurope.co.uk**

Notes

* In the making of sparkling wine, *remuage* is where the bottles are kept tilted and are turned at regular intervals. This allows the sediment to settle in the neck of the bottle so that it can be disgorged later.

** *Dégorgement* is the practice in sparkling wine making where the neck of the bottle is placed in an icy brine or glycol solution, when *remuage* is complete, which causes the neck's contents (mainly sediment) to freeze into a solid plug. During disgorging the cork (or cap) is removed, and the pressure in the bottle causes the frozen plug of sediment to pop out. The procedure is followed by the remaining *méthode champenoise* steps, including adding the dosage, topping off the bottle with additional wine (or in

this case beer) and re-corking it.

There's also the tingly effect of CO2 to take into account. The tingly sensation is actually low-level pain on the tongue from the CO2 – just see how long you can keep your tongue in a glass of cola!

Beer jargon debunked: Your beer glossary by Melissa Cole

The ingredients

- Yeast: no yeast, no alcohol! Alcohol and carbon dioxide are – rather unglamorously – the by-products of yeast eating sugar at the right temperature.

- Hops: the female cones of the hop plant are used in beer to add aroma and bitterness, but they also have a natural antibiotic effect that favours the activity of brewer's yeast over less desirable micro-organisms. Hops are also part of the same family as cannabis and have many uses in alternative medicine, including natural sleeping remedies.

- Malt: toasted and roasted grains are used to provide the yeast with enough food to make alcohol. The colour of your beer will depend on the amount of darker or lighter 'roasts' used in the process, very much like stronger or lighter coffee blends.

- Water: this may sound mad, but water has a profound effect on the flavour of your beer. The softer Czech Pilsners, for example, owe a lot to the water they are brewed with, whereas in the UK we have something called Burton, after the spiritual home of brewing Burton-on-Trent, which adds a slightly sulphurous edge to beer (not as bad as it sounds!).

The brewing process

• Mashing in: the first stage of the brewing process where the brewer adds hot water to lightly crushed, toasted (malted) grains to make a porridge and to obtain a sweet liquid called the wort.

• Copper: more often made from stainless steel these days, this is effectively a great big vessel like a kettle, where the wort goes to be boiled with hops.

• Early/late hops: this simply refers to when the hops are added in the boil. As a general rule, early hops are the varieties that offer the required bitterness and late hops are added for aroma and lighter flavours.

• Pitching the yeast: chucking in enough yeast to make beer – it's really not any more complicated than that!

• Fermentation: when the yeast gets to work on all the food it's been given at the right temperature, it's time for a positive procreation and respiration party!

• Maturation: a vital part of the process, this allows the (very) rough alcohol to mellow out and develop more delicate flavours. This is generally a shorter time for ales at a higher temperature and

a longer time for lagers at a lower temperature.

Other phrases

• Real/cask ale: this is beer that has gone through a secondary fermentation in a barrel or cask, which adds more complexity to the taste and ensures it's a very fresh product and generally only available in the pub.

• Bottle conditioned ale: as above, except it goes through the secondary fermentation in the bottle rather than the barrel.

• Bottled ale: beer that's been brewed, no extra yeast.

• Lager: real lager should actually be aged or stored at very low temperatures, not the case with the majority of big brands you see on supermarket shelves, so keep an eye out for high-quality Czech and German brands, as well as other artisan lager products.

• Hoppy/malty: these are nonsense words used by people too lazy to put true descriptions on their beers, or who fall into one of two camps – total beer snob or total beer ignoramus, both of which are generally to be avoided!

• Light strike: generally it's wise to avoid beers in clear glass bottles. The nature of hop oils is such that they degrade very quickly in the light, leaving a damp newspaper/wet shaggy dog smell and unpleasant flavour in the bottle … and that's why

C

Cocktails & Confectionery

lime is so necessary for your bottle of Sol or Corona!

• W: www.girlsguidetobeer.blogspot.com
and www.lovebeeratborough.ning.com

Pull your own pint

Leeds Brewery offer kegs of beer to purchase so you can set up your own bar at home, complete with a hand pump, pump clip, beer runners and beer mats for an authentic look. The beers on offer include the brewery's three regular ales – **Leeds Best**, a full-flavoured bitter, **Midnight Bell**, their award-winning rich dark ale, and **Leeds Pale** for a lighter option. If you've ever fantasized about having your own bar, and let's face it, we all have at some point, this is a step in the right direction – that, or just for a bit of fun. Don't blame me if you can never get your friends to leave, though.

• 36, 72 and 144 pint kegs are available
• T: 0113 244 5866
• W: www.leedsbrewery.co.uk

Champagne

We all know that *Which?* magazine is famed for its efforts to get a fairer deal for all consumers and publishes expert, unbiased information to help you make the right choice, whatever you're buying. Editor Martyn Hocking tells us ladies how to appreciate a good Champagne…

Storage tips

Heat and bright light are the things that are most likely to damage your hoard of Champagne – in the long term. It's wise not to keep your bottles by the radiator, or by a sunny window. If you're buying some bargain bottles now for future drinking, find a cool, dark spot for longer-term storage. And unlike still wines, you don't need to lay bottles of fizz on their sides.

Keeping upright

Research in the Champagne region has shown that Champagne and sparkling wine bottles are fine stored upright, even for months and years. In fact, some Champagne companies choose to store bottles upright in their own cellars.

While the corks in upright bottles of still wines can dry out and shrivel, the trapped carbon dioxide in a bottle of fizz forces wine vapour up against the cork, keeping it moist and therefore fitting snugly.

Some sparklers are best drunk right away

Does it improve? It's impossible to generalize. Some Champagnes will keep for years after purchase; some need drinking soon. Some will improve, developing more interesting flavours; some will deteriorate, losing fruitiness and developing flavours reminiscent of sherry.

It's also a matter of personal preference. If you offer a choice of Champagnes at any gathering of wine experts or wine buffs, there'll be disagreements over which wines are getting past it and which might benefit from more ageing.

Many of the non-Champagne sparkling wines mentioned in a report in a past issue of *Which?* were types of **Cava**, from the vineyards around Barcelona. These do not benefit from ageing, but most will keep for a few months.

By Martyn Hocking, editor, *Which?* magazine

• W: www.which.co.uk

…It's true, Cava and Prosecco are so now – far trendier and, in my opinion, lighter, on both the palate and the bank balance! Vinopolis offer a fantastic hen party package, where one of their wine guides will greet you and your party with a glass of Prosecco, while you learn a little more about the provenance of this elegant drink.

Your guide will then teach you and your guests how to sniff, swirl and slurp like a professional in a private 'How to Taste Wine' session. The chief hen will be challenged to a blind wine tasting of red and white wine now that she's an expert on the stuff, then you'll all learn how to shake and stir your own cocktail under the guidance of a **Vinopolis** cocktail expert.

A great way to start your celebrations (you're bound to be on the road to tipsy after this lot) and learn new tricks!

• W: www.vinopolis.co.uk ('Hen Parties')

Wine

It's impressive when a girl knows just enough about wine, but it's not always that easy to show you know a thing or two without looking like a plonker. I ask Richard Brierley – head of Fine Wine at Vanquish Wine Ltd, London, wine expert and auctioneer – to share his wine wisdom on how to purchase the ideal wine for certain key occasions…

Know your wine merchant

Treat him like your personal shopper, butcher, cheesemonger or travel agent: the more you ask, the more he will tell. Tell him what you are eating, how much you want to spend, ask about any recent arrivals and what he's drinking!

Get good glasses

No point having a killer dress without the shoes to match! Good glasses should be simple, long-stemmed and of the best quality. Riedel, Spiegelau and Peter Steger are some of the best. One for white, a larger one for red and a champagne flute should be any girl's minimum.

Two situations where the right wine can set you apart!

First date

Let's face it, everyone needs a glass of wine on a first date – and your choice should ooze class and understanding but not be snobby! Asking the wine waiter or bartender for recommendations is the way to go. Use sensual words: 'something delicious'. Stick with a crisp white, but stay clear of Pinot Grigio! My fave would be a Sauvignon Blanc from New Zealand or Chile.

Dinner party wines

Champagne is the only way to start a dinner party and every girl should have a couple of bottles permanently in the fridge for impromptu occasions. The real stuff from France's Champagne region sets the right impression. Choosing a smaller Champagne house shows an understanding of the region. Nicolas Feuillatte is a stellar choice that will please the most discerning guests.

Having red and white available is non-negotiable, but proposing the wine by its name and not as 'red or white' is the key to fabulousness. The white should be nicely chilled, but not overly cold. The red should be open as your guests arrive – that way, by dinnertime it will have had time to breathe. An un-oaked or lightly oaked Chardonnay will please most guests and is unobtrusive to match most dishes. Chablis or a Chilean Chardonnay may fit the bill.

For the red, the fresh raspberry and cherry fruit aromas of Pinot Noir are pleasing to the most discerning of diners. Pinot Noir from New Zealand is fresh and uncomplicated. In Burgundy, France, things are much more complicated – but your wine merchant may have a favourite to wow your guests.

Want to go a step further?

Having a wine collection sounds pretty daunting, but with the right friends and a sense of adventure it can be fabulously rewarding. The best way to start is to learn as much as possible about what you like. I like to taste with a group; it divides the cost and allows you to learn from others. Tasting evenings allow us to share our newly found passion. Choose a theme, invite people to bring a bottle and taste together. Six or eight people works well – any more wines and it gets too complicated. Taste them together, swap your impressions about what you like or dislike, and try to remember the ones you liked most! As you get better, you can do it 'blind' without knowing what the individual wines are. Voting for the group's wine of the night will help you remember the best ones.

- **Vanquish Wine Ltd, 16 Kingly Street, London W1B 5PT**
- **T: 020 7478 8950**
- **W: www.vanquishwine.com**
- **E: richard@vqwine.com**

Unwind with Entwine

One of my favourite lighter options is Entwine Wines, the lighter way to enjoy alcohol. Does that sound like a Maltesers advert?

You can watch your waist as well as your alcohol intake with a range of pre-mixed, low-calorie wine spritzers from Entwine. Full of natural ingredients and less than half the calories and alcohol than traditional wine, Entwine satisfies your need for treats without the guilt.

The range includes a Shiraz Rosé Spritzer – an attractive blend of fruity Shiraz Rosé and pure sparkling water, and a Sauvignon Blanc Spritzer – fresh Sauvignon Blanc spritzed with pure sparkling water.

• W: www.entwinedrinks.com

Confectionery

Girls crave chocolate because of the mood-elevating properties. Think about when you crave chocolate the most – when your period starts, when you feel down, when you're stressed, right? All these things affect our mood, but chocolate helps to even out these fluctuations chemically. Yes, that's why we love it, though I'm not sure that justifies my cake and pastry cravings … hey-ho!

Check out my round-up of the most fabulous sweet treats and show your man how to handle moodiness in the most enjoyable way…

Hotel Chocolat

Decadent chocolatiers Hotel Chocolat have opened a concept café where chocolate drinks are served in jugs with china cups and long-handled spoons. 'The Macho' is a great substitute for your daily cup of coffee, made with pure 100% cocoa solids, and the delectable range of chocolate dishes give you pleasure with every mouthful. Try the 'Dipping Pot Duo' – two bowls of melted chocolate served with sliced banana, mini breadsticks and marshmallows.

•163 Kensington High Street, London W8 6SU
• T: 020 7938 2144
• W: www.hotelchocolat.co.uk (N)

Crumbs and Doilies

A palace of cupcakes, every one is freshly baked and topped with a range of globally sourced sprinkles. Only organic free-range eggs, organic Doves Farm flour and other top-quality ingredients are used. The coffee cupcake is their most sophisticated, flavoured with real Arabica espresso coffee and topped with coffee, vanilla or chocolate icing and then finished with a chocolate-coated coffee bean, walnuts or dark chocolate shavings. *Mmm…*

• W: www.crumbsanddoilies.co.uk

Hummingbird Bakery

The Hummingbird Bakery offers American home baking to Londoners. You can also personalize cupcakes with your own message, piped in a huge number of different icings, toppings and even shapes and sizes. With freshly baked cupcakes, cookies, cakes and traditional American pies (the Mississippi Mudpie is to die for!), you'll be in confectionery heaven.

• W: www.hummingbirdbakery.co, plus three shops in London

Retro sweets

It's somewhat unnerving to see that the sweets I used to gorge on as a child are now being referred to as 'retro'! However, I'm exceptionally pleased to find that I can get my grown-up mitts on them. If Alphabet Letters, Anglo Bubbly Bubblegum, Candy Shrimps and Black Jacks take you back, buy a bag and enjoy!

• W: www.bagsofsweets.co.uk

British Candy

British Candy has got to be the best virtual sweet shop for retro sweets such as WHAM bars, Fizz Wiz Space Dust popping candy, Dib Dabs and Flying Saucers. I had a field day reminiscing about my younger years when browsing through, recalling the days of Sugar Paper, Rainbow Sugar and Halfpennies … am I showing my age?!

• W: www.britishcandy.com

Groovy Chocolate

Chocolate bars, chocolate boxes, chocolate coins – in short, this is chocolate heaven. They claim that they can make 'almost anything you can think of'. The chocolate Oscar is perfect for any budding little film starlet or film buff and the printed chocolate facility is great for weddings, corporate events or to impress your loved one. Using edible food dyes, they can reproduce virtually any image directly onto the bar (even photographs). Bars are individually packed into a handy pocket-sized box, which can also be personalized in a number of ways. Hmm, Brad Pitt printed onto

a chocolate bar might make it even tastier!

• W: www.groovychocolate.com

Mr Bunbury

Mr Bunbury's range of luxury, but affordable, chocolate brownies and cakes are the perfect indulgent teatime treat. Mr Bunbury describes his Madagascan Brownies as 'rich as Croesus and packed to the gunwales with highly superior Madagascan 66% cocoa chocolate'. His Chocolate Biscuit Cake – five satisfying digestive biscuit cakes enrobed in Belgian chocolate – is a chocolate-lover's dream.

• W: www.mrbunbury.co.uk

Dining & Domestic Bliss

Cafés

I love sitting in cafés watching the world go by and indulging in one of my favourite pastimes – people-watching. Sometimes there's nothing better to clear your head than sitting alone in a little café with a huge pot of tea and a slice of cake. Dine in one of these wonderful venues, each chosen for being most fabulous for a reason unique to them, and while away the hours…

• •

Most fabulous for escaping the hustle and bustle: Raoul's Café and Deli

• •

Raoul's Café and Deli is located in the

heart of Maida Vale in Little Venice, with a fine food delicatessen, and a second trendy eatery in Notting Hill. I visited the Notting Hill branch. This splendid location brings a touch of Parisian café culture to the Bohemian style of Notting Hill with its new 60-seat restaurant and 16-seat outdoor terrace.

I chose to walk down Portobello Road on a sunny Saturday afternoon (not recommended if you're in a hurry), but I was so pleased when I reached Raoul's as it's the perfect resting place after a shopping trip, long walk or hard day. Serving delicious Mediterranean cuisine, you can expect a wonderful all-day brunch and lunch menu, Mediterranean Plates, an extensive wine list and fresh puddings, and even a chicken kebab (this dish has never been so glam). Sit back and enjoy on the outdoor terrace as the sun shines.

- **Raoul's Café and Bar, 105–107 Talbot Road (between Westbourne Grove and Ledbury Road), Notting Hill, London W11 2AT**
- **T: 020 7229 2400**
- **W: www.raoulsgourmet.com**

Most fabulous for treating yourself: The Cake Café

I love the mismatched crockery and floral tablecloths and the genuine simplicity this café has to offer. This is the perfect place to kick back and savour a cupcake and glass of Prosecco, best enjoyed in the leafy courtyard. If you call them during the week with your 'Saturday cake orders' they will have your treat boxed up and

ready for you to take away.

The coffee is also notable, made with ethically sourced and fully traceable beans imported and roasted by Michael from Ariosa, who blends his coffee every week and delivers to The Cake Café the next day, so it's always full of flavour.

- **The Daintree Building, Pleasants Place, Dublin 2**
- **T: +353 (1) 478 9394**
- **W: www.thecakecafe.ie**

Most fabulous for a unique shopping and dining experience: Piazza by Anthony

Celebrated chef Anthony Flinn has chosen The Corn Exchange in Leeds, West Yorkshire, for his most ambitious venture to date – The Piazza, a ground-floor restaurant embracing the circular dome architecture with its magnificent 'sky at night' domed roof that lends an alfresco feel.

The buzzy restaurant sits in the middle surrounded by separate coves and areas that each offer something different. One cove houses a bakery where you can witness the bread, cakes and muffins being made and baked in front of you. Another cove presents chocolatiers making their own chocolate treats, next door to a deli of cheeses and hors d'oeuvres. The best bit? You can try these freshly made foods and buy them so you can continue to enjoy the experience at home. There is also an über-cool bar area; a more relaxed café area to stay in or take away, serving fresh meats, salads and snacks; private event and meeting rooms, and my favourite, the wine cellar. A truly original offering with truly amazing cuisine.

....

• **Piazza By Anthony, The Corn Exchange, Call Lane, Leeds LS1 7BR**
• **T: 0113 247 0995**
• **W: www.anthonysrestaurant.co.uk/piazza**

••••••••••••••••••••••••••••••••••••••

Most fabulous for seaside pleasure: Judges Bakery
••••••••••••••••••••••••••••••••••••••

Judges Bakery is owned and run by Green & Blacks founders Craig Sams and Josephine Fairley, with Soil Association award-winning baker Emmanuel Hadjiandreou – so you already know you're dealing with some of the most delicious baked goods around.

From jam tarts to white bloomers, sausage rolls to Madeira cakes, rye bread to their famous pink meringue pigs, the quality is second to none, so much so that the food-hunters at Selfridges have hand-picked their breads and cakes to offer to discerning food-lovers in London. The entire scrumptious experience is best enjoyed at their seaside venue, so ditch the no-carb diet and relish.

....

• **51 High Street, Hastings, East Sussex TN34 3EN**
• **T: 01424 722588**
• **W: www.judgesbakery.com**

••••••••••••••••••••••••••••••••••••••

Most fabulous for comfort food: Gruel
••••••••••••••••••••••••••••••••••••••

Gruel is a centrally located popular Dublin café famous for its 'Roast in a Roll', served daily. Each day diners can enjoy a different roast with some well-chosen garnishes in an ample crusty roll. There is also a fab salad bar in the centre of the room, along with homemade soups and an array of other gorgeous dishes, should you not fancy this roasty treat, but let's face it, you will!

....

• **Gruel, 68a Dame Street, Dublin 2**
• **T: +353 (1) 6707119**

••••••••••••••••••••••••••••••••••••••

Most fabulous for fresh food: Indulge Deli
••••••••••••••••••••••••••••••••••••••

Indulge is a modern continentally-influenced deli bar offering very high quality sandwiches, soups, baked potatoes and salads for eating in or taking away. It's a small café and always packed, but that's because the food is so good. There are boards of ingredients for you to choose from, drool over and even combine, plus a good offering of Italian coffees, fresh juices and healthy smoothies.

....

• **51 Station Parade, Harrogate**
• **T: 01423 851555**
• **W: www.indulgedelibar.co.uk**

••••••••••••••••••••••••••••••••••••••

Most fabulous for quick bites and chilling out: Embankment Café
••••••••••••••••••••••••••••••••••••••

There's a little bandstand in Embankment Gardens, London, that offers fresh sandwiches or salad with a choice of crisps or cookies and a drink for under £3 (prices subject to change). Entitled 'Grab a Bag', the concept gives you a quick healthy snack in a bag that you can take away or (my favourite) enjoy on the grass or in a deckchair as you sunbathe in the beautiful surroundings. If you fancy a main meal and a larger selection,

D

Dining & Domestic Bliss

Cake anyone?

walk along to Embankment Café and sit outside. The sausage sandwich is suitably generous in size, using herby sausages and soft white bread.

• **Victoria Embankment Gardens**
• **T: 07751 340 616**

Most fabulous for an afternoon rendezvous: Coffee Cake and Kink

This stylish, upbeat little café was situated down a quiet lane in the otherwise bustling Covent Garden, London. Though they have now moved and are looking for new premises, this is one café worth keeping an eye out for. The owner says it's based on the three things he enjoys most in life – what a wise trio of delights to place as priority! Surrounded by erotic art

and literature, sex toys and with a mixed crowd, your senses will be stimulated and stirred with the delectable array of homemade cakes, global coffees and teas and top-quality kink! Check out the website for updates and the home-order facility in the meantime.

• **T: 020 7419 2996**
• **W: www.coffeecakeandkink.com**

Restaurants and food halls

Dining out is one of my favourite things to do, and with so many fantastic restaurants to choose from, I'm never short of options. I adore food halls too, where you can savour the food at the onsite restaurant, then buy the produce to take home with you. However, so much choice brings bewilderment, so I took great pleasure in separating the so-so from the sensational just for you...

Most fabulous for indulgence: Fortnum & Mason

This book would not be complete without F&M. It is a haven of fabulousness: not only a food and drink emporium, offering everything from rose petal jelly to gourmet takeaway and bespoke Peggy Porschen wedding cakes, but Fortnum & Mason also sports an unrivalled wine department and is home to five dining experiences, a beautiful Ladies' floor, Beauty à la Carte treatment rooms and more ... phew!

The second floor offers a treasure trove dedicated to perfumery, handbags, jewellery, bed and bath ranges and the sort of accessories you simply don't find elsewhere. The Beauty à la Carte treatment rooms take you from express manicure to indulgent full-body massages.

Dining experiences include a wide range of cafés and dining rooms, taking you from breakfast to afternoon tea. My two favourites are The Parlour, a 1950s ice cream parlour, and 1707 Wine Bar with a wine list voted one of London's best by *Tatler* magazine. This is not a place to count calories (I *never* have), it's a place to indulge in style.

• 181 Piccadilly, London W1A 1ER
• T: 020 7734 8040
• W: www.fortnumandmason.co.uk

Most fabulous for breathtaking views across the city: Saltwater

Based in the cosmopolitan city of Nottingham, the stunning Saltwater Rooftop Bar and Restaurant presents flavoursome British food at affordable prices, as well as a selection of tastes from around the globe. Its real selling point though, comes from the rooftop bar and terrace, which offers breathtaking panoramic views across Nottingham.

• Saltwater Rooftop Bar and Restaurant, The Cornerhouse, Nottingham NG1 4AA
• T: 0115 924 2664
• W: www.saltwater-restaurant.com

Most fabulous for nostalgic glamour: Bob Bob Ricard

At last, quality English food served with the authenticity and eccentricity we all know and love.

Bob Bob Ricard, or 'BBR', is a two-floor restaurant designed by David Collins (The Wolseley). Tucked away in Soho, London, I expected the usual modern, urban eatery, but as I entered I felt as though I'd stepped back in time and entered a 1950s diner. Oozing nostalgic glamour, Cubist chandeliers hang from a high Venetian-mirrored ceiling. Marble panels, animated patterns and bold colours contrast and complement each other, while the elegance of the curtained booths adds intimacy and pays homage to the luxury of trains such as the Orient Express.

There is a secluded private dining section with dark wood-lined walls,

D

Dining & Domestic Bliss

housing eccentric antiques, and downstairs has more of an intimate late-night bar feel with a deep red booth-style layout and a dark wooden floor, designed to resemble a backgammon board.

My favourite detail was the champagne buttons at every table, which, when pressed, summon a champagne trolley. Can I arrange to have one of these at my bedside, please?

The restaurant at BBR is run by Francois Valero (formerly GM of The Ivy), seats 140 and offers 'traditional British comfort food with a twist'. Quirky options such as Jelly and Champagne sit happily with more traditional fare such as Beef Wellington. You must try the mini selection, including delights such as mini shepherds pie, mini beefburgers and mini macaroni cheese. All food is sourced from quality British suppliers and you can taste the freshness in every bite. Scrummy. The service is also worth a mention – you don't half feel special here! Love it!

• **Bob Bob Ricard, 1 Upper James Street, Soho, London W1F 9DF**
• **T: 020 3145 1000**
• **W: www.bobbobricard.com**

See also T: Tea for afternoon tea delights at Bob Bob Ricard

Most fabulous for non-fussy excellence: Tom Aitkens

Tom Aitkens (The Restaurant) won a Michelin star in January 2004 and three stars in the revered *Egon Ronay Restaurant Guide* 2005. The relaxed décor of this 75-seat brasserie is reflected perfectly in the laid-back menu choices such as Vanilla Belgian Waffles with Blueberry Compote or Homemade Strawberry Jam, Scottish Smoked Salmon with toasted bagel and cream cheese, and their tasty fry-ups and bacon sarnies. I'm sold.

• **Tom Aitkens, 43 Elystan Road, Chelsea, London SW3 3NT**
• **T: 020 7584 2003**

Most fabulous for celebrity spotting: The Cuckoo Club

The Cuckoo Club spreads glamour and exclusivity over two floors, visited by the likes of Mick Jagger, Leonardo Di Caprio, HRH Prince William and HRH Prince Harry, Kate Moss, Orlando Bloom and David and Victoria Beckham.

The Cuckoo Club committee is perhaps what sets this members' club apart from others, since it includes Bryan Ferry, Jemma Kidd, Jools Holland, Alice Temperley, Joseph Fiennes, Guy Chambers and Dougray Scott, amongst other respected figureheads.

I visited the ground-floor restaurant serving European contemporary cuisine. At first it can seem daunting, dimly lit and terribly fashionable, but the friendly and knowledgeable staff soon make you feel at ease and you realize that the initial elitism you may have smelt was actually excellence. Head Chef Fernando Stovell insists on a '*mi casa es tu casa*' approach, taking the time to interact with and serve his diners personally, sourcing all his own ingredients, and ensuring that his wine and food complement one another perfectly. It's a claim and an approach that he certainly achieves, since my request for a wine that brought out the flavours of my perfectly pink beef was exactly met, and the *amuse bouche* expertly cleansed my palate for the mouth-watering dessert. If you want to spoil yourself or impress a date, you will definitely accomplish that here.

If you fancy working off all that delicious food, boogie in the rock-chic club afterwards.

....

• **The Cuckoo Club, Swallow Street, London W1B 4EZ**
• **T: 020 7287 4300**
• **W: www.thecuckooclub.com**

See also E: Entertainment.

●●●●●●●●●●●●●●●●●●●●●●●●●●●●

Most fabulous for sushi: Crazy Bear Members Club

●●●●●●●●●●●●●●●●●●●●●●●●●●●●

Crazy Bear is a group of eateries and hotels that offer some of the most elaborate, eclectic and elegant interior design I've ever seen, combined with fresh food, experienced staff and an intimate atmosphere. The latest addition to the group is their private members' club in Covent Garden, London. It is easy to miss, as there's no signage and you ring the doorbell to gain entry, but this just adds to the exclusivity. Inside you will find flamboyant décor – with every wall a different texture, from suede and velvet to leather studded with Swarovski crystals. I couldn't help but stroke my way through the venue as I walked down the stairs to the private booths and laid-back eating area. Here, I listened to Brazilian beats and noshed on the best sushi I've ever had! Chef Jirayu Tungchuwong (Bird) was head chef at the acclaimed

Kyoto restaurant in Israel for twenty years – and you can certainly tell! Though cool and quirky, they don't do conventionality or pretentiousness, so members wanting fun and quality should apply. Various packages are available.

....

• **Crazy Bear, 17 Mercer Street (corner of Shelton Street), Covent Garden, London WC2H 9QJ**
• **T: 020 7520 5450**
• **W: www.crazybeargroup.co.uk**
(see the website for other venues across the UK)

●●●●●●●●●●●●●●●●●●●●●●●●●●●●

Most fabulous for trying a bit of everything: Pesto

●●●●●●●●●●●●●●●●●●●●●●●●●●●●

Pesto is about experiencing traditional Italian food in a new and exciting way – tapas style. Their menu is made up of lots of small dishes, with different flavours from around Italy, so you get to try a little bit of everything that you fancy. This is a great way to sample new dishes for the first time, or simply to have your cake and eat it (quite literally if you like)!

....

• **Two branches in Manchester and one in Liverpool**
• **Manchester: 115 Deansgate, Manchester M3 5NW**
• **T: 0161 831 9930**
• **W: www.pestorestaurants.co.uk (N)**

●●●●●●●●●●●●●●●●●●●●●●●●●●●●

Most fabulous for foodies: nahm

●●●●●●●●●●●●●●●●●●●●●●●●●●●●

nahm is an incredible Michelin-starred Thai restaurant situated in The Halkin Hotel, Belgravia, London, and the first Michelin-starred Thai

D

Dining & Domestic Bliss

restaurant in Europe, no less. The cuisine is based on ancient royal Thai traditions, spiced by Australian chef David Thompson.

Thai dishes, as well as updates on the theme using British ingredients, make the delicious range of food simply unbeatable. The fish soup is a triumph, with a blend of intoxicating flavours fighting for attention in your mouth. Michelin-starred? Absolutely.

• The Halkin, Halkin Street, London SW1X 7DJ
• T: 020 7333 1234
• W: www.halkin.como.bz

Most fabulous for theatrics: Min Jiang

Min Jiang is the minimally elegant Chinese restaurant on the tenth floor of Kensington's Royal Garden Hotel, affording spectacular views of Kensington Park. Dim Sum, spicy Sichuan treats and the famous Beijing Duck are served, which you simply must try.

The ducks are cooked in a wood-fired oven and presented in the traditional multi-course manner. Eating the duck here is something of a ritual. The chef carves it at your table and offers you the crispy skin to enjoy first, followed by pancakes served with a variety of dipping sauces and flavours including shredded spring onions, cucumber, hoisin sauce and strong minced garlic paste. The rest of the duck meat is prepared according to your taste. You can choose from an accompaniment of soup, noodles, rice or stir fry to help you devour the rest of it!

• Min Jiang, Royal Garden Hotel, 2–24 Kensington High Street, London W8 4PT
• T: 020 7361 1988
• W: www.royalgardenhotel.co.uk

Become a food critic

If you love dining out so much you wouldn't mind turning pro at it, then why not become a mystery diner? Mystery Dining gives you the opportunity to enjoy reimbursed restaurant meals frequently, in return for completing a detailed questionnaire about each visit. To be a successful mystery diner, you'll need to show your commitment and interest in giving detailed, fair and objective feedback. They provide initial training and a tailored briefing for each visit you undertake to get you started on the right path.

The performance of mystery diners is monitored and those producing the best reports secure the earliest choice of available dates. The budget for the dining experience will be pre-agreed, so there's no ordering a bottle of Krug alongside your sirloin steak and ten side orders! This is a professional opportunity for keen foodie contenders.

• W: www.mysterydining.co.uk

Dinner parties

If you lurve the whole dining experience and fancy yourself as a top-notch chef in your own kitchen, then why not host your own social gathering? Dinner party etiquette, however, can be a minefield of trip-

ups and it's important to get such an intimate affair right. So that you can be the hostess with the mostest, I ask Damian Clarkson to divulge his expert advice on how to avoid a disastrous dinner party.

Damian Clarkson is managing director of Red Snapper Events, and has catered for some of the most prestigious private parties and large-scale events of the social calendar. Damian has worked alongside clients including Fashion Fringe, Aston Martin, *OK!* magazine and the S. Pellegrino World's 50 Best Restaurant Awards, as well as being official caterer for Ian Fleming's Bond Bound Exhibition and many private dinners – and I've picked his brain for you...

Top 10 ultimate dinner party faux-pas by Damian Clarkson

1 Time management: Be as prepared as possible; do as many of the kitchen preparations as possible beforehand, leaving you free to socialize.

2 Dietary requirements: You must try to cater for any dietary requirements; ask guests beforehand, they will appreciate your thoughtfulness.

3 Airing your laundry in public: Make sure the house is tidy with all washing, etc. put away. No one wants to look at your underwear drying while they eat dinner.

4 Unexpected guests: Finalize your guest list. Ensure you know exactly how many people are coming; having an empty seat is just as bad as squeezing in one extra.

5 Hitting the bottle: Being drunk is never glamorous, but a drunken host is sinful, especially when it leads to serving burnt food. Don't be tempted by a tipple before people arrive.

6 Mystery diners: Ensure that you introduce people. Everyone around the table should know who they are dining with.

7 Nipping to the shop: Make sure you have food and wine to last the evening – nothing is worse than leaving your own party and no guest should go home hungry or be searching for a drink.

8 Chained to the kitchen: Although it's important to make sure the food is delectable, it's just as important to spend time with your guests. So don't spend the majority of your time back of house.

9 Let me entertain you: Dinner party entertainers such as magicians are very old hat and just plain tacky. Spend the money on some extra bubbles to ignite conversation.

10 Shutting the door: Don't rush your guests out of the door at the end of the night. Even if you are exhausted, be a welcoming host till the very last guest leaves.

• **Red Snapper, Unit 10, Bermondsey Trading Estate, 235 Rotherhithe New Road, London SE16 3LL**
• **W: www.redsnapperevents.com**

Try before you cry!

Another top tip comes from *iLoveMyGrub's* editor, Helenka Bednar, who has written for the BBC, Time Out, EasyJet, Virgin Media, Ryanair and AOL. Aimed at complete foodies, the team at *iLoveMyGrub.com* review great places to eat out, devise fabulous ways to eat in and keep readers abreast of the best recipes, food products and news around.

Helenka says, 'Whenever you throw a dinner party (no matter how casual), ensure that you've tried out the recipes you're using beforehand. There's nothing worse than that dreaded feeling of pulling something out of the oven that looks more like a car crash than a culinary showpiece. Cooking a dish you've mastered before will leave you confidently attending to your guests, instead of flapping about in the kitchen in a frenzy.'

• W: www.iLoveMyGrub.com

The finishing touches

Being a fabulous cook does not guarantee a fabulous dinner party. Detail is also key, so ensure you make your table look beautiful too, with tableware from entertaining dynamo **Scarlett Willow**. Choose from their selection of placemats, coasters, serving mats, glass platters, napkins and more.

For that extra special touch which is bound to set the table talking, design your own – you can guarantee your guests won't have seen them anywhere else, and to mark a special occasion this is a truly personal approach to a dinner party to remember.

Co-founder Clare Gradidge says, 'I'm not a fan of the paper napkin. In my opinion, no table is complete without beautiful cotton or, better still, linen napkins. It makes all the difference.'

• **Scarlett Willow, 1b The Village, 101 Amies Street, London SW11 2JW**
• **T: 020 7751 0865**
• **W: www.scarlettwillow.co.uk**

Also try **Talking Tables**, provider of stylish and coordinated accessories – full of ideas for fun finales, post-meal success and little gifts for your loved one. Try the sexy red heart-shaped sparklers – they're like the modern upgrade to footsie!

• **W: www.talkingtables.co.uk**

See also **V: Vintage** and **S: Shopping** for more ideas.

Picnics

Lulu Gwynne is the founder and owner of Betty Blythe, a beautifully designed and resplendently stocked fine food pantry in Brook Green, West London, that sells homemade cakes and specialist foodstuffs, all in gorgeous and quirky surroundings.

Born in Worcestershire, Lulu Gwynne blossomed in the Hereford countryside. Her passion for tea and cakes grew from evenings spent drinking tea from the pot and chatting about starting a glamorous life in London.

An award from the Queen as one of Britain's Young Achievers gave Lulu her first taste of being in London, and she became an avid fan of the capital from then on. In starting up her own shop, Lulu wanted to create a character that would spark customers' imaginations, and she used the shop's street name to come up with 'Betty Blythe'. She was pleasantly surprised to discover that the character actually existed and was a wonderfully glamorous 1920s film star! Lulus then took inspiration from some of London's finest food and drink establishments and added her own touch, to create an elegant but fun environment filled with her favourite foodstuffs, designs and trinkets with tea and cakes served from beautiful porcelain.

The glamour and charm of the shop spreads into her outside catering service, so who better to ask for advice on how to throw a resplendently decadent, charmingly English picnic but Lulu Gwynne?

How to have a fabulous picnic

Spontaneous picnics are fabulous! When the weather is gorgeous and you have emptied the pantry of goodies, pack everything and off you go! Sometimes it does help to be a little prepared. So here are the Betty Blythe tips on how to be ever-ready for a perfect picnic…

Dress for the day

It should be a sunny day for your perfect picnic, so to choose the perfect dress to spend the day in, think about how comfortable the dress is to sit in – anything tight around your waist is bad news for digestion, and don't choose anything too short, as the chaps don't need a flash of your undergarments while enjoying their eats.

Don't forget a blanket!

Genteel folk who picnic in the outdoors must show a commitment to a day of lazing and indulging by having the essential summer luxury of a wool or cashmere blanket. Don't forget fans, pillows and sun hats. One's delicate skin can be saved by having a sun umbrella – choose a light colour shade and decorate with pretty bows and frills!

Cool bag/box

Picnic hampers are beautiful for keeping all your eating equipment in, but the food itself is best stored in a cool bag or box. Do not turn up with plastic bags! If in doubt, borrow these types of things from a kind neighbour.

Games

Taking games to your picnic is so much fun! Think boules, a pack of cards, or, if you want to frolic with lawn games, a croquet set is key to an afternoon well spent.

Beverages

On your picnic, it's essential to bring beverages. White and rosé wines are very good. Champagne is to be encouraged, as it's perfect to accompany things like smoked salmon and other picnic foods.

For cool drinks, try a refreshing lemonade or ginger beer. Much needed after all that exertion and exhilaration from the lawn games.

Food choices

For a period picnic, use your vintage china packed safely away with your linen napkins. Betty Blythe food favourites are sandwiches with salmon and cream cheese, thin slices of ham or chicken with asparagus and vinaigrette, rice salad with celery, nuts and raisins, a fruit and cheese plate and, to complete your picnic, plenty of fresh strawberries, a Victoria sponge and lashings of good cheer!

Composed by Lulu Gwynne of Betty Blythe.

• **Betty Blythe, Fine Food Pantry, 73 Blythe Road, Brook Green, London W14 0HP**
• **T: 020 7602 1177**
• **W: www.bettyblythe.co.uk**

Back to the garden

A great place to host your first picnic is Back to the Garden. In a stunning, vast barn, the owners of Back to the Garden sell a range of organic meat, fruit and vegetables – all from their thousand-acre organic farm, which has the ancient woodland of Swanton Novers National Nature Reserve at its heart. Make a day of it and set up your picnic on the green – and be sure to try the homemade cakes!

• **Letheringsett, Holt, Norfolk NR25 7JJ**
• **T: 01263 715 996**
• **W: www.back-to-the-garden.co.uk**

Domestic bliss

If you're more of a Gabrielle Solis than a Brie Van de Kamp, don't sweat it – fake it! There's nothing wrong with hiring help; besides, faking is much more realistic than trying to be all things at once. It can be tiring acting the perfect housewife, chef, wife, career woman and friend, so take a break and put these Godsends on speed dial...

Junk and Disorderly rubbish removal service

Order a van from Junk and Disorderly to remove the rubbish you can't/won't shift. They'll happily tow away anything from unwanted books to old furniture and general trash. Just fill in the online questionnaire to get a quote, select a time, and a handy helper will get their hands dirty for you.

• **T: 0800 191 0055**
• **W: www.junkanddisorderly.com**

Yes, I did it all myself: The Christmas Dinner Company

What a find! If you tend to stress out over the Christmas dinner or want to impress your in-laws minus the strain, The Christmas Dinner Company delivers a complete, chilled and traditional lunch to your door on 23 December, catering for 6–8 or 10–12 people.

Everything is prepared as much as

possible for you – the vegetables are peeled, sauces made and there's even cooking instructions and a time planner to take the stress out of preparation so you can enjoy the day. Genius!

Oh, and be sure to take all the glory on this one – it will be our little secret.

• W: **www.christmasdinnercompany.co.uk**

Bring in the cleaners: Absolutely Spotless

Absolutely Spotless cleaning company undertakes professional cleaning of homes, flats and offices in London and the Home Counties, offering a 7-day/24-hour service, which can be arranged at short notice. The team erase years of sloppy housework to restore the shine and sparkle in your home.

• T: **020 7839 8222 or 020 8932 7360**
• W: **www.absolutelyspotless.co.uk**

Magnetic doorganizer, perfect for the kitchen or office

This magnetic 'doorganizer' will stick to the fridge/filing cabinet and has pockets for your essentials like keys, takeaway menus, iPod, remote controls – stuff you always need to hand but always end up losing! Well, not any more!

• W: **www.giftlab.co.uk**

One machine does it all: Thermomix

It sounds too good to be true; a single machine that can replace virtually every other piece of kitchen equipment and takes up hardly any space. Really?

Chef Simon Daniel says, 'With this wonderful technology, I make bread dough in less than two minutes and don't raise a sweat. I create sorbets, sauces, curry, cakes, dressings and much more, all using this single machine. The Thermomix can weigh, chop, crush ice, whip, blend, steam, slice, dice and even cook – just follow the steps, load up the machine and put your feet up while all the work is done for you.'

At last, a glimpse into the future of advanced technology turning kitchen chores into no-hassle bliss! On delivery, you'll get a two-hour demonstration and will become a whizz in the kitchen in no time.

• **UK Thermomix, Pinehill, Sunning Avenue, Sunningdale, Berkshire SL5 9PW**
• T: **01344 622 344**
• W: **www.UKThermomix.com**

Too much to do? Cushion the Impact!

With endless commitments to work, family, friends and clients, it can be difficult to accomplish everything you set out to do each day. Cushion the Impact step in and take care of every hassle you may have, from clearing clutter to researching a holiday, or the mundane yet time-consuming tasks such as putting photographs into albums. They'll also take on larger tasks such as organizing an event for you. You'll start to wonder how you lived without them.

• T: **020 7704 6922**
• W: **www.cushiontheimpact.co.uk**

Do you need a house-sitter or pet-sitter? Call Animal Angels!

Animal Angels House-Sitters and Pet-Sitters provide a professional pet-sitting and house-sitting service while you are away. The pet-sitter will also administer medication and follow special diets or food regimes where needed, take the pets for as many walks as you request, feed them at their usual times, groom them and, most importantly, give them lots of love and cuddles while you are away, giving you total peace of mind by providing a trustworthy, experienced and reliable service.

• W: www.professionalpetsitting.co.uk

Dog trainers

If your pooch has a habit of lifting his leg and leaving his 'musky perfume' on your Gucci handbag, gnaws at your upholstery or takes *you* for a walk, then your furry little friend needs training. There are some excellent dog trainers out there, including Robert Alleyne who has tamed some of Britain's worst dogs on BBC3's *Dog Borstal* programme.

• For more information on one-to-one behaviour consultations and dog training classes, see www.thedogownersclub. co.uk or call 020 8355 4836

Doggie hotel: ALLDOG

ALLDOG will care for your pooch in their private home setting, where love and affection and optimal exercise are guaranteed. Their services include walks, day-care, grooming and overnights at the ALLDOG Ranch. They can create bespoke programmes that include fitness and nutrition and when it comes to grooming and beauty, they have a selection of all-natural and organic products. They even bake their own dog biscuits with flavours such as 'Salmon Snacks', and 'Herbal Treat' for the vegetarian doggies!

• W: www.alldog.co.uk

Pooch Palace

Pooch Palace is exactly that. Their 'Home from Home' boarding is for those who don't like the idea of putting their pet into kennels. Your pooch will have all the comforts of home by actually living with the owners of Pooch Palace, in their home, though the five kennels are also exceptional. Equipped with underfloor heating and attached covered runs, the kennels provide spacious settings, plus there's also an enclosed half-acre secure paddock for dogs to 'socialize' and exercise at their leisure.

They board only ten dogs at any one time, stating that 'smaller numbers of dogs lead to less noise and stress'. All dogs are walked three times daily for 40 minutes at a time, being taken out at different times or in small groups.

It's enough to leave you envious!

• **Pooch Palace, Patley Bridge, Harrogate HG3 5QQ**
• **T: 01423 715 823 or 07598 561534**
• **W: www.pooch-palace.co.uk**

Get organized ... with The Holding Company

The Holding Company specializes in providing stunning ideas for storage and organizing things, in a range of finishes from natural woven materials to recycled fibreboard, from moulded acrylic to fabricated metal. With clever storage that looks good if left on show, you can transform your space room by room, making it clutter free. From bedroom to bathroom, kitchen to garage they have numerous methods that help give our lives structure and organization. I'm terribly organized and have a place for everything – after all, a clutter-free, organized life is an easier, less stressful life. The Holding Company's acrylic drawers and open cubby storage system with 'easy view' are both great for storing your accessories and cosmetics in perfect order. They enable you to see everything at once, so you can pick out your accessories in double-quick time and remember what you actually have!

• **The Holding Company, Unit 2, Finchley Industrial Centre, 879 High Road, London N12 8QA**
• **T: 020 8445 2888**
• **W: www.theholdingcompany.co.uk**

Dining & Domestic Bliss

D

Eco-living

If you find it a challenge to recycle at times, let alone find space for the three bins required, you can do your bit to help the environment, improve lives and communities, save energy and have a fabulous lifestyle with my pick of the best eco-chic products and places…

Eco-delicious: Water House

Water House aims to be the greenest, most ethical restaurant in London. Fitted with sustainable materials and a solar-panelled roof, the space uses renewable hydro-electricity. They compost kitchen waste and the menu is shown on a board, eliminating the need for paper menus. Oh, and the food is pretty scrummy too.

• Water House, 10 Orsman Road, London N1 5QJ
• T: 020 7033 0123
• W: www.waterhouserestaurant.co.uk

Want to save time and save the planet? You need Eco Concierge

Eco Concierge is a hands-on lifestyle management service for people who are interested in being greener but don't have the time or know-how to make the change.

The *Quick Fix* programme is for people who want to tackle their most significant impacts in one hit. You'll have a free assessment of your current footprint, then, if you want to take it further, a personalized solution will be created for you by their experts.

So, if they're assessing your home, they won't turn round and say, 'Get some loft insulation,' they'll actually organize a quote for you, make sure you understand the process and benefits, and even be at the house to let the builders in.

Your starter pack contains loads of exciting freebies to help you begin your journey – what an easy way to help save the planet!

- T: 0118 9591088
- W: www.ecoconcierge.org

Eco beauty: Green People

Green People products offer excellent value, they are effective and concentrated, containing a very high level of active plant extracts, and they are expertly formulated using certified organic ingredients. The quality means that only a small amount is needed, so the products will last you ages. Also, the fact that their skincare products contain over 90% active organic ingredients – compared to 'high street' products which normally have an active ingredient level (non-organic) of below 6% – means you know you're doing your bit to go green too.

- W: www.greenpeople.co.uk

Eco-logic: Thequietriot

Thequietriot.com showcases products, services and experiences which are well designed and energy efficient or sustainable. If you really don't know where to start, this is your shining light.

- W: www.thequietriot.com

Fabulous energy-saving products

This lot will help you save money and reduce your carbon dioxide emissions without compromising on style.

Pure DAB radio

We all know DAB is a fabulous improvement on FM radio quality. But did you know digital radios are inherently extremely energy hungry, because they work in perpetual standby mode? Well, Pure Radios are the first range to be accredited by the Energy Saving Trust. The Mio, which comes in five fab colours, reuses a few design ideas from the 1950s for chic vintage appeal, yet the technology is bang up to date.

- W: www.pure.com

Osram candle-shaped low-energy lightbulbs

Energy-saving lightbulbs have always been a fabulous idea – for your pocket and the environment – because they use up to 80% less electricity than a standard bulb, but produce the same amount of light. The initial ugly, gigantic bulbs have been replaced with stylish energy-saving equivalents.

Visit the Energy Saving Trust's website to discover how a bright idea has got even better.

....

• W: www.energysavingtrust.org.uk/lighting

• •

Smeg retro appliances (dishwashers and fridge-freezers)

• •

The average dishwasher is used for 247 cycles. An energy-efficient dishwasher uses around 40% less energy than an old, inefficient model. Thanks to its AAA rating, Smeg's retro-style dishwasher (DF6FABRO) has been endorsed by the Energy Saving Trust. Now for the science bit: this machine uses just 15 litres of water and the unique Aquatest function means that the dishwasher uses electronic infrared sensors to measure the clarity of incoming water, thus keeping water and energy consumption to a minimum.

UK households use £1.8 billion worth of electricity every year on cooling/freezing food and drinks. An energy-efficient fridge-freezer uses only 40% of the energy to do the same job as a ten-year-old appliance, and could save a home up to £34 a year by reducing CO_2 emissions by 142kg! The Smeg FAB28 fridge-freezer is A+ rated for energy efficiency, offering a superbly stylish appliance that looks fabulous and also operates on an ultra-efficient level.

....

• W: www.smegretro.co.uk
• For information about Energy Saving recommended appliances and products, see www.energysavingtrust.org.uk/recommended

• Sort through over 3,000 products and compare prices at www.energysavingtrust.org.uk/compare
• For more advice about Energy Saving recommended products, and about energy saving in general, call your local advice centre: 0800 512 012

• •

Swig with SIGG

• •

The reusable and recyclable bottles, made from a single piece of pure aluminium, help to reduce landfill waste caused by disposable plastic water bottles. In Europe 30 million plastic bottles are dumped into landfill every day. With plastic taking over 1,000 years to biodegrade, purchasing a SIGG bottle helps consumers to be proactive for the planet!

SIGG are tested to be 100% safe, light, durable and leak-proof, they are good for the environment and come in fashionable designs: hydrate in eco-style!

....

• W: www.sigg-aluminium.co.uk

• •

Pure Design

• •

A luxury online ethical gallery presenting a range of ethical products, from fashion accessories and decorative art to home and garden products and private commissions from a range of artists.

....

• T: 020 7193 2885
• W: www.puredesigncompany.co.uk

• •

Reuse

• •

We All Reuse encourages and

publicizes the work of designers and manufacturers who reuse both industrial and consumer waste, showcasing interesting ideas and events, and provides a members' network with forums and resources. Edited and maintained by volunteers and the designers themselves, We All Reuse promotes efforts to reuse, stating that this is one of the most effective ways of reducing our consumption and therefore our impact on the environment.

• **W: www.weallreuse.com**

Eco-bride: Hennumi

Hennumi bridal and special occasion hair accessories combine recycled and off-cut fabric with freshwater pearls, Swarovski crystals, feathers and vintage mother-of-pearl buttons.

Tosin Trim, Hennumi's designer, aims to promote an appreciation for the value of unwanted fabric and clothing by reusing such material in the creation of desirable accessories. Subtle hints of previous uses of fabrics can occasionally be seen, such as the reuse of buttons and buttonholes from men's shirts on the cushions.

• **W: www.hennumi.co.uk**

See also W: Weddings for more bridal inspiration.

Tote-ally eco-stylish: Envirosax®

Envirosax® shopping bags are the original, designer reusable bags.

Envirosax® have a huge collection of totes to enhance pretty much any outfit, from the springtime florals of the 'Botanica' range to the bold and funky, black and purple hues of the 'Candy' series.

Envirosax® bags can be folded to the size of a mobile phone and stored in your handbag – ideal for those plentiful spontaneous shopping days – and they are so lightweight, just 40g, yet with stamina. I didn't really notice I was carrying it, despite it being crammed full of goodies.

• **W: www.envirosax.com (N)**

Energy saving

The latest eco-bling technology for the home is Smart Voltage Management. Any smart girl about town should be aware that simply reducing the amount of voltage coming into your home can save you 10% off your electricity bills and reduce your carbon emissions. Installing a **VPhase** VX1 in your home even makes energy-saving lightbulbs 10% more efficient! Ask your energy company, or visit the VPhase website to find out how you can save energy and save money at the same time.

• **W: www.vphase.com**

Natural Collection will help you to go green at work with their range of stationery, all recycled from old goods. For instance, their pens are made from car parts, electrical goods and crisp packets!

• **W: www.naturalcollection.com**

If you want to recycle, but fear the

Eco-Living & Entertainment

E

massive bins don't quite complement your worktops, then choose a funky design from **EcoCentric**. There's also a range of bags and cosmetics to choose from, so you can go green with ease.

• W: www.ecocentric.co.uk

Eco-rain: Mira Showers

The Mira Eco showerhead from Mira Showers is the ideal way to do your bit for the planet. It uses innovative technology to aerate the water droplets from your shower, thereby saving 75% of the water normally used, but without impacting on your brilliant and refreshing shower experience. Available in white or chrome and in two showerhead styles.

• W: www.mirashowers.com

Clear Water: design and build experts for natural swimming pools

Whether you are looking for a new pool build, have a pool or pond conversion or a derelict pool to renovate, Clear Water Revival has superior filter systems to meet your design requirements – no chemicals, no salt, just clean and clear water, filtered naturally, all year round.

A natural swimming pool offers a completely natural alternative to chemical pools/ozone or salt pools. They are chlorine-free and harness nature's processes, with micro-organisms and plants balancing the water chemistry and maintaining clean, clear and hygienic conditions.

• **Clear Water Revival, The Hub Bristol, Bush House, 72 Prince Street, Bristol BS1 4QD**
• **T: 0117 370 1360**
• **W: www.clear-water-revival.com**

Car boot sales

Car boot sales are officially cool. I have picked up no end of genuine vintage clothing, china tea sets and bargain CDs, and reusing someone's unloved and unwanted goods is a great way to recycle, since you're not making waste but instead giving a new lease of life to something. It's a very ethical way to shop and if you host your own car boot sale you're not only getting rid of old goods, you're giving them a new home *and* making lots of cash!

• **To find a boot sale near you, visit www.yourbooty.co.uk**

Entertainment

Whether you wish to be entertained solo or in a group, or are doing the entertaining yourself, this section is jam-packed with merry-making ideas...

Bars

From gigantic piss-ups to family days out, there's a bar certain to entertain you. Modern bars come in all shapes, sizes and styles. Frankly, we're lucky

to have so much choice. I've laid out a selection of bars to suit every mood and occasion.

Most fabulous for laid-back lounging: MOJO, Leeds

If Johnny Depp lived in Leeds, he'd frequent MOJO. I love this place. It knows what it's good at: serving delicious drinks, playing great music and providing a comfortable yet electric atmosphere. A place where you can totally be yourself. If it's a rock-fuelled atmosphere you're after, mixed with a cocktail list long enough to floor even the most experienced of drinkers, then look no further than MOJO. It's a regular celebrity haunt, with the likes of Chris Martin, Chris Moyles and the Kaiser Chiefs all spotted at some point.

• 18 Merrion Street, Leeds LS1 6PQ
• T: 0113 244 6387
• W: www.mojobar.co.uk

Most fabulous for the novelty factor: belowzero

belowzero is a luxurious, stylish bar and lounge hidden underground in the wine vaults once used by the British monarchy.

Located on bustling, cosmopolitan Heddon Street, London, belowzero is maintained at a constant -5°C. Everything in the bar is made from crystal-clear ice, including the walls, tables, chairs and even the glasses that the cocktails are served in, making this literally the UK's coolest bar. Be warned, though, the UV light ain't too flattering!

• belowzero restaurant and lounge / ABSOLUT ICEBAR LONDON, 31–33 Heddon Street, London W1B 4BN
• T: 020 7478 8910
• W: www.belowzerolondon.com

Most fabulous for original design: LoungeLover

LoungeLover is one of those super-cool places that make you wonder if the staff got the job purely on looks. Yes, everyone is super-glam in this establishment, but also surprisingly laid back. There is little pretence and the staff are gorgeous *and* experienced (how about that), happy to recommend a tipple from the extensive drinks list. This is one of three in a series of themed bars in London, alongside Annex3 and Les Trois Garçons. If not just for the whacky interior, you must go for the cocktails.

• 1 Whitby Street, Shoreditch, London E2 7DP
• T: 020 7012 1234

Most fabulous for understated cool: Smokestack

The Smokestack cocktail menu harks back to a bygone era of classic drink-making using one of the most extensive collections of Vermouths in Leeds. Among many impressive drinks on the list are the 'Medici Martini', giving a nod back to the quintessential 'Speak Easy' style of cocktail-making which informs the menu as a whole, and the stylish 'Snug Harbour', which takes its name from New Orleans' premier jazz club.

I asked for one of my favourites,

E

Eco-Living & Entertainment

a Bloody Mary – so good when it's mixed right, but bloomin' awful when it's wrong! Mixologist Tom Vernon confidently blended it to perfection and I'm now a regular purely for the cocktails. Well, maybe not just for the cocktails, since this small but perfectly formed bar offers one of the coolest vibes I've encountered.

• **Smokestack, 159a Lower Briggate, Leeds**
• **T: 0113 245 2222**
• **W: www.myspace.com/smokestackleeds**

Most fabulous for an all-inclusive night out: Bar 166 & Bistro

Managing directors Matthew Jones and Richard Hawley of Bar 166 & Bistro, The Shed and Bar SixtyToo have created a concept that is a welcome stroke of genius. A lot of people do the 'Horsforth Crawl', sampling a different atmosphere in a number of bars on the same street, before heading into Leeds on a Saturday night. Most people start at Bar 166 & Bistro at around 7 p.m. for drinks, often a meal too, and work their way to Bar SixtyToo around 9 p.m., further down the road. It usually costs around £15 for a taxi into town thereafter, yet Jones and Hawley offer a free service for their customers – a double-decker bus which picks up at 10 p.m. and 11 p.m. from outside Bar SixtyToo. If you get on the bus, you're given a token for a free shot of Jagermeister when it drops off outside the Shed Bar in Leeds city centre; your entire night out sorted!

I have to put emphasis on starting your night with a meal at Bar 166 &

Bistro, boasting simple British food with a contemporary twist. I was surprised and delighted to savour the presentation and taste of big-city bites with cosy-town prices.

To guarantee space if you have a large party of people, you can pre-book your free seats on the bus beforehand by calling or emailing the bar.

• **Bar 166, 166 Town Street, Horsforth**
• **T: 0113 2582661**
• **W: www.bar166.co.uk**

Most fabulous for jazz and fizz: Matt & Phred's Jazz Club

Matt & Phred's is open six nights a week, Monday to Saturday, 5 p.m. – 2 a.m. Enjoy great jazz in a relaxed atmosphere with fine wine or a glass of fizz at the Champagne and Cava bar.

• **64 Tib Street, Northern Quarter, Manchester M4 1LW**
• **T: 0161 831 7002**
• **W: www.mattandphreds.com**

Most fabulous for a hidden surprise: Socio Rehab

This cutting-edge cocktail bar oozes exclusivity due to its elusiveness. With no name on the door, tucked away 'somewhere on Edge Street in the Northern Quarter', Manchester, it's worth finding as it's run by a team from the Players Consultancy, who specialize in the very best of fresh-fruit concoctions. Find it if you can!

• **W: www.beautifuldrinks.com**

Most fabulous for alfresco glamour: Baby Blue

This trendy, intimate bar is based downstairs in the gleaming waterfront restaurant Blue on Liverpool's Albert Dock. It's something of a celebrity spot and the fantastic alfresco terrace is one of the coolest hangouts for the young and beautiful in the summer.

- **The Albert Dock, Liverpool L3 4AE**
- **T: 0151 702 5840**
- **W: www.blue-venue.co.uk**

Most fabulous for live music: Dry Bar

An urban, cool café bar, Dry Bar reminds me of a barn with its laid-back, no-fuss open space. The ground floor offers a very relaxed atmosphere where you can't hear the music, but if you fancy discovering the next Oasis, venture downstairs for a very intimate and personal experience with bands playing anything from punk to rock. Apparently Liam Gallagher and Shaun Ryder have both visited (and been barred!) from this buzzy establishment.

- **28–30 Oldham Street, Manchester M1 1JN**
- **T: 0161 236 9840**

legendary dance music spectacular caters for the modern woman a lot more precisely, with boutique camping, pamper trailers and shops. Partying until the early hours need not leave you looking like a mess any longer, and if you're in flip-flops but the sun turns to rain (likely), you can go shopping for some new wellies! Hey, any excuse…

- **W: www.creamfields.com**

Standon Calling

Leading boutique lifestyle festival, Standon Calling is where everyone is a VIP. Forget your snotty VIP entry cards, all types get together for the best in indie and electro vibes. There's a few innovative surprises too, such as the underwater disco!

- **W: www.standon-calling.com**

Magic Loungeabout

This is a family-orientated 24-hour musical picnic 'up north'. You can order breakfast in bed if you book into the VIP area – it's a festival of food and fun-loving.

- **W: www.themagicloungeabout.net**

Festivals

Creamfields

Creamfields is the world's biggest festival team, with festivals in 13 countries. This

Clubs

Most fabulous for celebrity spotting: The Cuckoo Club

The interior of the club is designed

by Blacksheep, the team behind the London headquarters of Hermes. Blacksheep describe the interior of the reception as 'jewelled-cigar-box-like', and these fashionably louche surroundings grace the entire club. With an alternative music policy, celebrities and royalty as their customers, and a committee that reads like a who's who of the fashion, music and society worlds, this is one hot members' club to be seen in.

- **The Cuckoo Club, Swallow Street, London W1B 4EZ**
- **T: 020 7287 4300**
- **W: www.thecuckooclub.com**

See also: D: Dining for details of their glam restaurant.

Most fabulous for stylish intimacy: The Valmont Club

The Valmont Club is based on Fulham Road, Chelsea, London, and presents a comfortable and somewhat private setting split into four main areas. Banquette seating areas are separated by gold-beaded curtains and a series of private velvet-curtained booths with individual music volume control are the real individual touch. If you hire a booth, you will have your own waitress service to bring you the most delicious cocktails served in a vintage Chambord bottle. You can choose your own glassware from a range including shooters, tall, Martini and Dom Perignon Sniffers (for two people).

Surrounded by a juxtaposition of neon, black glass bars, velvet drapes, art deco statues and antique lighting, you will have as much to look at as to

enjoy in this out-of-town venue, ideal for an intimate night out.

- **The Valmont Club, 266–266a Fulham Road, London SW10 9EL**
- **T: 020 7352 6200**
- **W: www.thevalmontclub.com**

Most fabulous for partying hard: The Sub Club

This intimate basement club has been a firm favourite among Glaswegian party princesses for 20 years. You'll find a mix of up-and-coming musicians and resident and guest DJs who have made this venue the popular party haunt it is today. Steel beams, exposed brickwork and low lighting make for an effortlessly easy-going yet thriving atmosphere.

- **22 Jamaica Street, Glasgow G1**
- **T: 0141 221 1177**
- **W: www.subclub.co.uk**

Most fabulous for making a day of it: The Factory Club

Situated next to the Ornamental Lake, in the trendy Custard Factory, Birmingham, The Factory Club is a 500-capacity music venue with two floors above the ground floor bar and club areas. The small bar on the ground floor leads to the club/gig room, which boasts a balcony overlooking the lake, and the second floor proves a popular choice for the VIPs. In the past, The Factory Club as been host to artists such as Amy Winehouse, Steve Lawler and Groove Armada. I'd advise making a day of it since The Custard Factory has a lot to offer and the Factory Kitchen Café and entire lake area comes to life in the summer with cocktails and barbecues aplenty.

....

• **Factory Events, Custard Factory, Gibb Street, Digbeth, Birmingham, West Midlands B9 4AA**
• **T: 0121 224 7855**
• **W: www.factoryclub.co.uk and www. custardfactory.co.uk**

Your access to entertainment

often extortionate entry fees, then join a members' club that offers you privileges. Innerplace membership provides the smart way to go out in London. Not only do members hear about the best places to go and the hottest new openings, but they are rewarded for being the ideal hip clientele with privileged access and amazing value-added benefits. These include free entry to the coolest members' clubs, complimentary champagne when dining at the finest restaurants, and the opportunity to attend film premieres, VIP events and Innerplace's own free monthly members' parties at the hottest venues in the capital. There is a very reasonable monthly fee to pay for all of that, so members can continue to enjoy the best London has to offer while actually saving money and staying in the know. I won't go out in the 'Big Smoke' without first consulting the knowledge of the team at Innerplace, and I trust them to get me into the right places, no questions asked.

....

• **T: 020 3167 0077**
• **W: www.innerplace.co.uk**

Girls' night out: GLM

GLM is the answer to the ultimate girls' night out, taking away the hassle of picking where to go and how to dress. After signing up for free membership, you'll receive a cheery email each week with the latest parties, events and special offers going on around London. All you need to do is pick which party

You're not on the list, you're not coming in: you need Innerplace

If you want to experience all the best places in London, but you don't want to queue or pay the you want to go to and you'll receive a confirmation email or text almost straight away. As well as free entry to selected nights, you'll be able to take advantage of drinks promotions as well as a full personal birthday planning service from Lola's cupcakes to a champagne reception – all you need to do is turn up! With surprisingly friendly door hosts to welcome you in (this makes a change), GLM allows you to feel fabulous and enjoy your night in style.

• T: 0870 042 3521
• W: www.glm.uk.com

Fun stuff

Blistering Barbeques

Blistering Barbecues supply all-weather barbeques of varying types for any occasion. They are the party planners of choice for alfresco dining and provide all sorts of unique ideas. They can come to you, or you can hire a venue through them – ideal for a social gathering or wedding with a difference.

Their blistering spit-roasts are a novel idea, providing delicious meat and a spectacle simultaneously. The blistering spit-roast comes with all the other Blistering services, including full menus for starters, side dishes, salads and puddings. If you're having a wedding, check out their legendary pavlova.

To top it off, chef Nigella Lawson says it's good enough for her: 'Blistering Barbecues cooked in my

garden this summer, and I long for an excuse to book them again.'

• W: www.blistering.co.uk

Electric Cinema

Electric Cinema, based on Portobello Road, London, had the great idea of two-seater sofas for you and your date to snuggle on. The bar serves every tipple you require and food is served in cones. The fish and chips are lip-smackingly delicious! Other typical cinema snacks are also served, and you can choose a spacious comfy leather armchair with a footstool all to yourself if you like. That's how cinema should be!

• 191 Portobello Road, London W11 2ED
• Box office: 020 7908 9696
• W: www.electriccinema.co.uk

The Camelot Theme Park

For families and big kids alike, The Camelot Theme Park will take you to a time where dragons roam free, King Arthur rules and knights do battle on horseback. The day starts in style with the Pendragon's Plunge wet and wild water slide that drops you off right in the heart of the action. What an entrance! The best ride is the 'king of the rollercoasters', Knightmare. At a bold 87ft high, the half-mile, two-minute experience of turns, loops and steep drops is sure to fulfil your thrill-seeking side. There are gentle rides for little ones too, and the daily jousting tournament is a magnificent presentation of skill and horsemanship. Merlin's School of Wizardry exhibits a spectacle of sorcery and magical illusions. There is a real mix of activities, adventure and entertainment for an active day out. The park's season usually runs from late May to early September, but call for up-to-date information.

• **Camelot Theme Park, Chorley, Charnock Richard, Lancashire PR7 5LP**
• **T: 0871 663 6400**

Blue Planet Aquarium

Blue Planet Aquarium boasts a 70m moving underwater walkway through Caribbean waters. Home to some 20 different species of sharks, they are fascinating to watch as you sit safely in your seat in the Aquatheatre! The Wobbegong Shark is a species renowned for its ability to blend into the background with its specially camouflaged body, and there is plenty of other marine life too – over 450 species in fact. There's more to experience outside with the Otter Enclosure, housing two families of Asian Otters, and the Octopus Adventure play area which is an ideal way to entertain children under 10 as you sip a frothy cappuccino at the outdoor café.

• **Blue Planet Aquarium, Ellesmere Port, Cheshire Oaks, Cheshire CH65 9L**
• **T: 0151 357 8800**

Ludlow Food Festival

Ludlow hosts an annual festival presenting top-quality small independent food and drink producers from the Marches, the England–Wales border country.

From demonstrations, talks and trails to some serious food tasting, a fun day out can be had – whether you're a foodie looking to sample the latest and best supplies, or just want to try something different and appreciate the good things in life.

• **W: www.foodfestival.co.uk**

Virgin balloon flights

Surprise a loved one with a romantic balloon flight – a different way to entertain yourselves, that's for sure! After a full pilot briefing, you'll enjoy a champagne toast and take to the air to see the sights with a bird's-eye view.

• **W: www.virginballoonflights.com**

See also O: Outdoor Pursuits for other entertainment and adventure ideas.

E

Eco-Living & Entertainment

Fashion

Ah, fashion ... an illustration of your personality, a status symbol, a form of therapy (of the retail kind). Fashion today offers a wealth of diversity and expression. There are numerous new designers emerging each year, along with dedicated shows, events and entire weeks across the globe, plus varying ways to shop – virtually and actually. With so many new businesses opening,

closing, succeeding, failing – one can get dizzy with the offering. I come to the rescue and seek out some fabulous fashion finds, some known, others not so well known, but each sensational, naturally.

Fashion care

Practical Princess is all about bringing complete wardrobe organization to your life, creating order where there is chaos, simplicity where there is clutter. They say, 'A badly hung wardrobe and overstuffed chest of drawers inevitably means that you are only wearing about 20% of your clothes,' so a correctly hung and organized wardrobe allows you to see, at a glance, what you have and – crucially – what you don't have. They claim that with their help 'selecting an outfit will become a pleasure'. They even sell the essential tools to help you achieve total wardrobe heaven, including specially designed hangers, shoe drawers and bikini bags.

Knowing she would be bursting with practical advice, I asked Practical Princess founder Elika Gibbs to share her top tips on how to organize our clothes, and therefore our lives a little! Today, Elika is linchpin to some of the world's most influential women, whose lives would not begin to work without her organizational input. Here she offers her advice on key areas such as how to care for your cashmere and how to make the most of each shopping trip...

How to declutter and get the ideal wardrobe by Elika Gibbs

Empty your wardrobe completely and clean it. Then go through all your clothes, shoes and accessories and section items into resale/charity/archive/keep. Relocate all items to be archived to a separate wardrobe section, or use a storage solution such as vacuum-packing, or wrap in acid-free tissue and box. Be firm with yourself; don't hang on to dated or tired items unless they have sentimental value. If you are unsure about a particular item, try it on. Box any sentimental items and store them elsewhere.

Streamline your wardrobe by rehanging everything on matching hangers. Practical Princess rubberized hangers are perfect, as they are specifically designed for each garment and reduce any damage or misshaping that could occur.

Rehang your garments in sections, i.e. all jackets together, all shirts together, and colour-coordinate your garments. If possible, keep seasons separate and cover all your out-of-season garments to protect them from dust. If you don't have the space for this, store items with a specialist garment storage provider.

Template-fold all of your vests, t-shirts and fine knits and section them by colour and type. Line your drawers with scented drawer liners for fresh-smelling clothes, and use drawer dividers to section underwear, tights, belts, scarves and ties. Make sure that drawers only have vest tops, t-shirts, underwear, scarves, belts, etc. inside them: don't ever mix up your drawers.

Photograph and store all your shoes in shoe drawers, as this protects them and will mean that you can see on the front of each box which pair of shoes is inside. Use Practical Princess bespoke shoe software to create a clear photographic image label for quick reference, and Practical Princess shoe drawers which can be stacked while the shoes remain easily accessible.

Take handbags out of their protective covers and use them for travel or to retain the handbag's shape, and store your handbags by size and colour somewhere that you can see them.

It's always good to have movable shelves, so that when the season changes and your wardrobe expands or shrinks, you will be able to cater for this.

Dressing tips

Once your wardrobe is organized, you will be able to see what you have, and by giving your wardrobe that 'boutique-like' feel, you will also be more likely to find forgotten treasures.

It is important each season to try on the contents of your wardrobe, so that you only have clothes in your wardrobe that you know fit, and to make sure that you have things that will work together. Also, you might find that by changing lengths and getting rid of pieces that no longer work or no longer fit, your wardrobe seems more uniform.

Each season, pull everything out and start again. If you aren't wearing certain items but want to keep them, put them away/archive them. These will seem much more exciting when you then go back to them the next season.

Only ever have in your wardrobe the clothes that you are currently wearing; this will make it much quicker and easier to get dressed every day. And remember that classic pieces can always be updated with accessories or a new pair of shoes.

Make a list of what your wardrobe is lacking. Having already organized everything will stop you repeat-buying. If you see, for example, that you have five black pencil skirts in your wardrobe, you don't need any more

black pencil skirts!

The content of a wardrobe is the most important. Sometimes big wardrobes can be overwhelming and it's rare that people use all the pieces. People tend to be more creative and get more looks when they have a smaller wardrobe with great foundation pieces, beautiful classics, fabulous accessories, i.e. shoes, handbags and jewellery, and some key pieces from the current season to update and lift it.

If you use a folding template to fold sweaters, everything will all be the same size when folded, making it easier to see and locate the one you want to wear when things are on top of one another.

The more visually appetizing your wardrobe is, the more it will inspire you to wear your clothes, to mix and match and to be inventive – so keep it organized, keep it tidy and keep it colour-coordinated. You wouldn't make a beautifully prepared meal, put it in a blender, then eat it off a dirty plate; treat your wardrobe the same way.

Remember, sometimes less is more.

Shopping tips

When you go shopping, always look at your existing wardrobe first and try to work from this. Have a look at what you already have and the good foundation pieces in your wardrobe, and go on from there to work out the gaps that need filling.

You can then go out shopping with the aim to buy what's missing and items that will complement your existing pieces. This way you will also prevent any repeat buys or mistake purchases that will not go with anything in your wardrobe.

Don't buy 'campaign pieces', as they will date.

Make sure you go shopping with a good list of exactly what you need, and stick to it.

People always forget to buy those essential generic items such as a white t-shirt. Replace basics such as vests, t-shirts and everyday shoes regularly.

Bring along any items that you need to match something up with.

Always shop according to lifestyle and not desire. If you are a stay-at-home mum, for example, you won't need a power suit. But do try to make sure that you have an outfit for every occasion that might come up, i.e. a dress for a christening, a wedding or the races.

Before you shop, think about your budget, and then stick to it.

Always check out the high street and secondhand stores to grab some great bargains.

If you are shopping for a mixture of high street and designer pieces, always start with high street and then move on to the designer stores.

It's important to have a great pair of jeans, as these can be dressed up or down, and it's also important to make sure that they are a great fit. It's always worth spending more to get that great pair of jeans.

It's also worth shopping for great accessories that you will be able to mix and match with outfits and that will update your wardrobe.

Always check the returns policy in stores, so that you know you can return items if you later change your mind or find that they don't fit.

Make an effort while you're shopping to imagine what the clothes will look like when you wear them, and always wear a strapless bra so you don't have to imagine what strapless items will look like without the bra straps.

How to care for your clothes and wardrobe

- Regularly empty and clean the inside of your wardrobe, including the hanging rails, using a mild bleach-free cleaning fluid, to avoid dust collecting and sitting on your clothes.

- Dry-clean your garments.

- Make sure that all the garments in your closet are ironed, as this will make getting dressed easier.

- Use boot inserts for your boots so that they don't wrinkle.

- Store all shoes in cardboard boxes

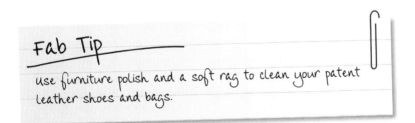

Fab Tip

Use furniture polish and a soft rag to clean your patent leather shoes and bags.

or drawers to protect them from dust and sunlight.

- If your shoes are not in shoe boxes and are on shelves or racking, it's essential that you use a feather duster every other day to keep them dust-free, especially on satins and suedes.

- Use shoulder covers for occasional wear and light-coloured garments to prevent dust settling on them.

- Good hangers are essential: never use wire hangers as these damage your clothes, and also be careful of padded and wooden hangers as these can also damage clothes, as well as taking up more space in your wardrobe.

Top ways to care for cashmere

- Handwash in tepid water with a good mild liquid soap.

- Dry flat and reshape while damp.

- If bobbles appear, lightly shave these and use a lint roller to remove any dust.

- Out of season, store in a cool dry place with moth repellent such as a lavender-scented product.

- Template-fold all cashmere sweaters and cardigans and store them on shelves together.

- **Practical Princess Ltd, 39 Stephendale Road, London SW6 2LT**
- **T: 020 7371 0276**
- **W: www.practicalprincess.com**

Where to buy your cashmere: my pick of the best

Caring for your cashmere is one thing, but where do you buy the best?

The classics that have years of experience in providing luxury are **Brora** and **The Cashmere Company**.

- **W: www.brora.co.uk (N) and www.cashmerecompany.com**

One of my favourites and one of the most comprehensive cashmere brands available is **Pure Collection**.

- **T: 0844 848 1030**
- **W: www.purecollection.com**

One of the most modern ranges out there, created by designer Maggie Hu, is **Simply Cashmere**. The range presents a collection of party pieces, simple separates and evening wear, plus there's a great fashion trends section to inspire you. The garments use 100% fine cashmere yarn, designed for modern women in mind – so much choice!

- **W: www.simplycashmere.com**

Fashion must-haves

The miracle jeans: Tummy Tuck

Dubbed the 'wonder jeans', Tummy Tuck Jeans by Not Your Daughter's Jeans have been celebrated by the fashion press and women the world over. With an invisible, patented corset-like structure hidden in the front of every pair and the use of 4% Lycra (regular jeans usually only use 2%), Tummy Tuck Jeans flatten the stomach, lift the bottom and smooth the thighs. Surprisingly, they feel so comfortable – like wearing your joggers but with all those added benefits. Twiggy is among the celebrity fans – and I'm happy to take a leaf out of her book! You are advised to go down a dress size too, due to the stretchiness, and it's better to squeeze in for the best results, but don't worry, this won't give you an unsightly muffin top.

• W: www.tummytuckjeans.uk.com and www.tummytuckjeans.org.uk (N)

You should also check out the originals in offering well-fitting, figure-fixing denim, **French Dressing Jeans** ('FDJ'), quite simply offering great-fitting jeans that work well with everything, in a choice of styles and with tummy-slimming, 'butt-lifting' properties.

• W: www.fdj.ca and www.fdjjeans.com (N)

The jewellery designer: Babette Wasserman

Classically trained at Central St Martin's College of Art in London, Babette Wasserman launched her own jewellery label and cufflink collection in early 1997.

Widely regarded by the fashion industry as the most progressive designer of stylish, fashionable and innovative jewellery, Babette Wasserman can be found in some of the most exclusive stores around the world. She is renowned for her original and versatile designs, which include the popular Saucer (reversible) cufflinks and her 'reversible' pieces of jewellery.

Personally, I don't think you'll find anything that compares in the same market: every piece sparkles with grandeur.

• T: 020 8964 9777
• W: www.babette-wasserman.com (N)

The one to watch: Kate Tailyour

Stylish and ethical, you will look amazing and feel great wearing Kate Tailyour. All the garments are made in England, many using British cloths, so the carbon footprint of the clothes is kept to a minimum, while those made using fair trade and organic cloths from India and Nepal help to support the growers and weavers there.

The fabrics are sophisticated and simple, incorporating silk, satin, jerseys and gorgeous prints and weaves. The range includes contemporary separates, with sports-inspired details, unique panelling and fabric combinations. Her signature wearable separates are always a big feature in the collection. I can only see great things ahead for this designer.

• T: 020 8968 5570
• W: www.katetailyour.co.uk

The novelty: Heidi Seeker

Heidi Seeker offer a huge array of unique, casual clothes and fun accessories, most of which are designed and handmade in their studio.

Two years ago, hip girl group

F

Fashion & Food

The Pipettes asked Heidi Seeker to design some personalized cardigans and necklaces for them to wear on tour. The response from The Pipettes fans was so overwhelming that they started offering a personalizing service online. Now there are six necklace styles to choose from and two cardigan designs, as well as the option to add a personalized charm to any of their bags. I've got a Pink Lady cardi with 'too fabulous' on the back – I couldn't resist!

For ladies on a budget faced with the mass-produced fashion dictates of the high street, Heidi Seeker offer an alternative without the huge price tag.

• W: www.heidiseeker.com

Old-school glamour: After Six

The Medici Ltd showroom off Oxford Street, London, is perfect for a touch of old-school glamour.

Imagine walking into a treasure trove of dazzling dresses, classic two-pieces and fascinators. Each time I go in, I want to dress up and be whisked off to the races, a grand ball or a glamorous cocktail lounge! If you're super-special, they arrange private viewings and offer previews of collections, private fittings and alterations so you can get fitted and walk away with your purchase that day.

Their label After Six is a stunning on-trend occasionwear label that offers clear flair – think sequins, tassels and flattering lines – and is adored by the likes of model Caprice.

• Medici Ltd, 17–18 Margaret Street, London W1W 8RP

• T: 020 7436 2882
• W: www.aftersixcollection.com

The street stylist: Kit'n'Kaboodle

If street style is more your thing, or you opt for the cosy look on occasion, try Kit'n'Kaboodle Clothing by Sallyanne McCrory. Providing a range of hoodies that are all individually customized by hand, Kit'n'Kaboodle work with you to find ideas and inspiration that will make your hoody unique and individual to your own style and personality.

I experienced the direct personal service with the founder Sallyanne, who asked me about my interests and ideas for the design of my very own one-of-a-kind hoody. I shared my love for peacock feathers and butterflies, while Sallyanne sketched and brainstormed with me, and she promised that the real thing would be in my hands in two weeks. I was delighted with the result and never knew hoodies could be so glam.

Each one comes with handwritten washing instructions and its own character name.

• T: 07815 917394
• W: www.knkclothing.com

The swimwear designer: Melissa Odabash

Melissa Odabash lived in Italy and modelled there for top Italian designers. As a former catwalk and swimwear model, she is experienced in what makes good and poor swimwear. She says, 'I was modelling suits that were sparkly and tacky and I just thought: I can do better than this.' So she did – creating her first bikinis by hand and taking them around the boutiques of Milan. Within two years her zebra-print bikini had become the best-selling item in the Victoria's Secrets catalogue. Another became the most popular swimsuit in America after it appeared on the cover of *US Glamour*. Odabash suits are now best-selling styles in top stores across the globe and I think her secret is down to the detail. For instance, Odabash does not use underwire or padding which can be uncomfortable or look unnatural. Instead, she uses fine twisted elastic, discreetly sewn into the delicate lingerie material used for lining. The look is softer and there is no feeling of it digging into your skin. Collections are often adorned with buckles, beading, shells and embroidery and there are styles to suit all body types.

Celebrities including Kate Moss, Jennifer Lopez, Paris Hilton, Elle Macpherson, Victoria Beckham, Catherine Zeta Jones, Teri Hatcher, Beyoncé, Uma Thurman, Sarah Jessica Parker, Heidi Klum, Halle Berry and Cindy Crawford all choose Odabash when holidaying themselves. Ah! So this is why they look so good in those swimwear shots (well, that and a fleet of make-up artists and clever lighting)!

....

• W: www.melissaodabash.com (N)

●●●●●●●●●●●●●●●●●●●●●●

The modern woman's man: James Lakeland
●●●●●●●●●●●●●●●●●●●●●●

James Lakeland has gone from strength to strength, offering women a complete capsule wardrobe. With a

luxurious collection all made in Italy, dresses are James's passion, with a vision that creates cutting-edge designs, sculptured to flatter and be versatile enough to suit a number of occasions.

....

• T: Stockist enquiry line 020 7636 7130
• W: www.jameslakeland.net

●●●●●●●●●●●●●●●●●●●●●●

The international favourite: Eley Kishimoto
●●●●●●●●●●●●●●●●●●●●●●

Eley Kishimoto is a husband-and-wife partnership forged in the early 1990s, and they are now one of the biggest names on the fashion scene, deemed the 'patron saints of print' and offering quirky collections for women. Various collaborations have produced footwear, hosiery, sunglasses, leather belts and other 'flash' collaborations, under the umbrella of 'womenswear mainline'.

In addition to this, numerous products such as wallpaper, furniture – upholstered and printed – and furnishing fabrics, glassware and crockery have been developed.

....

• 215 Lyham Road, London SW2 5PY
• T: 020 8674 7411
• W: www.eleykishimoto.com

●●●●●●●●●●●●●●●●●●●●●●

The stylist: Francesca Marotta
●●●●●●●●●●●●●●●●●●●●●●

Dubbed 'the new *enfant terrible* of fashion', Francesca Marotta is part of the new crop of young designers creating a buzz among fashionistas with her own award-winning collection, and she has also worked with celebrities such as The Scissor Sisters. A fashion designer by trade, Francesca

Fab Tip

Always carry a pair of flat ballet pumps in your bag and avoid wearing heels every day. I know it's tough if you love them as much as I do, but if you look after your feet, they'll look after you. You have to know when enough is enough. Most flats today fold in half, so they're small enough to fit into the chicest of clutch bags. **Coco Rose** has some gorgeous ballet pumps that fold and come in their own little bag.

W: www.cocoroselondon.com

says it is this talent that gives her styling abilities a more aesthetic edge than your average stylist, as she has the designer's eye.

Her design background gives her thorough knowledge of fashion history and all its eras, making her completely versatile and

knowledgeable about all the details that matter – from colour palettes to what actually works on the model and what will work on print.

But her style savviness doesn't stop at commercial genius. Francesca offers personal shopper packages where a consultation will first address your

Fab Tip

If you've got gorgeous leather shoes or handbags and they're looking a little tired, revive them by using a damp cloth lathered up with soapy suds. Use gentle circular motions to buff the leather and then wipe clean with a soft cloth and leather polish. Good as new!

needs. The all-important shopping trip then takes place, during which Francesca takes you around the relevant places, teaching you how to shop according to your body shape and lifestyle and for whatever occasion you require.

Her little black book of the fashion set also means that introductions can be made to a variety of fashion designers, bespoke tailors and even hair and make-up experts if you want to go for the full works. We should all have one.

• W: www.francescamarotta.com

The shoe designer: Charlotte Olympia

Charlotte Olympia shoes make me *drooool* … like Homer Simpson over doughnuts. They're works of art for the feet, beautiful to look at and so sexy to wear. Each shoe is finished with the signature gold spider web on the sole for extra individuality and detail. Using a mix of arresting colours, metallic and the most riveting platform designs, Charlotte Olympia heels are easy to salivate over.

• W: www.charlotteolympia.com

Fashion godsends

The ultimate dress hire (and my saviour): Girl Meets Dress

Girl Meets Dress is today's version of a dress hire shop but with the added bonuses of having the dress of your dreams delivered right to your door and then having it picked back up – no dry-cleaning, no shopping and no messing!

Hire casual and evening styles in a variety of sizes by the likes of Fendi, Marc by Marc Jacobs and Chloe. Some are also for sale. The selection is updated weekly, but if you're looking for something particular, drop them an email and they'll try to track it down. If this is not already a necessity in your fabulous life, it soon will be!

• W: www.girlmeetsdress.co.uk

The ultimate shoe hire: Cinderella-Me

Cinderella-Me was conceived following the success of designer fashion hire in the USA as exemplified by handbag hire companies like Bag Borrow or Steal, which featured in the film *Sex and the City*. The founders conducted market research in the UK which identified a new niche market for designer shoe hire. As a result, *Cinderella-Me.co.uk* is the first designer shoe hire portal in the UK, making many designs accessible. In the current economic climate, hiring is also a more sensible option. It allows women the freedom to alternate and vary their wardrobes without breaking the bank.

• W: www.Cinderella-Me.co.uk

How to turn a wobble into a wiggle

I'm a bit of an expert on how to walk in heels. In my earlier years, I assisted my older sister in her career as a global model, backstage and at fashion shoots, and picked up an awful lot of trade secrets on how to walk in skyscrapers minus the face-grimacing pain they can sometimes bring.

Since Carrie Bradshaw pranced around in her Manolos with Big, and Victoria Beckham decided high heels should be worn on every occasion (even to a theme park!), stilettos have become the ultimate fashion statement.

They're also a legendary weapon of mass seduction. One of the most celebrated sex symbols of all time, Marilyn Monroe, once said, 'I don't know who invented the high heel, but all women owe him a lot.' They're sexy and provocative, and they make the wearer appear taller and slimmer thanks to the added height they give.

However, heels can be a challenge to walk in. Limping, wobbling or feeling any pain neither looks good nor is it good for your health. It is important that you learn to walk in them with care for happy feet and a healthy you.

So, how do you turn that wobble into a wiggle?

Get fitted

Try on different heel heights, pick the one that's most comfortable for you and ensure that you have the right size. A size too small will hurt your feet, while a bigger size is likely to make you wobble and fall, so get your feet measured properly at a footwear boutique.

> **Fab Tip**
>
> If you are having the hem of your trousers taken up, be sure to get measured with your shoes on! Take the shoes you intend to wear with your newly tailored trousers with you, or you could risk getting ankle-swingers. Not a good look!

Prepare the shoe

Score the bottom of your shoes with a key or penknife to create rifts and a rough surface that will make them less slippery and afford you better traction.

Protect your tootsies

Grimacing in pain at chafing shoes does *not* look or feel sexy, so if you find it tough to break in your new pair of stiletto high heels or thigh-high boots, try aids like small gel cushions for the balls of the feet and heel inserts to help minimize rubbing at the back of the shoe. Prevention is the best cure.

Carry spares

Wearing high heels for a long time can result in a visit to the podiatrist, so you need to know when enough is enough. Carry some flat ballet pumps in your bag to change into before the potential pain hits.

Perfect your posture

Walking with ease in high heels all stems from your posture. If you don't find your centre of gravity, your weight will be distributed unevenly as you walk and this affects your balance, hence the common wobble.

Improve your sense of balance by standing first on one leg and then the other. Repeat this as many times as you like until you wobble less. Practise makes perfect!

The added height that heels give you can also cause stiff knees, causing you to tilt forward and grip your thighs. This posture is all wrong, making you look sorry for yourself and causing your ankles to wobble.

First, stand up straight, with your shoulders rolled back and down. Point your chest to the sky to lift your ribcage and look super-confident (there's a difference between sticking your breasts out and lifting your bust)! This engages your lower abs and strengthens your lower back to stabilize you and improve balance.

If you catch yourself slouching, correct yourself by practising this move regularly. It can be performed standing or whilst sat at your desk so there's no excuse for poor posture!

Finally, relax through the hips and knees to help you slide through the foot and step from heel to toe.

Make them look pretty

Finally, ensure that you treat your

tootsies to a monthly pedicure, at home or in your favourite salon. After being tucked away in shoes all day, they deserve a little pampering.

Keep them looking good with little effort with **Bio Sculpture Gel**, used at various salons nationwide. It comes in various colours from clear to hot pink. The gel is applied in thin strokes over your natural nail or acrylic tips just like an ordinary nail varnish, and each coat is set under an ultraviolet lamp. The gel dries incredibly fast, is non-sticky and will not smudge or chip! The colour will last until it grows out with your natural nails. For long-lasting nail colour, this is the only way to go.

Bio Sculpture Gel is available at Jo Pallan at Nicky Clarke, Leeds (www.NickyClarke. com) and selected Nails Inc. Bars across the nation. See www.nailsinc.com for your nearest salon.

Tailored to you: Evangeline Belle

Don't you just hate looking like everyone else? And don't you just hate finding the perfect dress, yet off the hanger and on you it gapes at the back or is slightly too short? Evangeline Belle is a luxury service for individual made-to-order fashion from the main line Evie Belle.

You can expect to be guided through your fashion choice with the head designer to establish what clothing items you require and for what occasions. Entire wardrobes, capsule collections or sensational one-offs can be created according to your tastes, lifestyle and your body, giving you tailored

clothing that fits you like a second skin.

Services include a style, design and fit consultation, and a made-to-order service covering dresses, coats and tailored suits – and the result is a range of individual pieces that will never be replicated, with individual fabric and colour choices or a bespoke design, which can be created by the client and guided by the designer.

**T: 020 8986 8608 or 020 7193 2381
W: www.eviebelle.com**

Fashion fixes

Clean Heels

Clean Heels are flexible heel-stoppers for stiletto heels in a plain clear or crystal rose design to stop you sinking in the mud at weddings, barbecues and the races, or being stuck between decking at garden events.

Simply put on a pair of Clean Heels stoppers, enjoy your day, then either dispose of them or rinse them off and pop them in your bag, ready for another day. I'm not sure about the street cred, but if you love your practical solutions, this is a fun one to try!

• **W: www.cleanheels.co.uk**

Classic Shoe Repairs

From reheeling to buffing shoes and mending a beloved handbag, you can do it all here. Surely a speed-dial must-have?

- **23–25 Brecknock Road, Islington, London N7 0BL**
- **T: 020 7485 5275**
- **W: www.classicshoerepairs.co.uk**

Tailors: Apsley

Apsley Tailors were founded in 1889 and are still owned by a member of the founding family. They are a solely bespoke tailoring company with no off-the-peg clothing, and all garments are made by hand.

Presenting a vast range of the finest fabrics from Scabel, Holland & Sherry, Ermenegildo Zegna and Loro Piano to Charles Clayton, Dormeuil and Wain Shiell, Apsley will give you fantastic quality for your money, reasonable prices and with speed. Suits you, Sir.

- **13 Pall Mall, London SW1Y 5LU**
- **T: 020 7925 2238**
- **W: www.apsleytailors.com**

Light relief: Love Your Shoes Gel Cushions

Why do beautiful shoes hurt? It could be a situation of 'no pain, no gain', but I even curse my beloved Manolos after a long day of teetering in them. If you ever suffer from that burning sensation on the ball of the foot or rubbing on the back of your heel, and you want to don your shoes minus the unsightly blisters, then get yourself some 'Love Your Shoes' gel cushions. The gels are specially designed to give you long-lasting relief on your feet. The well-cushioned, slimline gels are adhesive, washable and reusable, plus they come in a handy protective case, so you can store them easily and hygienically while on the move.

There are four types of gels in the Love Your Shoes range:

Ball of Foot Gel Cushions provide blissful relief from burning ball of foot pain.

Invisible Gel Heel Cushions provide soothing relief for heel pain.

Invisible Gel Heel Guards provide relief from sore heel rubbing and stop shoes from slipping.

Invisible Gel Spots provide extra relief for any sensitive spots on your tootsies.

- **Available from Superdrug (N)**
- **T: Thornton & Ross, 01484 842217**
- **W: www.loveyourshoesforlonger.com**

Air your laundry with The Laundress

Fashion experts Gwen Whiting (former fashion designer) and Lindsey Wieber (former head of sales for Chanel) are the co-founders of The Laundress™, a luxury fabric care and speciality detergent line. They saw the necessity of caring properly for their clothing and homes, but were unable to find products on the market that met their standards of delicacy, fragrance and sophistication. Then came the creation of their detergents and fabric care products with their uniquely developed fragrances of Cedar, Baby, Lady and Classic. My necessities include the Cashmere Shampoo and Denim Wash.

- **W: www.thelaundress.com**

Fashion sense

Bargainista is hosted by *koodos.com*, the leading online discount fashion boutique headed up by Miriam Lahage, who has over 20 years' senior buying experience for TJ Maxx, the huge US clothing discounter. Miriam posts advice on securing bargains and the news content is contributed by Susannah Barron, ex-*Guardian* and award-winning fashion journalist. So, with all this experience under their oh-so-fashionable belts, Bargainista share their top tips with *The Modern Girl's Guide to Fabulousness*...

Connecting with your favourite shop

You love that shop. It's the best curated, best edited, lovely shop with all the wares you adore. It has your favourite big names along with the beautiful brands you have just discovered. It's way too close to your flat. If you spend any more money there, you know you'll be in trouble. What to do? Apply to work there! Even if it's only for a few hours a month, it's well worth it.

- Staff discounts make a huge difference to the price you pay.

- You will know about sales ahead of time.

- If there are items that are slightly damaged, you could buy them and mend them.

- You will be on the list when they have special events or shows.

- Who could ask for a better employee than someone who already loves the shop?

- You might even get a chance to connect with some of the designers.

- Even if there are no openings now, establish yourself as a friend of the shop. You could get trained up so that they could call on you when they do need help.

Bargainista's holy grail in fashion sense

- Learn to sew. After all, those designer jeans are no bargain at all if they sit in your wardrobe for months waiting to be taken up.

- Stop being such a wuss about haggling. Everyone's at it these days – the salespeople expect it.

- Read the care labels and wash accordingly.

- Invest in rainwear. If we're talking cost per wear, a great trench is worth all last summer's unworn maxi dresses put together.

- Start saving. You want those McQueen heels by May? Better sacrifice that morning latte then.

- It's not a bargain if you have an item in the back of your drawer you've never worn; chances are, you bought it in a sale. Why is it that we so often go out to save money and actually end up wasting it by buying something we wouldn't normally pick, just because it's reduced?

Bargainista's five warning signs to help you avoid dodgy purchases

1 It's too small. If it doesn't fit properly, don't buy it. Be especially careful with items you think will stretch – sure, jeans will give a little, but not so much that if your flesh is bulging over the top this will disappear. The flipside of this, but probably much rarer, is: *don't buy something that's too big* and needs substantial alterations. In other words, if an item isn't flattering, put it back on the rail.

2 It's uncomfortable. This may be because it's too small, but alternatively it could be the cut, e.g. a pair of trousers fit on the hips but pinch on the waist, or shoes have straps that rub. Or maybe the fabric is scratchy.

3 It's expensive to clean. Tot up those cleaning bills before buying something that's dry-clean only – it could cost you £3 or £4 a time and double the price of the garment over its lifetime.

4 It's faulty or soiled. A loose button or hem is a simple job to rectify; a rip is not so easily dealt with. Likewise, are you confident that stain can be removed?

5 It doesn't blend in *with anything else in your wardrobe*. If you can't think of anything in your wardrobe

to match with a so-called bargain, then it isn't one. Either you are going to have to make a load of other purchases to create an outfit, or, more likely, the reason why it doesn't fit with your stuff is that it's not your style.

Finally, if it passes all these tests and you're still undecided, ask yourself … if you could afford to pay full price for it, would you still buy it? Or, given a bigger budget, would you opt for something else?

• **W: www.bargainista.co.uk**

Favours

Favours are a unique fashion collection created entirely by people who want to support a good cause. Basically, you can do your bit by saving old clothes from the bin and turning them into stylish new outfits, then donating them to raise money for charity. For the truly fashion conscious, customized clothes have never looked better.

All of the clothes donated to the Favours fashion collection are sold online to raise money for Body & Soul, a charity helping children, young people and families affected by HIV in the UK.

W: www.vinspired.com and www. bodyandsoulcharity.org

Fashion saviours

Sample sales have been known to turn the normally sane citizen into a fierce, frenzied fanatic with oversized

expensive handbag and sharpened elbows at the ready. However, I have fought whitened tooth and manicured nail to find the best ones out there for you, including online sample sales so you can shop till you drop in the comfort of your own home. The sales are on and your money's precious, so make sure you hit only the most worthwhile...

Sample sales

Brand Alley offers up to a whopping 80% off designer clothes, make-up, shoes and homeware products. Discounts are only available to registered members, but membership is free and it's easy to sign up. Each sale only lasts for a few days while stock lasts, but you'll always get an email notifying you of when the sales start so you can pencil in the time. You also get access to discounted homewares and beauty products for holistic style for less, and the blog is worth a read for its informative lifestyle articles. One of the best of its kind, for sure.

• W: www.brandalley.co.uk

DSUK give you designer clothes at amazing prices. They hold five fashion sales a year, each one lasting for four days and providing a range of womenswear, menswear, some childrenswear and accessories from over 100 different labels. Once you are registered on the mailing list, you will receive invitations to all of the events.

• W: www.designersales.co.uk

Fashion Confidential presents a myriad of fashion advice, inspirational buys and up-to-date gossip in the fashion and beauty world. Their VIP events, exclusive discounts, expert advice and must-have sales will keep you ahead of the fashion game – and it's all free!

• W: www.fashionconfidential.co.uk

Vente-privee.com is the original and biggest online private members' shopping club, which launched in the UK at the end of 2008 and has already celebrated its billionth visitor to a sale! Having first launched in Paris in 2001, vente-privee has since opened its virtual doors in Spain, Germany, Italy and the UK and is now the sixth biggest online retailer in Europe, with 7 million members and a 2008 turnover of approximately £450 million. Vente-privee has a cult following wherever it goes. Offering amazing sales with savings of 50–70%, women across the globe are poised at their computers waiting for a sale to go live. Sign up and see what all the fuss is about for yourself.

• W: www.vente-privee.com

Useful stuff

The Laden Showroom gathers independent designers from across the UK and also sells a selection on *www.asos.com*. They have a list of cool celebrity shoppers, including Noel Gallagher and Victoria Beckham. Great for when you want to discover something original.

• 103 Brick Lane, London E1 6SE
• T: 020 7247 2431
• W: www.ladenshowroom.co.uk and www.asos.com

Bedecked specialize in everything from attention-grabbing buttons and fastenings to exquisite ribbons, lace, braid, flowers and feathers. If you love fashion and frippery and customizing your clothing, you'll find a finishing touch here.

....

• 5 Castle Street, Hay-on-Wye, Herefordshire HR3 5DF
• T: 01497 822 769
• W: www.bedecked.co.uk

Fashion support

Fashion Enter Ltd

Fashion Enter is an industry-based specialist that offers real support and advice for today's talented designers and manufacturers. Its full guidance and networking opportunities, combined with an online presence and two retail boutiques, make Fashion Enter a unique company.

The website at *www.fashioncapital. co.uk* is a major business tool for all connected to the fashion industry. The members' only sections give specialist advice from over 15 leading industry experts on all major areas of the industry, including legal, accounts, patterns, production, design and intellectual property.

The two retail boutiques are situated in Croydon's Centrale shopping centre and in Vicarage Fields shopping centre in Barking, giving retail space to new and up-and-coming designers for a small fee. Fashion Capital and Fashion Enter also offer members a free online boutique via the websites at *www.enter-boutique.com* and *www.fcboutique.com*.

The **Showroom** combines designs from highly talented, up-and-coming designers and top retailers associated with Fashion Enter with designs by fashion students at Kingston College. Situated in Kingston upon Thames, next to the Bentalls Centre, the Showroom includes clients such as ASOS and Topshop, as well as overseas buyers, top retailers and a host of smaller boutiques. It's strictly invitation only and provides an exclusive gallery concept for today's diverse and dynamic fashion market. To date, over 17 designers have been selected by both Topshop and ASOS.

Profile is a static trade show and catwalk theatre, showcasing the very best ladieswear, menswear and accessory designers. It's a much-needed platform between Graduate Fashion Week and London Fashion Week. The late Isabella Blow stated, 'It is just amazing to see such vibrant talent here tonight. Having shortlisted the entries with Gerry DeVeaux, the total event has been a huge success for everyone. This Profile event has my full support for young designer talent of today.'

There's loads more on offer, too, from workshops and courses to events and public relations support.

....

• Fashion House, 1st Floor, 28 Station Approach, Hayes, Bromley, Kent BR2 7EH
• T: Fashion House, 020 8462 9620
• T: Croydon boutique, 020 8681 5014
• T: Barking boutique, 020 8507 3454
• T: The Showroom, 020 8546 8209
• W: www.fashion-enter.com

If this section gets you going, see also S: Shopping.

F

Fashion & Food

Food

There is so much variety on offer today – not just the type of food you have, but how you have it: in a restaurant, prepared at home, or delivered to you. From masterclasses to home delivery, from the health kicks to the indulgent, this section is sure to get your mouth watering…

Masterclasses

Passionate about fish: Billingsgate

Get enthused about the wonderful variety of seafood available with a masterclass. Fresh sea bass, bream, mackerel, sardines, plaice, cod, salmon and our absolute favourite, red gurnard, are a few of the species you could be working with. You'll learn to fillet, scale, clean, skin and pin bone – in fact, everything you need to know to give you more confidence with fish. You also take home the fish you've prepared, so make sure you bring a cool bag!

- Office: 30 Billingsgate Market, Trafalgar Way, London E14 5ST
- T: 020 7517 3548
- W: www.seafoodtraining.org

Create a week's worth of meals with a Michelin Star chef: The Kitchen

Since new retail food concept The Kitchen opened its doors in June 2008, it has captured the imagination of thousands of Londoners as the perfect meal-planning service and the only place in the capital where one can batch-cook Michelin Star meals for the whole family for less than £6 per head (prices subject to change).

The ethos is maximum effort in The Kitchen, minimal effort at home, and its daily sessions, designed and led by Michelin Star chef Thierry Laborde, have provided countless homes with the finest gourmet meals.

The Kitchen works by providing you with the finest fresh ingredients (washed, peeled, chopped and measured), an abundance of cooking utensils and all the equipment you could possibly need to create your very own culinary masterpieces. The shopping, chopping and pot-washing is done for you, leaving plenty of time to relax with a glass of wine!

It's all fabulously simple: choose your meals online, prepare your dishes at The Kitchen (inclusive of expert advice from Thierry and sous chef Claudio), and dazzle your friends and family with a Michelin Star meal at home.

- W: www.visitthekitchen.com

Butchery skills: Allen's of Mayfair

If you'd love to know where all the cuts come from, what's good for different cooking methods, where to find aged beef, how to French-trim lamb … then this team of butchers offers courses covering all of this information and more, specially devised to show you how to produce a selection of meats ready for the oven. The talented team will teach their students a range of cuts which are both interesting to prepare and easy to master.

....

If you would like to book tickets for the Butchery for Beginners class at Allen's of Mayfair, phone 020 7499 5831 for more information.

....

Barbecue perfection with Gaucho
....

If, like most men, your fella comes over all Gordon Ramsay when he gets a barbecue and a pair of steel tongs before him (but ends up burning all the meat), then send him to the award-winning Gaucho's weekly masterclasses. And why not go too? They will teach you how to barbecue the perfect Argentine Asado, the technique used for grilling meat to perfection. You will learn about different cuts of beef, lamb and pork, so you can impress your guests, or finally train up Mr Wannabe BBQ Chef of the Year…

....

• **64 Heath Street, London NW3**
• **T: 020 7431 8222**

....

Claridge's Masterclass Programme
....

With a long-standing reputation as the best of the best, Claridge's Masterclass Programme shares the secrets and skills of its own cooking team as well as renowned international chefs and guest experts.

The secrets of buying, preparing and cooking food are revealed as their executive chefs take you through the year, offering tailored classes to suit various occasions, including Christmas.

Along with a series of classes by Claridge's chefs, other highlights include the art of designing flower bouquets, and champagne masterclasses with tips on how to complement dishes with the correct champagne.

....

• **T: 020 7409 6307**
• **W: www.claridges.co.uk/masterclasses**

Food delivery

....

Tapas in a Box
....

For convivial stress-free home entertaining, you can't beat the handmade authentic dishes from Tapas in a Box. Order online, receive your beautifully packaged selection, put it in the oven to heat and let everyone think you've turned into a Spanish domestic goddess. *Olé*!

....

• **13 Smallbrook Business Centre, Waterloo Industrial Estate, Bidford on Avon, Warwickshire B50 4JE**
• **T: 01789 778844**
• **W: www.tapasinabox.com**

....

Graze
....

Graze is a new delivery service from Graham Bosher (founder of LoveFilm) that sends healthy snackboxes in the mail. There are more than 128 things to choose from, including nuts, rice crackers, dried and fresh fruit, vegetables, seeds and olives. Your goods are sent by first-class post (to anywhere in the UK, be it a home or an office) in cool cardboard packaging

F

Fashion & Food

that's slim enough to fit in a standard-sized letterbox.

They deliver nationwide – any address that can receive post in the UK can receive a Graze box. The food in your box is selected according to your own tastes. Just tell them what you like, love, or would like to try, then they put together your box based on these ratings, ensuring that you always receive the food you like.

You can add as many addresses to your account as you like, so you can send boxes to whoever you like or wherever you are, and you don't have to wait around to sign for it, since all Graze boxes fit through normal-sized letterboxes.

• W: www.graze.com (N)

It's pukka: Pure Pie

Pure Pie offer a delicious range of pies made by hand in Kent using locally sourced ingredients. Choose from fillings like steak, horseradish and ale; lamb, mint and potato; Thai chicken with lemongrass; smoked cheese and mushroom; or butterbean and mixed veggies. If it's something sweet you're after, the apple and blackberry version should do the trick.

Pop your pie in the oven for a hearty supper, or, if you've got company, order a box of 8 or 24 Little Pies and serve as substantial canapés.

• T: 01622 840200
• W: www.purepie.co.uk (N)

Abel & Cole

Abel & Cole is a home-delivery company for really good food. You can place your order online or by calling their award-winning customer service team, and select from a wide range of organic fruit and veg, as well as fish and meat, kitchen cupboard essentials, prepared meals and gifts. It's all delivered to your doorstep and you don't have to be in. They deliver to each area the same day every week, to minimize emissions, and they use as little packaging as possible. They source local British food wherever possible, and if they have to import (for example, oranges and bananas), they *never* airfreight.

Abel & Cole make it easy to support British farmers, minimize your effect on the environment and budget your weekly shop: no trawling the aisles chucking things in your trolley that you don't really need. They also have a superb range of recipes on their website, to help you make the most of seasonal veg.

• T: 08452 62 62 62
• W: www.abelandcole.co.uk

Snacks

Caviar: Arënkha MSC

Arënkha MSC is a gourmet treat reminiscent of caviar, made from wild, sustainably fished herring. Subtly spiced, warmly smoky in flavour and equally suited to hot or cold dishes, the little black pearls add an especially tasty touch to canapés, party nibbles, starters and main courses. It's a perfect product for the modern girl who wants high impact, big flavour and glamour in one quick, easy package. And with the feel-good fact that Arënkha MSC has a Marine Stewardship Council certification, you know they are doing their little bit to ensure the future of our world, while maintaining a high luxury quotient at an affordable price.

Chef and restaurateur Mark Hix is a huge fan, stating, 'Arënkha MSC is a delicious, really good and viable ethical alternative to caviar made from smoked herring with a few other natural flavourings added, and I use it in the same way I use caviar, by combining it with a jacket spud.'

If Mark says it's cool with a jacket spud, then it is, so follow his recipe:

. . . .

Mark Hix's baked potato with sour cream and Arënkha MSC

. . . .

- Serves 2
- Who can resist the humble baked potato, its insides made smoothly creamy with butter and crème fraîche, then lavishly topped with Arënkha MSC?

Ingredients

- 4 medium baking potatoes
- 75g (3oz) butter
- 2 heaped tbsp crème fraîche
- 2 x 55g jars Arënkha MSC
- Salt and freshly ground black pepper

Method

Preheat the oven to 190°C/375°F/gas mark 5.

Wrap the potatoes in foil, place on a baking tray and cook on the middle shelf of the oven for 45 minutes. Remove the foil and continue cooking the potatoes for a further 20 minutes or until soft when poked with a fine skewer. Cut the tops off the potatoes, scoop out the centres into a bowl and mash well with a fork.

Mix in the butter, crème fraîche and a generous amount of seasoning. Refill the skins, reheat in the oven until piping hot and serve topped with Arënkha MSC. Delicious!

Mark always had a love of food from a young age and his early career saw him in a succession of top hotels under some top chefs: The Hilton, The Grosvenor House Hotel under Anton Edelman and Vaughan Archer, and The Dorchester under Anton Mosimann. At only 22 he was made head chef of The Candlewick Room.

After four years, Mark took the position of head chef at Le Caprice. In 1990 he was appointed as executive head chef overseeing both Le Caprice and The Ivy and subsequently J. Sheekey. Company expansion led to Mark eventually overseeing further sites – Daphne's, Bam-Bou, Rivington (Shoreditch and Greenwich), Scott's and Urban Caprice.

Mark started his own venture in December 2007 after 17 years at Caprice Holdings. 2008 saw the opening of Hix Oyster & Chop House in Smithfield, London and Hix Oyster & Fish House in Lyme Regis, Dorset. His first West End restaurant, HIX, opened to critical acclaim in October 2009 in Soho, London. His latest restaurant, HIX Restaurant and Champagne Bar, opened in Selfridges, London in March 2010.

. . . .

- **Arënkha MSC is available from Waitrose, www.waitrose.com (N) and Ocado, www.ocado.com(N)**
- **W: www.restaurantsetcltd.co.uk**

F

Fashion & Food

Canderel recipes by Lorna Rhodes

Canderel is the UK's number-one low-calorie sweetener, available in handy tablet dispensers and granular jars. A teaspoon of Canderel granules contains only two calories compared to 20 calories in a teaspoon of sugar, so if you do count calories, it makes perfect waistline sense to switch where possible and dramatically reduce your calorie intake the easy way. To kickstart your use of this healthier alternative, Canderel share some of their delicious recipes…

Chocolate Cheesecake

- Serves 12
- Preparation time 20 minutes
- Cooking time 50 minutes, at 150°C or gas mark 2

Per portion

- Fat: 13.7g (of which saturates 6.6g)
- Cals: 245
- Carbs: 22.7g (of which sugars 13.7g)

Ingredients

- 75g Amaretti biscuits
- 25g cocoa
- 100g reduced-fat digestive biscuits
- 40g reduced-fat butter
- 150g plain chocolate
- 3 large eggs, separated
- 500g ricotta cheese
- 150ml fat-free plain yogurt
- 2 tsp cornflour
- 10 tbsp granular Canderel
- 1 tsp vanilla extract

Method

Line the base and sides of a 20cm non-stick springform cake tin. Put the biscuits into a plastic bag and bash with a rolling pin to reduce to fine crumbs, add the cocoa and shake together. Melt the butter in a medium bowl in the microwave for 20 seconds, then add the crumb mixture and stir together. Tip into the cake tin and press evenly over the base. Chill while preparing the filling.

Melt the chocolate in a small bowl over a pan of simmering water, or place in the microwave and cook on high for 1½ minutes. Stir until smooth, then set aside to cool completely.

Whisk the egg whites until softly peaking. Place the egg yolks, ricotta, yogurt, cornflour, Canderel and vanilla in a large bowl and beat with an electric whisk until smooth. Whisk in the cooled chocolate, then carefully fold in the egg whites. Turn into the prepared tin. Level the surface, then place on a baking sheet and bake in a preheated oven for 50 minutes.

Turn off the oven and leave the cheesecake in the cooling oven for 1 hour. Chill until ready to serve. Peel off the lining paper round the side and slip the cheesecake onto a plate, leaving the base lining paper behind.

Halve a few strawberries and decorate the top if wished, sprinkling with extra Canderel.

New York Berry Pancakes

- Makes 8
- Preparation time 15 minutes
- Cooking time 15 minutes

Per pancake with berries

- Fat: 3.6g (of which saturates 0.7g)
- Cals: 128
- Carbs: 19.2g (of which sugars 3.4g)

Ingredients

- 250g mixed berries, thawed if frozen
- 1 tsp cornflour
- 4 tbsp granular Canderel
- For the pancakes:
- 100g plain flour
- 1 tsp baking powder
- ½ tsp ground cinnamon
- 40g porridge oats
- 4 tbsp granular Canderel
- 120ml fat-free plain yogurt
- 5 tbsp skimmed milk
- 2 medium eggs
- 1 tsp vanilla extract
- 2 tsp sunflower oil

Method

Put the berries into a pan with 2 tbsp water, and slowly bring to a simmer. Blend the cornflour with 1 tbsp water, add to the berries with the Canderel and stir over a medium heat until the juices thicken. Remove from the heat.

To make the pancakes, put the flour, baking powder, cinnamon, oats and Canderel into a bowl. Whisk the yogurt, milk, eggs and vanilla extract together, then add to the dry ingredients and beat together to make a smooth batter.

To cook the pancakes, heat a large non-stick frying pan on a medium heat, and brush the base of the pan with oil. Drop 3 tbsp of the batter into the pan, leaving a little space between each one: Cook for about 2 minutes, while bubbles come to the surface. When the underside is golden, flip the pancakes over and cook for a further 2 minutes.

Remove from the pan, brush the pan with oil again and continue to cook the pancakes. Serve topped with the berry sauce.

••••••••••••••••••••••••••••••••••••••

Champagne Jellies
••••••••••••••••••••••••••••••••••••••

- Makes 4
- Preparation time 15 minutes plus chilling

Per portion

- Fat: 0.0g
- Cals: 97
- Carbs: 12.8g (of which sugars 8.2g)

Ingredients

- 4 leaves gelatine
- 3 tbsp granular Canderel
- 100ml pomegranate juice (sugar-free)
- ½ bottle pink champagne, sparkling white wine, Cava or Prosecco
- Extra Canderel

Method

Put the gelatine leaves into a pan, add 100ml cold water and leave to soak for 5 minutes. Heat gently and stir until melted. Remove from the heat, stir in the Canderel, pour into a large jug, and leave to cool. Put 4 glasses in the fridge to chill.

Stir the pomegranate juice into the gelatine liquid, then carefully pour in the champagne and stir gently. Allow to settle, then skim off the foam.

Pour into chilled glasses, then place them in the fridge to set for several hours or overnight.

Just before serving, sprinkle a little Canderel on each if wished.

Tip: Use 2 x 200ml (mini bottles) if a half-bottle is unavailable

Chocolate Martini

- Serves 1
- Preparation time 5 minutes, plus cooling

Per portion

- Fat: 1.4g (of which saturates 0.8g)
- Cals: 189
- Carbs: 20.1g (of which sugars 16.8g)

Ingredients

- 4 tbsp hot Italian coffee
- 3 tsp Canderel
- 1 heaped tsp cocoa powder
- 3 tbsp semi-skimmed milk
- 1fl oz shot vodka
- 1 fl oz shot Kahlua
- Crushed ice

Method

Mix the coffee, Canderel and cocoa powder together. Allow to cool.Pour into a cocktail shaker, add the milk, Vodka and Kahlua, and shake. Place some crushed ice into the cocktail glass, then strain over the Martini and serve.

- **W: www.canderel.uk.com (N)**

Higgidy

A chicken and mushroom pie is so last year, sweetie. Indulge in simply gorgeous pies with Higgidy, proving that English people really can cook! There are a variety of flavours and fresh ingredients. One of my favourites is the British Beef, Stilton and Ale Pie. However, if you're watching your figure or want something lighter, then choose from one of their 'skinnies', offering lighter and altogether healthier options, such as Skinny Mushroom and Leaf Spinach Pie and Skinny Butternut Squash and Red Pepper Pie. The latter uses butternut squash roasted with spices and tossed with red pepper pieces on a creamy ricotta custard base in a caraway seed pastry, light and totally moreish.

- **Available in stores nationwide – use the locator on the website to find your nearest.**
- **W: www.higgidy.co.uk (N)**

Popina

Popina (meaning 'tavern' or 'eatery' in Latin) bases its ethos around the idea of 'supercreativity', offering unique, handmade treats such as Ginger and Caramelized Chilli Biscuits and wafer-thin Fig, Apricot and Pistachio Biscotti.

All the products are made daily from scratch and the ingredients are sourced from the UK and around the world. You must try one (or several) of their award-winning range of handmade sweet and savoury tarts, biscuits, crackers and brownies. You will taste the freshness in every mouthful and adore the visual appeal of the products too, each one like a work of handmade art. You will soon understand why they have won awards every year since 2004.

Available in the fresh bakery departments of the UK's finest food halls and delis, in Popina Farmers' Market stalls across London, and online
- **T: 020 3212 0110**
- **W: www.shop.popina.co.uk and www.popina.co.uk**

Gadgets

Every girl needs a little high-tech modernity, and there's a gadget for every need. We're not all frills and lipgloss, right? From the domesticated to the dynamo, check out this round-up of gizmos to make your busy lifestyle more efficient...

• •

A laptop that does your make-up – one day

• •

HP and a pool of cool designers have created some very original laptop ideas. The **HP Makeup** has its very own pull-out make-up set and a printing device to give your nails an individual design, and the screen switches to mirror mode at the push of a button. The **HP Nobag** has a touch sensor with hard OLED technology, so that the laptop can be rolled up and stored easily in your McQueen tote, or clutch for that matter. With the **HP Fitness** you can control your weight and a bracelet is included so you can keep track of your progress while working out. All concepts are from the industrial designer Nikita Buyanov for HP and Intel... Sorry, but they don't exist just yet. I just wanted to give you a heads-up on some gadgets I think every modern girl will love some day. Watch this space!

• W: www.hp.com (N)

Perfectly poached eggs

If your poached eggs often resemble sloppy meringue, if they fall apart, or if you achieve a chalky rather than a runny finish, then **Lakeland's** twenty-first-century solution to the problem of wandering whites will ensure perfection every time. Coat the silicone lightly with oil, crack your egg into the pod, and float it in boiling water. Once cooked, flip the pod inside out to release the domed egg. This has revolutionized my breakfasts!

• W: www.lakeland.co.uk

Bathtime drinks holder

If you enjoy a tipple in the tub, the **Limpet** drinks holder will safely hold your beverage of choice while you indulge in a hot soak. The super-secure clamp system grips the bathroom tiles like a limpet, hence the name – can you see what they've done there? Choose from white, pink and blue.

• W: www.giftlab.co.uk

On-the-go power

The **powermonkey-eXplorer** has proved to be an invaluable piece of kit, providing essential power in the most remote locations. Incorporating the new solarmonkey, the powermonkey-eXplorer lets you charge wherever, whenever.

Compatible with the majority of mobile phones, iPods, MP3/MP4 players, PDAs and portable games consoles, powermonkey-eXplorer will recharge your devices – giving you 96 hours of standby on your mobile, 40 hours on your iPod, 5 hours on your games console, 48 hours on your PDA and 6 hours on MP3/MP4 players. Available in four colours, blue, grey, pink and yellow, it's stylish and essential!

So how does it work? The solarmonkey draws power directly from the sun – giving you free power wherever you are. Make sure your powermonkey-eXplorer has full power at all times by charging it with the handy solarmonkey, which can be attached to a rucksack, hung from a window, left in a car or taken anywhere the sun shines!

Ultra-compact, tough and powerful, the powermonkey-eXplorer is water-resistant and made from rubberized casing, so it can take whatever life throws at it, yet it remains the lightest, most versatile charger available today. With the powermonkey-eXplorer and solarmonkey, you always have two reusable sources of power so you need never run out again!

• W: www.powertraveller.com

Portable media player

This portable media player allows users to watch video, on a five-inch screen, on the move! It's complete with easy, instant access to the internet, email, TV, music, photos and much more. With an ultra-thin, stylish design and touch-screen technology, the crystal clear, high resolution screen of the **ARCHOS 5** offers a superior viewing and internet experience in a stunning, design-focused package. With so many options available, the new ARCHOS Internet Media Tablets are perfect for any situation – whether on the train to work, on holiday lounging by the pool or even just when your boyfriend insists on watching the footie!

• W: www.archos.com

Other desirables

An **Insinkerator Hot Water Tap** can be built into kitchen sink designs and dispenses hot water up to 98°C so there's no need to boil the kettle each time you fancy a brew. It also dispenses cold filtered water and is cheap to run, overall saving you time, money and energy!

• W: www.magnet.co.uk (N)

Sennheiser CX 300-ll precision headphones are the Rolls-Royce of earphones. They reduce background noise, improve the quality of the bass and the clarity of the sound, they look sharp, they're comfortable and come in different colours and ear sizes.

• W: www.sennheiser.co.uk (N)

If you don't want your man to keep all the James Bond-style accessories for himself, bag yourself the **Camden** by **Storm Watches**. It's a man's design, but I couldn't resist the LED touch screen and hi-tech sleekness – and a chunky oversized watch on a slender wrist oozes confident style. It comes in black or slate. Just don't start wearing his boxers, as that might be a nod to masculine style gone too far…

• W: www.stormwatches.com (N)

If your car won't start and you're stranded, you don't have to fear flagging down a stranger for their jump leads or not being able to contact your car rescue provider, as there's a high-power starter unit that plugs into your 12V cigarette lighter socket that will charge you up and have you on your way in ten minutes – phew!

• T: 0871 855 16127
• W: www.expertverdict.com

Wheel of shoe-fortune: tszuji

tszuji is home to the very best shoe storage solutions for your precious collection, and their Shoe Wheel is a great space-saving design that will store up to 30 pairs in 20 clear expandable pockets. I love the idea of having my Laboutins on display as well as having easy access to them all. Simply spin and make your selection.

• T: 0845 2246506
• W: www.tszuji.co.uk (N)

Rowenta® Ultrasteam Brush

Rowenta's hand-held Ultrasteam Brush delivers a continuous flow of steam, gently and efficiently removing creases and wrinkles from your clothes. I pack mine whenever I travel or holiday, as it's fabulous for rescuing your threads from that crumpled straight-from-a-suitcase look, and it comes with a travel bag. The variable heat settings deliver just the right amount of steam; it can be used on a range of fabrics, including curtains and upholstery.

• W: www.lakeland.co.uk

G

Gadgets & Gifts

In-car charger: Motormonkey

The world's smallest and lightest in-car charger, the motormonkey was inspired by a conversation with Aston Martin. This neat little gizmo will sit impassively in your cigarette lighter without draining the car's battery – a big issue with many in-car chargers – and it looks sleek too.

• W: www.powertraveller.com

Oregon Scientific Metal Weather Station

This weather forecaster will let you know when the snow will fall, featuring a radio-controlled clock to ensure that it's always accurate. The 12/24-hour Weather Station will let you know the indoor and outdoor temperatures and humidity as well as indicating the future weather conditions. You'll never again be stuck in your Hunters if the sun suddenly shines, nor be wearing flip-flops in the rain!

• W: www.oregonscientific.co.uk

Gifts

With modern technology taking over so many elements of our daily lives, it's important not to forget the intimacy of giving a tangible gift, full of personal thought. I resent getting 'virtual Bellinis' on my social networking page every birthday, and vouchers just don't cut the mustard. However, we're all guilty of it and as we get busier, quick-fix solutions are just convenient. Use these gift portals for inspiration and efficiency and make the effort – whether it's for a loved one, an occasion, to treat yourself, or just to let someone know you're thinking of them...

Send a thought

For when you want to send more than a card, but not go to the expense of flowers, sendathought has a selection of 'little thoughts' for every moment, from 'chin up' gestures to 'happy birthday' presents. Everything is beautifully wrapped, and overall a lot more thoughtful than your usual gift sites.

If you don't want the recipient of your thoughtful gift to open it until a specific day, let them know and they'll add a 'don't open until' sticker with this date to the outer packaging.

• W: www.sendathought.co.uk

Gift ideas

This has saved me hours of trawling round the shops looking for the perfect gift. If you're after a thoughtful gift but don't have time to search high and low or are just stuck for inspiration, *giftgen.co.uk* is a godsend. You select your budget (from £3 to £600 plus), then the age of the recipient, followed by specific characteristics. Giftgen then offer you a long list of suitable gift ideas, complete with where to buy them. Genius!

• W: www.giftgen.co.uk

Save time

Don't waste your lunchtime trekking

down the high street for gifts for your friends and family. Visit *www.postapresent.co.uk* and order from a wide range of affordable quality gifts for any occasion. You simply choose your gift, pay, and they will gift-wrap it and post direct to the recipient, or to yourself if preferred. The Pamper Box is super-girly and includes a pretty reusable box, Exfoliating Salt Scrub, Gorgeous Glow Luxury Face and Body Lotion, Relaxing Bath Oil, Goddess Pulse Point to soothe and calm your mood, a Face Cloth and a romantic CD. It makes a great gift for yourself or a friend in need!

- **Hawthorne House, Hull Road, Hemingbrough, North Yorkshire YO8 6QJ**
- **T: 0844 8845 463**
- **W: www.postapresent.co.uk**

Glimpse Online

GlimpseOnline.com is an emporium for unique design-led interiors, jewellery, furniture, fashion, art, ceramics, glassware, cushions and bespoke gifts by over 1,000 hand-picked and talented, emerging designers. Whether you're looking for the lavish and expensive, the affordable, the eco-friendly or something for your home, you'll find something cool and gorgeous here.

- **T: 020 8981 1180**
- **W: www.GlimpseOnline.com**

Your own unique bottle of bubbly: GettingPersonal

GettingPersonal.co.uk is your home

for personalized and unique gift ideas that cannot be purchased on the high street. Create your own personalized bottle of champagne with your own unique message. Their blend is Pinot Noir, Meunier and Chardonnay and it comes complete with a stylish champagne gift box. 'Bubbles au Fabulous' marked my bottle!

- **W: www.gettingpersonal.co.uk**

You don't have to be rich or famous to have your own biography: contact The Quince Tree

If you want to give a gift that will become the receiver's greatest keepsake, how about their own biography? A couple of guided sessions with an experienced interviewer are all you need to record your memories. The Quince Tree will turn those memories into a beautiful bespoke, handmade book. The final product contains hand-marbled paper inlays and a slipcase for protection. It can include photographs or original illustrations. They can also help you with writing support, editing, layout, printing and binding – turning stories into heirlooms.

- **W: www.thequincetree.co.uk**

For the adventurous: Thanks Darling

Thanks Darling has over 950 exciting and exhilarating gift ideas, from flying experiences to signed special edition books by sporting heroes such as Sir Geoff Hurst. Gift Experiences are also available, for hen and stag activities or corporate days.

• W: www.thanksdarling.com

Lost for Words

Lost for words is what you'll be when you receive any one of their gifts – from beautiful bespoke giftbooks and personalized calendars to personalized chocolate boxes, all containing photographs and a story, told in your words.

The books are simply beautiful. After a full consultation with the friendly team where they closely establish every important detail about the recipient, and gather images and memorabilia, the making of the book – dedicated to the recipient, complete with stories, memories and pictures – will create a keepsake that will never be forgotten.

• Lost for Words, Lancaster House, 237 Sussex Gardens, London W2 3UD
• T: 07802 815336 or 020 7262 2292
• W: www.sabadesigns.co.uk

Gift-wrapping made easy: the giftelope

If you've got your gift but can't be bothered/have no time to wrap it, then the giftelope is the stress-saving alternative to wrapping paper – a gorgeous boutique gift envelope made from recycled paper in Scotland with embossed ribbon and tag detailing. You simply write the tag, pop in the gift, seal, and go. A gorgeous gift, wrapped in seconds!

• W: www.giftelope.com

Say it in a film: Bespoke Films

Bespoke Films help you create a unique and compelling film where you can mix contributions from friends, family and colleagues with your own choice of music, photographs and home movie footage. Your film can feature celebrity contributors, historic newsreel footage of famous events and, if requested, secret filming. To retain the vital element of surprise, they can make the whole film in total secrecy; just don't say I suggested it!

• Bespoke Films Ltd, 350 Goldhawk Road, London W6 0XF
• T: 020 8834 7293
• W: www.bespokefilms.com

Pressies4princesses

Pressies4princesses is great if you're shopping for a girl specifically – which makes this the ideal gift site to show your other half so you can get what you *really* want (finally, no more thoughtless half-price flowers from the petrol station)! Divided into helpful areas according to whom you may be shopping for – girlfriend, wife, mother, sister, best friend, colleague and daughter – you'll find all the inspiration you need. Each gift has witty comments on the kind of person the product would suit most, so you're bound to find a thoughtful match.

• W: www.pressies4princesses.co.uk

Heavenly hair

Your hair is one thing that (unless you have none or live under a hat) you and the world see every single day. It is therefore important to look after it and keep it looking good. Bad hair days always make you feel naff, so get gorgeous locks by reading on...

Hair fragrance from James Brown

Daily pollution and grind, smoke and smog can make your locks pongy and lacklustre. If you want a quick revival, use a hair fragrance. James Brown London Shine and Fragrance Mist adds shine and perfume to otherwise less than impressive hair, so he can get close and you won't remind him of an ash tray!

• **Available from Boots the Chemist (N)**

Marc Jacobs Hair Shine

This is definitely one for the label lovers. The classic bottle makes a great handbag addition as well as getting rid of nasty dry ends, softening your hair. The scent is reminiscent of your favourite beach holiday, but use sparingly and spray onto your hands, then apply – if you

103

apply directly to your hair, you could end up smelling great but looking like a chip pan.

• **T: 0800 652 7661**

A load of bullocks?

A new, intense conditioning treatment at Hari's Salon uses organic pedigree Angus bull semen, fresh from Brooklet Farm in Cheshire. The substance's pure protein, combined with katera, a protein-rich plant root, penetrates each shaft and deeply nourishes the hair.

After a shampoo and head massage, your locks are slathered in a thick mask and placed under a steamer. Twenty minutes later, after a rinse and blow-dry, your barnet is bouncy and shiny and you'll look as if you just stepped out of a salon … oh, you just did!

• **Hari's, 305 Brompton Road, London SW3 2DY**
• **T: 020 7581 5211**
• **W: www.harissalon.com**

Quick fix: Batiste Dry Shampoo

Having clean, shiny and lustrous locks, whatever the length, can really make a difference in boosting your self-esteem. But if you're in a hurry or want perfect locks without having to wash and style your hair every day, then my secret weapon is Batiste Dry Shampoo, available in a range of fragrances. It cleverly zaps any grease and leaves locks bouncy and full.

With just one spray of this fine mist, your hair smells shampoo-fresh and wonderfully clean. Just spray it on as you would a hairspray, targeting the roots and greasy areas, comb through, and hey presto, bouncy, sweet-smelling hair in seconds!

• **Available from Superdrug (N)**

No appointment needed at The Blow Dry Bar

The Blow Dry Bar in TopShop's flagship Oxford Circus store in London is one for your address book. If you're in the area, just pop

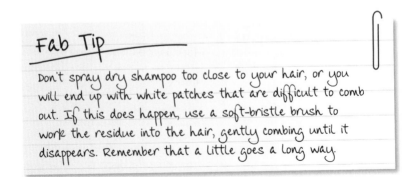

Fab Tip

Don't spray dry shampoo too close to your hair, or you will end up with white patches that are difficult to comb out. If this does happen, use a soft-bristle brush to work the residue into the hair, gently combing until it disappears. Remember that a little goes a long way.

in and get your locks transformed. No appointment is needed; all you need to do is choose one of the eight styles from the 'Hair Menu' – from the catwalk-inspired up-dos to groomed waves and super-sleek locks – and it will take the Hersheson team a mere 30 minutes. Though many of the styles look suitable for only long hair, this isn't the case, and you can have the looks tailored to you. Perfect if you want to look dazzling in double-quick time.

• **TopShop, Oxford Street, London**
• **W: www.hershesonsblowdrybar.com**

Bargain products: Cyvilian

One for the bargain hunters, Cyvilian is crammed with over 650 different products – including Sexy Hair, Scruples, Osis, Tigi and KMS California. All products are at discounted prices – some as much as 50% lower than the RRP, and first-time users are offered a 5% discount. Many of the products are eligible for free shipping – saving on postage.

• **Cyvilian Hair Store, Basement Shop, 57 Marchmont Street, London WC1N 1AP**
• **T: 0871 218 0027**
• **W: www.cyvilianhairstore.co.uk**

Hair extensions

Oh yes, gone are the years of straggly, embarrassingly detectable threads – luscious locks can now be yours!

Great Lengths

Great Lengths are the leader in premium hair extensions enjoyed by the world's most stylish women. They only use the finest 100% human hair of guaranteed origin and ethicality. Using their patented systems, their specially formulated bonds attach to your own hair and are kind to your hair and scalp, so don't worry about the horror stories you may have heard before. They are virtually undetectable by sight or touch, can be styled, curled or coloured, and they can be removed with no damage to your own hair.

• **T: 0113 216 3062**
• **W: www.greatlengthshair.co.uk (use the store locator to find your nearest provider)**

Tatiana Hair Extensions

Small, but highly specialist, this unique salon in Kensington, London, offers hair extensions, hair replacement and hair integration systems. The 'virgin' hair is carefully chosen and brought back from Russia by Tatiana herself and is of the highest quality. The method that Tatiana Hair Extensions uses is also revolutionary and unique. Using micro-rings instead of glue, this method doesn't damage the hair and allows the hair extensions to be tightened on a regular basis, meaning the hair lasts longer.

Tatiana's work has been featured in a 2008 BBC documentary called *Whose Hair Is It Anyway?*, presented by pop star Jamelia. The singer travelled to Russia with Tatiana and the BBC crew to find out how and where the hair came from, dispersing rumours of hair exploitation. Tatiana frequently visits Russia, carefully choosing hair for her clients to ensure the best quality, as well as cutting out the middle man, which allows her prices to be competitive.

- **27 Holland Street, London W8 4NA**
- **T: 020 7937 1989**
- **W: www.tatianahairextensions.co.uk**

Temporary solution: Additional Lengths

If you aren't sure and want to try out the look, or simply want longer, fuller hair on occasion, try the Additional Lengths 100% human hair clip-in hair pieces. They are applied by parting the hair and clipping them in, and are removed in the same easy way.

- **W: www.additionallengths.co.uk**

How to get glossy hair

New York über-hairstylist/colourist and cult beauty expert James Corbett offers tips on how to achieve glossy locks…

James Corbett's top tips for glossy hair

Glossy hair is healthy hair! I cannot stress that enough! When the hair is healthy, the hair cuticle lies flat. When

the cuticle lies flat, it allows the light to reflect off it, which gives you shiny, glossy and healthy hair.

My oil of choice is the **Philip B Rejuvenating Oil Treatment**. It is carefully and lovingly created to give optimum results on the hair. To create your own version at home, use sesame oil and almond oil, which you should be able to find in most supermarkets. Jojoba oil and lavender oil will make it even better, and you should be able to find these oils in a local health food store.

Remember, oil and water do not mix, so the oil must be applied to dry hair. The directions from the Philip B oil treatment can be used for any similar treatment:

1 Brush hair and scalp with a natural boar-bristle brush.

2 Take one-inch sections of dry, unwashed hair; apply the oil liberally to the point of saturation. Never apply oil to wet hair!

3 Work the oil in with your fingers, massage into the scalp and work through to the ends.

4 Comb with a fine-tooth comb.

5 For additional benefits, heat the oil with a blow-dryer, or use a plastic cap and go into a steam room for a few minutes or as long as you desire.

6 *Before* wetting, apply a clarifying shampoo directly on top of the oil. Do not wet the hair yet. Massage the shampoo into the oiled hair.

7 Slowly incorporate a small amount

of water to lather, and pull through to the ends.

8 Rinse and repeat if necessary.

If you have finer hair, it may take two shampoos to remove all the oil. The build-up from old products will be gone. You will have fed your hair and your scalp, thereby leaving you with shiny, glossy hair!

• W: www.jamescorbett.net

Paul Labrecque Luxury Hair Care

Paul Labrecque is hailed as one of 'today's top stylists' in New York, and has been named Manhattan's cult favourite 'Best Colourist', but you can get a taste of his superiority with the Paul Labrecque Luxury Hair Care, available in the UK exclusively in Selfridges across the country.

Understanding our needs perfectly, Labrecque says, 'Today's men and women are on the go. They need to look fabulous and well-groomed but rarely have hours to stand in front of the mirror. I created this line to provide high-quality salon results in a snap.'

He's not fibbing, either. His Color Finish Polish & Seal Droplets is one of the only serums ever to tame my hair without weighing it down and making it look greasy and lank. Invisible alcohol-free drops seal in colour, replenish moisture and eliminate static for a mirror-like shine. UV filters prevent fading and discoloration, and maintain the hair's natural lustre. I've ordered several bottles!

• **To look equally well-groomed, head to Selfridges (N), or go to www. beautyexpert.co.uk and check out the new Paul Labrecque Luxury Hair Care**

Fabulous salons

Most fabulous if you're short on time: RMUK

RMUK is one of L'Oreal's top 100 UK portfolio artistic salons and a flagship in the north, offering colour specialists, advanced and precision cutting and a variety of both permanent and semi-permanent hair treatments. Relaxing in the sumptuous surroundings of the salon, clients can take advantage of the many beauty treatments on offer, ranging from dermalogica face-mapping to 'true Brazilian waxing'. If you're short on time and want a manicure as your highlights lift, or a soothing facial after a not-so-soothing wax, you can have it. Proud owner Massi Moura can even handpick a bespoke package for hen parties that includes a light lunch and sparkling wine, starting in the upstairs bar and lounge area.

• **RMUK, 9–11 Eastgate, Leeds LS2 7LY**
• **T: 0113 243 6842**
• **W: www.rm-uk.com**

Most fabulous for no-fuss good results: Jam Hair

Jamie Shackleton is the eccentric owner of Jam, having opened his first

H

Heavenly Hair & Hotels

salon back in 1976 in Leeds. After a successful career spanning the 1980s and 90s, Jam Hair was established in 1991 and is now located in the vibrant and dynamic area of Headingley. Jam has a truly diverse clientele and the look of the salon is relaxed and funky. An antique dentist's chair takes pride of place in the window, with opposing wall surfaces of natural wood and stone. The secluded salon spa area, with its interchanging hypnotic lighting, is where you'll have your hair washed as you lie back in the soothing massage chair, experiencing a shiatsu back massage as part of your treatment. These little touches, alongside the laid-back and expert staff, make Jam Hair one to remember.

Oh, and if you want to try extensions with a reliable source, Jamie Shackleton has been specializing in hair extensions since 1981 when mono-fibre was first invented, and Jam Hair have been offering Great Lengths human hair extensions since 1991. Every aspect of the Great Lengths system is covered at Jam, including Fast Fusion, Cold Fusion and Heat Fusion methods, meaning they can totally tailor-make the experience to your hair type.

- **Jam Hair, 77a Otley Road, Headingley, Leeds LS6 3PS**
- **T: 0113 2786275 / 2743281**

Most fabulous celebrity chain: Nicky Clarke

We all know the famous Nicky Clarke, but despite his global fame, his nationwide salons have maintained

that personal, non-imposing atmosphere and expertise that some chains sadly lack. There are salons across the UK and all offer a range of top-notch treatments for the hair and body. Knowing we all want to look and feel good from our barnet to our tootsies, some salons offer beauty treatments so you can have your nails done as your colour sets, and the Mayfair branch offers reflexology with Andrea Hurst, who is listed as the top practitioner in her field by *Vogue* magazine. Now you can leave feeling completely revived, quite literally from head to toe.

I love the Leeds salon in particular, with their growing beauty services, top eyebrow expert Jo Pallan (a threading master) and the best catering a salon can offer, thanks to their collaboration with top restaurant chain *Anthony's*.

- **W: www.nickyclarke.com (N)**
- **W: www.andreahurst.co.uk**

Most fabulous for answering every hair prayer: Hari's

Located in the heart of shopping heaven, Chelsea at Brompton Cross, Hari's is a transformed London townhouse offering four floors of hair and beauty expertise.

The blow-dry and cutting floor has its own organic juice bar alongside a colour clinic and chic penthouse-style private hair spa for extra pampering – 'Hari's Hair Hospital'.

'Hair Doctors' will prescribe exactly what your scalp and hair need, followed by a prescribed treatment – all designed to inject stressed-out hair with gloss and volume. The pièce de résistance is that every treatment is applied with a mind-soothing Indian head massage. If you and/or your locks are stressed out – from too much sun, fun, product or straighteners – visit Hari's to get healthy, happy hair again.

....

- 305 Brompton Road, London SW3 2DY
- T: 020 7581 5211
- W: www.harissalon.co.uk

Most fabulous for a VIP experience: Sejour

Sejour is one of those salons that makes you feel like a VIP through the little luxury touches they offer. With a hugely experienced team of international stylists, the 'UKs Top 10 Recognized Hair Colourists', specialists in areas such as afro and extensions, a call-out service (if you need style help brought to you) and a chauffeur service, all offered as you sit on your Shiatsu massage chair in your silk kimono, Sejour clearly offers more than the average salon to create a totally personal experience bound to make you feel as special as you deserve to!

....

- 3–5 Bray Place, London SW3 3LL
- T: 08448 848 400
- W: www.sejour.co.uk

Hotels

Every fabulous girl needs a stylish place to stay. Whether it's to accommodate your jet-setting lifestyle, provide a naughty weekend away, or find a last-minute crash pad on a business trip, there's plenty of choice. Many hotels today offer more than just a cosy bed – think stylish bars, luxurious spas and award-winning restaurants. Whatever type of accommodation your fabulous self requires, I unveil my pick of some of the best – one for each mood...

Most fabulous for a dirty weekend: Hotel Pelirocco, Brighton

Hotel Pelirocco is Brighton's sauciest stopover, situated on the seafront of central Brighton. If you're looking for something totally different, try one of the 19 themed bedrooms – each inspired by pop subculture, musicians and inspired creative-types.

Their flagship suite, 'The Playroom', is their ultimate 'dirty weekend' room. Dedicated to all things indulgent, this is one heck of a sexy boudoir. There's an eight-foot round bed with mirrored canopy, a separate living area with a 42-inch plasma for PS2/TV/radio (well, you've got to cater for your fella's tastes!) and a luxury ensuite bathroom with a huge plunge bath and double monsoon shower heads for steamy moments. To up the privacy factor even more, you even get your own entrance from the street. Finally, to top it all off, there's a pole-dancing area with a fitted pole. The hotel can even arrange for you to have lessons prior to your stay so you can impress the pants off your partner – quite literally, I'm sure...

Other rooms include the frivolous 'Fancy Pants', a room themed around knickers, with 'bum art' adorning the walls and pantie-wearing mannequins; and 'Pressure Sounds', a Jamaican-style dub and reggae room with Lee Scratch Perry wallpaper.

....

- **Hotel Pelirocco, 10 Regency Square, Brighton, East Sussex BN1 2FG**
- **T: 01273 327055**
- **W: www.hotelpelirocco.co.uk**

● ●

Most fabulous for interior design: Haymarket Hotel

● ●

Just around the corner from Trafalgar Square, bang in the middle of the theatre district, nestles the spectacularly beautiful Haymarket Hotel with 50 bedrooms and suites and a townhouse of true glamour. Notably, the exquisite interior immediately inspires you in wanting to recreate the look for your own home, and this beauty hits you first from the outside. The building was created by John Nash (who designed Buckingham Palace). Then, as you walk indoors, the reception is contemporary yet with a classical elegance; a fusion which continues throughout the entire hotel.

I stayed in a one-bedroom suite and, all bull aside, I didn't want to leave. With the feeling of a luxury city apartment and the setting of a fashionably à la mode English cottage, the bold styles unify and distinguish from one another at once. The cosy pink sofa and rose-patterned cushions contrast with the other chairs, each of different tones and shapes, while expertly blending in style. Reclaimed bureaus and

closets add character next to the fashion mannequins and accented canvases. The bed was one of the tallest I've slept on: I felt like the Princess and the Pea! All bathrooms are designed with granite, oak and glass walk-in showers, double basins and flat-screen TVs over the bath. I needed little else, lying there in a bubble bath with a whole different kind of bubbles in my glass.

The shooting gallery on the ground floor is a vast, glamorous room with five-metre-high ceilings, the buzzy bar and restaurant Brumus is worth a visit, and the pool has a long pewter honesty bar where you can mix your own cocktails, admire the dramatic lighting installation, or lounge on the metallic gold leather sofas post swim.

This inspiring interior is designed by Kit Kemp, one half of the husband-and-wife duo Tim and Kit Kemp, who own Firmdale Hotels. This luxurious hotel group consists of six hotels and four bars and restaurants in London, and it is no surprise that Firmdale received the Queen's Award for Enterprise in 2000 and 2006. You won't be disappointed.

....

- **1 Suffolk Place, London SW1Y 4BP**
- **T: 020 7470 4000**
- **W: www.haymarkethotel.com**

● ●

Most fabulous for cocktails: Mai Yango

● ●

Mai Yango is a four-star-rated, 14-bedroom boutique hotel and perhaps the funkiest in Leicester. A blend of timbers, woods and vibrant colours are present throughout, with original finishing touches such as their timber wardrobes lined with hot pink felt. The award-winning restaurant offers á la carte fine dining two doors from the hotel lobby entrance. Styled around a Moroccan theme, intimate booths brimming with drapes, low lighting and oversized cushions provide a romantic and homely seating area next to small tables and laid-back sofas. There is the option of a taster menu, allowing you to sample a collection of some of the most popular dishes in a succession of six satisfying courses. The cocktails are a must-try and the top-floor Glass Bar is open to residents and members only, perfect for enjoying one of their finest tipples on the terrace.

• 13–21 St Nicholas Place, Leicester LE1 4LD
• T: 0116 251 8898
• W: www.maiyango.com

Most fabulous for down time: Black Swan Hotel

Escape to the historic Black Swan Hotel in the market town of Helmsley, North Yorkshire. This is a hotel where relaxation and decadence are high on the menu, with elegant and individually styled rooms and the award-winning three-AA-rosette Rutland Restaurant which uses the best seasonal ingredients, most of which are locally sourced. Head to the hotel's highly acclaimed tearoom to indulge in handmade cakes, pastries and chocolates, then work it all off in the Verbena Spa, just 200 yards away.

• Black Swan Hotel, Market Place, Helmsley, North Yorkshire YO62 5BJ
• T: 01439 770466
• W: www.blackswan-helmsley.co.uk

Most fabulous for relaxing after sightseeing across the capital: Malmaison, London

Malmaison hotels are one of my preferred groups, as they never fail to make me feel relaxed and cared for. They have 12 branches across the UK – each individual yet encompassing the opulent finish and vibrant personality of Malmaison. The London hotel is a short walk from Farringdon tube station, nestled among the many kooky cafés and restaurants in the area. It is perfectly placed to retire to after a little retail therapy or West End show, and the onsite destination brasserie is moody and intimate enough to unwind in. The 'homegrown and local menu' is both delectable and commendable, using locally sourced produce, from the best oysters farmed in the River Blackwater by the Malden Oyster and Seafood Company, to traditional ale from the Battersea Brewery Company. The cuisine and impressive cocktail list are as high in flavour as the décor is lavish, and a real treat for lovers is the suitably entitled Love Suite. Here you will be enveloped in glorious indulgence, with the provision of Champagne on ice, chocolate-dipped strawberries, aromatic oils and candles, a chilled Mal CD and that all-important champagne breakfast in your room the next morning. An ideal hotel for enjoying London at its best, and best shared with your significant other!

H

Heavenly Hair & Hotels

- **18–21 Charterhouse Square, London EC1M 6AH**
- **T: 0871 223 5000**
- **W: www.malmaison.com (N)**

Most fabulous for making you feel like royalty: Lumley Castle Hotel

If ever you feel that chivalry is dead – which, let's face it, most of us do these days – then Lumley Castle Hotel will bring a little Pride and Prejudice feel into your life. This fully converted and beautifully restored 600-year-old castle transports you into a bygone world of honour and luxury. From the 73 individually decorated bedrooms through to the elegant Black Knight restaurant, every room offers an element of romance and sophistication. Now all you need is your own Mr Darcy to emerge from the lakes in a wet white shirt…

- **Lumley Castle Hotel, Chester-le-Street, County Durham DH3 4NX**
- **T: 0191 389 1111**
- **W: www.lumleycastle.com**

Most fabulous for a luxury retreat: Cardington House

Sitting majestically above the picturesque harbour of St Aubin in Jersey, Cardington House boasts all the splendour and grandeur you would expect from a Victorian property. Set in beautiful, meticulously kept mature gardens, with steps leading down from the terrace to a large heated swimming pool and hot tub, steps at the far end

of the grounds lead to a secluded beach with views out to St Aubin's Fort, St Helier and beyond.

Cardington House offers five luxurious en-suite bedrooms, all of which boast magnificent sea views. The two master suites, King and Scott, feature their very own private terrace and dressing room for an ultimate lavish experience. Sigh…

- **Cardington House, Mont es Tours, St Brelade, Jersey JE3 8LP**
- **T: 01534 748000**
- **W: www.cardingtonhouse.com**

Most fabulous for rooftop pleasure: The Chambers, Park Place, Leeds

Situated in the heart of Leeds' business district, The Chambers at Park Place is a stone's throw from the town centre and train station and makes the perfect meeting place or event space, as well as boasting 58 super-chic serviced apartments and four penthouses.

Open-plan in design and offering lots more living space than a hotel room, each apartment has its own kitchen and living room, and one or two bedrooms complete with very comfortable king-size beds.

I stayed in a state-of-the-art two-bed/two-bath penthouse, with Aquavision TV that you can watch while you soak in the spa bath, and this baby boasts the only rooftop hot tub in Leeds with the most superb views across the city. Relax with a glass of wine or champers that the staff can supply for you.

This is great if you are commuting to Leeds for business or pleasure, or even if you fancy treating yourself and want a central overnight stay after a shopping spree and night on the town. I've even heard that people live here for months on end, so if you're flush enough – why not?

....

- T: 0113 386 3300
- W: www.morethanjustabed.com

•••••••••••••••••••••••••••••••••

Most fabulous for making you feel at home: myhotel Chelsea
•••••••••••••••••••••••••••••••••

Myhotels are an award-winning hospitality brand, with three hotels across the UK (two in London, one in Brighton). Each hotel uses feng shui 'to enable the senses to experience the harmony of sound, light, colour, aroma, texture and taste'. All babble aside, they really do appeal to your senses. My personal favourite is the Chelsea branch, themed around Sex and the City and perfectly combining eccentric English style with the cosmopolitan vibe of city living. You feel as though you're truly at home as you sit in front of the roaring fire on a cosy sofa with fresh flowers and natural light refreshing the air.

Designer James Soane of Project Orange aimed to make it feel like a refreshingly bright country house, and he's got it spot on. Located on a quiet residential street in Chelsea, it's peaceful yet only a short walk from some of the area's most sought-after labels and independent boutiques. The hotel serves chic afternoon tea delights with hoards of ladies who lunch attending each day, plus an extensive list of chic cocktails and delicious dishes. While you're there, you must visit the on-site spa too – girly heaven!

- **myhotel Chelsea, 35 Ixworth Place, London SW3 3QX**
- **T: 020 7225 7500**
- **W: www.myhotels.com**

•••••••••••••••••••••••••••••••••

Most fabulous for flamboyant eclecticism in the countryside: Crazy Bear Hotel, Stadhampton
•••••••••••••••••••••••••••••••••

This is no ordinary hotel. The reception is a lavishly restyled double-decker bus, so you know you're in for something different from the outset! Surrounded by tropical gardens, this sixteenth-century building has been bravely styled to mix the traditional with the outlandish yet super-stylish touches you expect from every Crazy Bear outlet. From oak beams, roaring fires and an eight-foot brown bear to a discreet Thai brasserie and dimly lit wine cellar, this is one extraordinary amalgamation of elegance, amusement and wit.

The English restaurant is bold – wine bottles form the ceiling, animal print covers the floor, and there's lots of padded leather, mirrors, chandeliers and impressive lighting. Modern British food is prepared using fresh produce from the Crazy Bear Farm Shop, including meats reared on the Crazy Bear Farm.

There are 17 bedroom suites, each individually designed, ranging from art deco to more contemporary and elaborately luxurious – think deep plunging copper roll-top baths at the foot of your gigantic four-poster bed, and very sexy textured wall coverings and clever lighting. This is an extravagantly plush yet wholly tranquil resting place. You'll love the individuality.

H

Heavenly Hair & Hotels

- Bear Lane, Stadhampton, Oxfordshire OX44 7UR
- W: www.crazybeargroup.co.uk

Most fabulous for doing business in style: Wyndham Grand

The Wyndham Grand, London Chelsea Harbour, is the flagship hotel in the Wyndham Worldwide family. Having undergone an extensive refurbishment plan, the new Penthouse Floor has three meeting rooms, an executive lounge and four exquisite penthouses overlooking the London skyline – a must to experience, each designed with a different theme.

Its unique waterside location in the prestigious Chelsea Harbour lends a peaceful location despite being in central London and is easy to get to, plus the business facilities are to a good standard, but it's the view that makes any long-winded tête-à-tête more enjoyable.

The new spa boasts seven treatment rooms, a nail bar and a swimming pool complete with juice bar to follow that hectic/boring/over-running business meeting. Perfect for mixing a little business with pleasure.

- Wyndham Grand, London Chelsea Harbour, London SW10 0XG
- W: www.wyndhamgrandlondon.co.uk

Most fabulous for its on-site restaurant: Park Plaza Sherlock Holmes

Park Plaza Sherlock Holmes is located on Baker Street. Although housing

119 rooms, the hotel has an intimate feel, but it's the AA rosette-awarded grill restaurant and buzzing cocktail bar that really makes this hotel. The staff are very knowledgeable in the food and drink departments, happy to cater to your tastes (which they do expertly), and I was most impressed with the cocktail list – so much so that I asked them to provide a recipe for my **C: Cocktails** section.

- Park Plaza Sherlock Holmes, 108 Baker Street, London W1I 6LJ
- T: 020 7486 6161
- W: www.parkplazasherlockholmes.com

The Park Plaza spa, **Aurora** (more accurately described as treatment rooms, in my opinion), is located downstairs in the hotel and is a cute little corner for pampering. Though tiny, there is a range of delicious treatments on offer, including the indulgent Chocolate Therapy for the face. Using 100% cocoa and natural cocoa butter, skin is nourished and hydrated with antioxidants and minerals. If you can resist the smell that makes you want to lick it all off, your skin will look luminous afterwards.

- Aurora, Park Plaza Sherlock Holmes, 108 Baker Street, London W1U 6LJ
- T: 020 7486 6161 or 07545 234220
- W: www.aurora-wellbeing.com

Most fabulous hotel bar: The May Fair Hotel

Holding 400 luxury hotel bedrooms, with some highly impressive suites, a spa, a restaurant, the London Casino and a truly funky bar, The May Fair

Bar serves what I refer to as 'proper food' – that is, generous portions and balanced meals. The menu offers a range of plates to make your mouth water and your tummy full, with classic dishes such as fish and chunky chips, sharing plates and gourmet burgers. Oh yes, I've never been one to graze! The bar has an electric atmosphere, heaving with trendy yet non-pretentious types – they do indeed exist!

I stayed in one of the super-swish duplexes with a private lounge area and upper-level bedroom. What struck me immediately about the hotel is the art work: collected from across the globe, this elegantly fashionable and über-cool hotel is as well known for its style as its legendary status, providing one of the best places to stay, dine, drink, dance or just gasp at. I have stayed where The Ratpack once stayed, and I recommend it highly to you.

• **The May Fair Hotel, Stratton Street, London W1J 8LT**
• **T: 020 7769 4041**
• **W: www.themayfairhotel.co.uk**

Most fabulous for rock-star cool: The Hard Days Night Hotel

The Hard Days Night Hotel in Liverpool is, inevitably, themed around the Beatles, with rock-star cool oozing from every one of their 110 bedrooms. If you want to go for the best the hotel has to offer, stay in the John Lennon penthouse suite complete with white interior and piano.

• **T: 0151 236 1964**
• **W: www.harddaysnighthotel.com**

Most fabulous for a restful treat pre-airport rush: The Chiswick Moran Hotel

Chiswick is a leafy West London riverside neighbourhood offering quick access to Heathrow Airport, so if you fancy chilling out and making the most of your London stay before your frantic trip or long flight, this is the place to enjoy.

Its position makes it ideal for touring the many attractions that London has to offer, if you have time – but as it boasts four-star accommodation, a retro-chic bar and restaurant and cosy, funky bedrooms, you may not want to leave.

All rooms have an airy feel, with lots of natural light pouring in through the picture windows that grant views of the green district that is Chiswick.

Napa Restaurant offers modern British cuisine in a chic setting and the palm-lined terrace makes an idyllic backdrop for a meal al fresco (weather permitting!), though the location is its high point.

• **Chiswick Moran Hotel, 626 Chiswick High Road, London W4 5RY**
• **T: 020 8996 5200**
• **W: www.moranhotels.com and www.naparestaurant.co.uk**

Most fabulous for catering for your ever-changing needs: The Zetter

The Zetter is a funky hotel with

an on-site destination restaurant, overlooking the fashionable St John's Square, London. The design overall, and in all 59 bedrooms, is light, airy, cosy and modern, and they're brilliant at adding luxurious detail, from the generous products to the seductive lighting and the private al fresco seating. There are rooms to cater for every mood and budget, the most positive feature of the hotel.

Stay with a friend in the Corner Deluxe, come back for a business trip and use the work station in the St John Superior, or, if you return for a rendezvous, there is a suite to suit. The 'ultimate Zetter experience' has to be the Rooftop Studio Deluxe where you'll delight in your own private outdoor patio area affording spectacular views of the London skyline, with so much indoor space on offer too. Toast your existence with one of their superb frozen cocktails by night, or enjoy the delicious breakfast on the patio by day. Not to be missed.

• **The Zetter, St John's Square, 86–88 Clerkenwell Road, London EC1M 5RJ**
• **T: 020 7324 4444**
• **W: www.thezetter.com**

See also C: Cocktails for their exclusive 6-Inch Stiletto cocktail.

Most fabulous for his and hers heaven: Oulton Hall

Oulton Hall is a stunning hotel converted from a mid-eighteenth-century mansion set amidst landscaped gardens and a 20-foot putt park course which is superb for golf fanatics and amateurs alike.

In fact, Oulton Hall boasts the north of England's leading golf performance centre, with buggy hire, a practice range for perfecting your putting, the Academy coaching facilities, staffed by four PGA teaching professionals, and a driving range with 18 covered and floodlit bays so you can practise at any time.

The 152 rooms maintain the elegant English charm and grandeur of the eighteenth century. In 1991 De Vere Hotels acquired the lease, spending some £20 million on restoration and expansion, and the Hall has been transformed into a truly luxurious hotel. Walls are adorned with proud portraits, staircases are winding and graceful, and the rich oak tones fuse with the full-bodied reds to create a sumptuous air of superiority.

The Spa at The Oulton Club is the latest addition and far more modern in style. There is a list of treatments from standard waxing and tanning to ESPA face and body treatments, and even 'ESPA for the boys', including 'Golfer's Tonic' to revive the most tired of gents.

After a day on the golf course, book the VIP Treatment Suite, which is a private room with your own hydro pool, steam room and shower and two reclining beds. The room is yours for as long as you require, so try a dual massage where you and yours are treated to a massage simultaneously, or hire it for a girly get-together and book in for treatments throughout the day as you sip champagne.

There is also a Drawing Room (ideal for afternoon tea), the Whisky

Room (stocking 300 whiskies from across the world), the Champagne Bar (in partnership with Perrier Jouet with over 50 champagnes) and two restaurants, The Claret Jug and The Calverly Grill, with the latter being awarded two rosettes.

It's the ideal retreat to keep both girly girls *and* men's men happy.

....

• **Oulton Hall, Rothwell Lane, Oulton, Leeds, Yorkshire LS26 8HN**
• **T: 0113 282 1000**
• **W: www.devere.co.uk/our-locations/ oulton-hall**

H

Heavenly Hair & Hotels

Ice Cream & Interior Design

Ice cream

Ice cream ... the only treat that can truly make us girls feel better after a break-up or bad day, and perfect for girls' nights in. From parlours to homemade brands and sugar-free varieties, stuff your face and get happy...

Hey Jude

As a family, they make homemade ice cream in their barn in Hampshire. It was all started in 2002 by the father of the family and is named after the mother. If that story is already too delicious, you'll love the flavours. Originally begun as a hobby, the ice cream was just sold to the village pub, but now the whole family have joined in and Jude's makes premium dairy ice cream that is available throughout the south-east of England, in addition to supplying well-known restaurant groups including Gordon Ramsay Holdings, Caprice Holdings, D&D Restaurants and Raymond Blanc's restaurants.

If you didn't think ice cream could be this cool (excuse the poor pun), well, you're wrong. *Harper's Bazaar* states, 'Jude's is the new name in ice cream,' and Simon Shama of *Vogue* magazine has a crush on the sorbet: 'Elderflower crush sorbet made by the terrific Jude's … is about as close to perfection as modern gelati will ever get.'

Using milk and cream from local cows, the family invest in their local community to create the likes of Peach and Champagne Crush, Winter Warmer and Ginger Spice. In addition, the company supports local causes, donating 10% of its profits to charity. Talk about honest family values! They even take on your suggestions for new flavours … Kir Royale ice cream, anyone?

W: www.judes.co.uk

Idyllic day out: Cheshire Farm Ice Cream

Set in a picture-perfect location overlooked by the twin peaks of Beeston and Peckforton Castle lies a farm with its own Ice Cream Parlour and adjoining Tea Room, seating 60 people. Start off at the under-sixes' play barn (only if you have kids with you, obviously), then visit the viewing gallery to watch the milking, and see the birds of prey and animal corner. There are 30 different flavours of ice cream in the parlour and five different types of cone to accompany your choice. Take-home packs of ice cream are also sold in the shop with freezer bags, cones and a range of other sundries to use at home. The farm also sells English Lakes Diabetic Ice Cream in Vanilla, Strawberry and Chocolate, so there's little excuse not to indulge.

• **Cheshire Farm Ice Cream, Tattenhall,**

Chester, Cheshire CH3 9NE
• **T: 01829 770446**
• **W: www.cheshirefarmicecream.co.uk**

Good since 1925: Winstones

Perched on the slopes of Rodborough Common in the Cotswolds, the Winstones have been making ice cream since 1925, originally made at the house adjoining the Greenacres site and sold direct to the public from a small shop there. The shop still exists, offering beautiful views as you slurp.

• **Winstones Ice Cream, Greenacres, Bownham, Stroud, Gloucestershire**
• **T: 01453 873270 or 873794**

Moo-licious

Mr Moo's ice cream parlour and coffee shop is most famous for their Cowpat Sundae and their six-scoop Mega Moo, a real treat for the brave! If you're all ice-creamed out, there's also a host of coffees, teas, smoothies and fresh, locally sourced snacks and finger sandwiches. They cater very well for children if you fancy a family day out.

• **Southfield House Farm, Skipsea, Driffield, East Yorkshire YO25 8SY**
• **T: 01262 469829**
• **W: www.mrmoos.co.uk**

Shaky Jakes

There are over 200 shakes to choose from at this nostalgic 1950s-style café – they've thought of everything,

Ice Cream & Interior Design

and you'll be staring at the menus for minutes on end, choosing anything from Jaffa Cakes, Wagonwheels, Oreo cookies and flapjacks to Iced Gems, Palma violets, Skittles and blueberries. You can make up your own concoction or choose from one of their creations. I loved the **Brown Owl** with marshmallow, chocolate brownies and their indulgent creamy ice cream.

With plans to open three more stores after just one year of trading, Shaky Jakes is set to satisfy sweet cravings nationwide. For now, enjoy their delights in Headingly and don't be put off by the queues: it's a sign of their quality and popularity.

- **Ground Floor, 2 Gateway House, 15 North Lane, Headingly LS6 3HG**
- **T: 0113 2179156**
- **W: www.shakyjakes.co.uk**

Fancy a Snog?

I've found a whole new way to snog, with all the fun and indulgence you desire from doing something naughty, yet with none of the shame... Snog is a delicious frozen yogurt that lacks fat and has hardly any calories, served with fresh fruit. The first brand to launch in the UK, Snog breaks new ground, offering an 'evolved version' of the frozen yogurt retail experience. They make their frozen yogurt fresh on the premises every day using fresh non-fat organic yogurt and organic skimmed milk. It's sweetened with organic Agave nectar, a natural plant extract with the same sweetness as refined sugar but with only half the calories.

The Natural Snog and Green Tea Snog have only 72 calories per 100g serving and miraculously, the Chocolate Snog has 79 calories per 100g serving. Knowing there's no fat, no artificial sweeteners or colouring, and a low calorific content and GI, there's no excuse not to Snog!

Snog South Kensington opened in May 2008 as the first in the UK and now in Soho. Snog Covent Garden and Snog Westfield are planned for the future.

- **W: www.ifancyasnog.com**

Made Fair ice cream

Feel fabulous when you indulge in Made Fair organic and fair trade luxury ice creams and frozen smoothies. Fair on the environment, fair to third world growers and fair to UK dairy farmers, Made Fair offers truly guilt-free pleasure. Made with British organic milk and cream, you can enjoy flavours such as Strawberry Pavlova, Cappuccino and Rich Chocolate.

- **Available at delis, independent retailers and other quality food stores across the UK**
- **W: www.creamogalloway.co.uk**

Interior design

'Home is where the heart is', 'staying in is the new going out', 'home sweet home' – with clichés like these there must be some truth in all of that, so take pride in your home and show it some love...

Hunky Dory Home

Hunky Dory Home specialize in 'gorgeous, quirky things for gorgeous, quirky people', having started out as 'an act of rebellion' aiming to produce bright, colourful home accessories as a backlash against the neutral products that saturate interior design shops. The handmade lampshades and cushions in bold prints, wall art, quirky clocks, kitchenalia and gifts will leave you spoilt for choice.

- T: 0191 6454004
- W: www.hunkydoryhome.co.uk

Sharon Marston

Marston is an extremely talented artist who creates bespoke handcrafted sculptural light installations using fibre-optic technology. Creations range from 'Azure', using hand-blown glass droplets in iridescent sea blue that cascade like a waterfall, to the elaborate and hypnotic 'Spiral' that weaves elegantly downwards. There are glorious centrepieces and more compact designs to suit any room. Simply stunning.

You can visit these works of art in the showroom by appointment.

- Studio F31 and F34a, Parkhall Road Trading Estate, 40 Martell Road, London SE21 8EN
- W: www.sharonmarston.com

Bombay Duck

Bombay Duck is the creation of two sisters on a mission to indulge the imagination with exuberant style, quirky design and a sassy sense of humour. Their printed hangers are great for displaying your Vera Wang creations in your bedroom – printed with words such as 'Belle of the Ball', 'Naughty but Nice', 'Footloose and Fancy Free' and 'Pretty as a Princess'. Their travel collection is also adorable, offering luxury passport holders and all-essential travel wallets to keep your tickets and documentation organized and looking chic. Well, it beats the tour operators' flimsy paper versions, doesn't it?

- W: www.bombayduck.com

Rockett St George

A purely online shop that aims to offer an eclectic mix of contemporary homeware and gifts with a strong emphasis on style. You'll find edgy, individual and modern yet timeless pieces here.

- T: 020 8350 5450
- W: www.rockettstgeorge.co.uk

Dotmaison

Dotmaison.com enables you to browse the collections of the world's leading home brands with designs inspired straight from the catwalks of London, New York, Milan and Paris. You wore this season's Missoni dress, and loved it. Now you can live in the style too. Versace, Vera Wang, Orla Kiely and Lulu Guinness collections can all be found on the virtual pages of Dotmaison.

- W: www.dotmaison.com

Ice Cream & Interior Design

Stickers get chic

Your home needs as much style consideration as your wardrobe, but is less easy and more expensive to change on a regular basis. A perfect way to change the look of your walls on a budget is by using stickers. Less fussy and more modern than stencils, stickers change the look of a room in minutes. The **Iron Vines** wall graphics pack from *abodeliving.co.uk* contains nine stickers to create your design, and there are some very fun and elegant designs available at **Sticky Ups**.

• W: www.abodeliving.co.uk
• W: www.stickyups.co.uk

The Nursery Company

The Nursery Company provides a truly exclusive, stylish and bespoke service to the discerning parent or designer. The luxury interior collections and accessories for children's rooms capture and inspire all imaginations. A wide range of colours, prints, textures and styles are available to create the perfect children's room. The Nursery Company also provides an ultra-speedy service, allowing for last-minute orders that only take 3–5 weeks to create, so there's no need to battle down the high street.

• T: 020 7228 3042
• W: www.thenurserycompany.com

Supernice

Supernice represents exceptional design-led products and brands, often bringing them to the UK market for the first time. Best for achieving a cool and original vibe.

• W: www.supernice.co.uk

Designers' showcase at 30elm

30elm is an online community for home owners and interior designers to network and collaborate on home design projects. You can also start your own project, choose the basic criteria, and blog about your process, adding items from your folder, which holds things you've collected from

Fab Tips

Vinegar is a household saviour! Use it to clean slatted blinds by donning a cotton glove and dipping your hand into a solution made of equal parts white vinegar and hot tap water. Slide your fingers across each slat and you will be amazed at the dirt removed. White wine vinegar also removes mildew from your showerhead, shower screens and windows, and if you put some in a spray bottle, a gentle mist of this wonder-stuff will prevent mildew on the bottoms of rugs and carpeting too.

around the site. Invite others to join your team for group collaboration, or find professionals to help you, and if you're a budding interior designer, you can let the professionals find you as well.

• W: www.30elm.com

my interior stylist ltd

My interior stylist offers an essential service to anyone who wants their home to look fabulous but doesn't necessarily have a fabulous bank balance. Specialists in home styling, all projects are catered for, from total refurbishment and project management to one-day makeovers or even just a day shopping for cushions! Experts in achieving a designer look without the price tag, they are worth their weight in shiny gold. For other services, check out the website or call creative director Zoe personally for some friendly advice.

• T: 07516 762 768
• W: www.myinteriorstylist.com

Ice Cream & Interior Design

Jet-Setting

J

& 'Just For Fun'

Jet-setting

There's plenty to see, do and experience in your UK-wide guide, but every fabulous girl travels frequently and there's only one way to do it – in style. This section has everything from luxury airlines to airport lounge access and chic getaways...

Travel in style

Luxury in the air: Jet Airways

India's premier international airline, Jet Airways, is one of only three airlines to fly to the UK with private suites in first class. The suite doubles up as a one-to-one meeting room, offers a one-to-one private dining experience, or just simply provides passengers with the ultimate in luxury, comfort and privacy.

Now get this: each suite includes a 23-inch flat-screen television and substantial storage areas that include a personal hanging wardrobe, dual credenza and an ottoman. The seats, manufactured by BE Aerospace, will convert to the world's longest flat beds at 83 inches and offer variable lumbar support and an eight-point massage system.

The state-of-the-art in-flight Panasonic eX2 entertainment system offers passengers over 200 hours of Hollywood and Bollywood movies, regional films, television and short programming, audio CDs covering every imaginable music genre and much, much more, all on demand and all heard through Bose noise cancellation headphones.

If you really have to work among all this luxury, laptop power and in-flight telephones are available with the unique ability to send SMS and email. A Bulgari amenity kit is provided for passengers, along with a luxury sleeper suit. The menu choices are extensive and served on hand-painted Bernardaud porcelain dinnerware. The Indian element of Jet Airways' in-flight menu is designed and catered for by Kensington's Bombay Brasserie (part of the luxury Taj group), while Michelin-starred chef Yves Mattagne has recently joined the Jet Airways catering team and will be designing the Western element of the food. The finest of champagnes, including vintage Dom Perignon and Krug, as well as the best wines from around the world and a library of single malt whiskies are served in Mikasa crystal glasses.

Right, that makes 'cattle class' look exactly that!

• **T: 0808 101 1199**
• **W: www.jetairways.com**

Meet and Greet

Meet and Greet is the ultimate parking service. A chauffeur meets you outside the terminal and drives your car to the airport car park. On your return, a chauffeur returns your car to you outside the terminal and all this is arranged with a quick telephone call. It takes so much hassle out of waiting around (most probably in the cold as you head back to Blighty) and it's comforting to know that it's all there waiting for you so you can head back home in a flash.

• **W: www.purpleparking.com**

Airport Angel

For the girl who likes to travel in style, Airport Angel is an airport lounge membership programme giving access to a network of over 300 VIP airport lounges worldwide. Irrespective of class of ticket, Airport Angel members can escape the hustle and bustle of airport departure areas and find a private space in a comfortable airport lounge, where they can relax away from the crowds and enjoy first-class facilities while the AirTexts service keeps you informed of boarding progress plus any changes or delays to your flight. Airport Angel has a dedicated customer care team open

Jet-Setting & 'Just For Fun'   **J**

24/7, 365 days a year, and members also receive preferential rates for other travel services such as car hire and airport parking. Available by paying a reasonable membership fee.

- **T: 08448 73 13 73**
- **W: www.airportangel.co.uk**

Mr & Mrs Smith

Boutique hotel experts, Mr & Mrs Smith have been producing guidebooks and selling stylish stays long before 'Brangelina' even thought of making contract-killer movies together. The London-based company now offers around 500 gorgeous hotels and self-catering properties, all of which are available to book via its expert travel team or award-winning website.

It also operates a membership scheme which entitles you to free gifts at check-in – from bottles of champagne to spa treatments – as well as huge discounts, room upgrades and

savings on fashionista-friendly brands that Mr & Mrs Smith love, including Myla, Coco Ribbon and Heidi Klein.

Its 'Get a Room!' gift cards, available in £50 denominations, also make the most perfect presents.

- **T: 0845 034 0700**
- **W: www.mrandmrssmith.com**

Holiday Extras

The UK's leading holiday add-ons provider for the savvy traveller, Holiday Extras offers airport parking, hotels and lounges at unbeatable rates. The earlier you book, the better the rates available. Also, all parking and hotel bookings are covered by the Best Price Guarantee, so if you find the same on offer cheaper elsewhere, they'll pick up the cost of your booking. Parking and hotels are available at all major airports nationwide.

- **W: www.holidayextras.com**

Fab Tip

Flights and travelling can dry out your skin, so remove your make-up en route and apply a nourishing cream to your face. **Elizabeth Arden's Eight Hour Cream** and **Prescriptive's Super Flight Cream** are my two favourites and they've been around for decades. They'll instantly revive parched skin, making them perfect to use in-flight.

- **W: www.prescriptives.com (N)**
- **W: www.elizabetharden.co.uk (N)**

Seat Guru

We all want the best seat on the plane when we travel, but unless you're in first class, it's difficult to know which seat will offer you the finest experience. Seat Guru rate almost every seat in a wide variation of plane models according to leg room, seat comfort and window alignment, so you can book in advance and fly in comfort.

• **W: www.seatguru.com**

Travel and learn

Learn to cook Italian food in Italy

In my pursuit of fabulousness, I simply couldn't leave out a week of learning how to cook authentic Italian food at a villa in the hills of Tuscany. Celebrity chef Maria Liberati, author of the best-selling book *The Basic Art of Italian Cooking*, is director of the ultra-elegant Cooking School in Italy which opens around four times a year. The programmes are six nights/ seven days and include a choice of lodging at the spacious villa or luxury suites at the local castle of Sismano, authentic hands-on Italian cooking classes, wine tastings at the local vineyards, tours of olive oil mills, an opportunity to meet with artisan food producers, a tour of the local pottery studio, nature walks in the hills of Umbria, all meals and wine, plus transport from Rome airport to the villa and back, and La Dolce Vita for the week.

The cooking school and villa are located in the region of Umbria and village of Sismano, a town that borders on Tuscany.

• **W: www.marialiberati.com**

Learning Holidays

Learning Holidays has over 1,000 holiday courses in 30 countries worldwide. Five of the most fabulous include cosmetic-making, perfume-making, cooking, wine tasting, and surf and yoga camps with an eco-twist…

Learn to make your own cosmetics in Paris

You'll learn from a Parisian how to create your own personalized products – lipstick, face and body cream using all natural ingredients. You take home recipes so you can easily recreate these back home.

Create your own signature scent in Grasse or Eze in France (the home of Chanel No. 5)

You can learn to create your own perfume on the Côte d'Azur. Learning Holidays offer a range of courses starting from under £50, but the two-day personalized course gives you your own Maître Parfumeur to help you create a scent that you can reorder in the future. This brings a new meaning to your 'signature scent'.

Dinner party cooking

Learn how to cook dishes to impress even the most serious of foodies. Cooking weekends are available in France, Spain and Italy. This would be fun to go to as a group of girls so you can sample the local talent – sorry, *culture* – too!

You'll learn how to cook traditional dishes and how to 'plate up' and serve food that makes a difference.

Discover luxury wine and relaxation in Bordeaux

Learn all about Bordeaux wines, from young wines to vintage, and have lunch at a Michelin-starred restaurant where you'll have a lesson on wine and food pairing.

Adventure/activity: learn to surf and practise yoga on an eco-friendly surf holiday in Seignosse, France

You will relax in a fabulous eco-friendly luxury surf camp in France, where you can chill out in the hydro pool and snack on organic foods as you hang out in the hammocks after your surfing and yoga lessons. Bliss!

• W: www.golearnto.com

Activity holidays

Many girls are getting into action sports these days – they're not just for the guys! Surfing, wakeboarding, kitesurfing and snowboarding are just a few of the adrenalin sports out there, and guess what, I've tried most of them so I can tell you what the best activities are.

Snow and Wake

A really fabulous idea for a week away with the girls is Snow and Wake in Bulgaria, such a fantastic place for girls to go now they have opened their new Dragushinovo Boutique Chalet Hotel. Activities range from wakeboarding to waterskiing, jet-skiing, sailing, fishing and mountain-biking. Between activities, you will be treated to massage and relaxation, or you can spend time sunning yourself on the beautiful lakeside beach with a mojito from the bar and restaurant, or, if you go in the winter, a hot toddy in front of the log fires.

• W: www.snowandwakebulgaria.com

Jingando

Jingando Holidays is a Rio de Janeiro specialist able to set up all kinds of holidays to the city within its tailor-made programme. The company particularly specializes in two types of Rio holiday: dancing and volunteering. Jingando uses its profits to support the Julio Otoni after-school children's club in Rio. Kids there learn English and computing, courtesy of an online computer room, and travel on group excursions to local sights normally inaccessible to them. A holiday with Jingando mean you automatically financially assist the club, so you can have fun and offer help where it matters.

Jingando offers a two-week trip combining samba lessons with sessions working on the Make Favela Art community project – a programme that is slowly painting the outsides of buildings in a hillside shantytown, transforming it into a luminous landmark of which locals can be proud … a mural to boost morale, if you like.

Volunteers are treated to fabulous views of Rio while they paint. In the mornings, learn the classic Brazilian dance courtesy of one-to-one lessons at Marinho Bras' renowned samba school, and put your new skills to use by night in Rio's lively bars and clubs (accompanied by a tour host). You can either spend 14 hours dancing and eight hours painting, or vice versa, and there are excursions to Sugar Loaf, Christos and Copacabana thrown in for good measure.

- T: 020 8877 1630
- W: www.jingandoholidays.com and www.jingandoholidays.com/community

Get a share in an aircraft: NetJets

NetJets Europe is the largest operator of business jets and private jets in Europe and they've worked out how to drive down the cost of flying privately through buying a share in a NetJets aircraft. This will buy you access to an entire fleet for a tiny fraction of what it costs to buy and maintain a single aircraft.

You are guaranteed an aircraft whenever you need it, anywhere in the world. You can fly as often or as little as you like and you only pay for the hours you use, no capital exposure, no long-term commitment. That's one cost-effective way of living the dream!

- T: 020 7361 9620
- W: www.netjetseurope.com

See Central and South America with Journey Latin America

Whether you want to relax in paradise on the beaches of Brazil, snorkel in the turquoise waters of Mexico, rub shoulders with the tropical penguins of the Galapagos or ride with the Gauchos of Argentina, Journey Latin America are 'the UK's No. 1' travel specialist to Central and South America. Every one of their 70 staff has lived, worked or travelled in the region and they are able to offer practical advice based on personal experience.

- Journey Latin America, 12 &13, Heathfield Terrace, London W4 4JE
- T: 020 8747 8315
- W: www.journeylatinamerica.co.uk

Luxury hotels and spas overseas

Chiva-Som, Hua Hin, Thailand

Located in the royal resort of Hua Hin on the Gulf of Thailand, Chiva-Som is Asia's premier dedicated health spa, offering a holistic approach to health and wellness that blends Eastern and Western philosophies. Chiva-Som, meaning 'Haven of Life', is world-renowned for the quality of its therapies as well as its delicious, healthy spa cuisine. Chiva-Som is the only destination spa to have been consistently ranked as one of the top three 'Best Destination Spas' at the Condé Nast Traveller Readers'

Awards, since the awards were launched ten years ago.

and opulence of the city's latest skyscraping hotels.

- **W: www.chivasom.com**

- **W: www.desertpalm.ae**

Cotton Bay Village, St Lucia

Enjoying a beautiful beachside location on the picturesque east coast of St Lucia, Cotton Bay Village is a cool Caribbean cocktail of private villas and a world-class destination resort, served in a tropical village setting that epitomizes barefoot elegance. With just 74 luxury suites, townhouses and villas, Cotton Bay Village is an oasis of peace, offering a refined yet relaxed experience and a warm, welcoming environment in which discerning guests can truly feel at home.

- **W: www.cottonbayvillage.com**

Desert Palm, Dubai

Set in the manicured surrounds of a polo estate, Desert Palm emerges from the desert landscape to provide a refreshing, avant-garde contrast to the conventional ostentation

Hotel Hacienda Na Xamena, Ibiza

Hotel Hacienda Na Xamena is located on an unspoilt coastal plot of San Miguel in the north-east, sitting 180 metres above sea level amid a two-kilometre stretch of coast and wild Mediterranean pine tree forest.

Every inch of this luxurious property is breathtaking, from the grandiose entrance to the harmony of the freshwater outdoor pool. Everywhere you look, you are surrounded by hilltop greenery and the hypnotic glint of the turquoise sea, making the view the finest element of the venue, yet there is a host of tempting treats to occupy you otherwise.

There is a total of 65 rooms and suites, many equipped with a private jacuzzi, sunken hyrdo bathtub and panoramic views over the cliffs and sea. Each room is comfortably modern and oozing the same atmosphere of relaxation as the entire venue.

A must-try is the thalassotherapy

★ Fab Tip ★

The poolside bar at Hotel Hacienda Na Xamena is perfect for watching the sunset with a cocktail. Also try the exclusive trip by yacht to Formantera to discover this upcoming, nearby and terribly chic island. The Workshop Na Xamena is worth a try too, where you can learn cooking skills alongside demonstrations in their specialized kitchen.

saltwater treatment pools with sea views and cascades, nestled on the side of the hilltop for ultimate tranquillity. Each pool uses water in a distinct way, pumped from the Mediterranean and heated to 37°C to massage and stimulate different areas of your body (the powerful therapeutic water jets work wonders for stiff shoulders).

The hotel has five gourmet restaurants, each with a different atmosphere, taking you from a chilled-out breakfast to a magical evening meal – and what exquisite cuisine!

This is an unforgettable romantic getaway that's simply stunning, both gastronomically and aesthetically.

• **For more information on Hotel Hacienda Na Xamena, visit www.preferredboutique.com**

Huvafen Fushi, The Maldives

Nestled within its very own private lagoon, Huvafen Fushi is the Maldives' most stylish resort. Huvafen Fushi showcases the world's very first underwater spa and the most spacious accommodation in the Maldives, with 43 'island chic' bungalows, each boasting a vast private plunge pool. Highly exclusive.

• **W: www.huvafenfushi.com**

Paresa, Thailand

Situated on the western coast of Phuket, Thailand, Paresa is a deluxe five-star resort, located in the area often referred to as 'Millionaires' Row'. Perched high on the clifftop, surrounded by tropical forests and

131

the blue waters of the Andaman Ocean, Paresa's unique architecture and elegant interiors are inspired by traditional Southern Thai homes in both the design and the use of natural materials which complement the surroundings. Each of the 49 spacious rooms and suites has a spectacular outlook, boasting uninterrupted sea views, most offering private infinity pools from which guests can enjoy the magnificent surroundings.

• **W: www.paresaresorts.com**

Wellbeing Escapes, UK

Try searching the net for a 'health holiday', and you'll find hundreds of confusing, conflicting options. Wellbeing Escapes search for the rare, the wonderful, the best-kept secrets and the ultimate escape, meticulously researching and reviewing everything they offer. Working with specialists to provide a wellness experience that delivers what it promises, whether it's an introduction to yoga in the Himalayas or a stress-free day in a top spa in London, the aim is simply to make sure clients come back feeling fabulous.

• **W: www.wellbeingescapes.co.uk**

Holiday extras

Price Plummeting Villas

A great excuse for groups of girls to snap up a top European villa on the cheap, Belvilla's 'Price Plummet' sees

the price on a selected villa plummet, with the price you end up paying becoming cheaper by the second.

Belvilla's 'Price Plummet' takes place daily, every week, and if you are the lucky one, you can end up renting a villa for as little as £1! But don't wait too long, they only have one villa on offer per week and the first to bid gets it.

Belvilla are the only company in the travel industry to operate such an exciting scheme, and they decided to start it in order to celebrate their 20-year anniversary. It's proved so popular that it's now a permanent fixture, and one I want to share with you – aren't you lucky!

• **W: www.belvilla.co.uk**

TripAdvisor.co.uk

You may have the ideal destination in mind, but what if it turns out to be a disappointment? If your 'five-star deluxe hotel' has ever ended up being more like 'an ant-ridden two-star hell', avoid this nightmare recurring and bid farewell to disappointing hotels with *TripAdvisor.co.uk* – the ultimate companion to planning a fittingly fabulous trip.

Featuring over 20 million reviews penned by real travellers, TripAdvisor gives you insiders' opinions and candid photos, revealing what hotels are really like. Search by town to compare an array of options in a particular spot, or look up individual hotel names for the low-down on a specific place.

• **W: www.TripAdvisor.co.uk**

Holiday gear: Tica London

You have the destination down, the flight booked and your place in the airport lounge booked, but planning your holiday wardrobe is just as essential! If you like to travel but often struggle to find gorgeous swimwear year-round on the high street, shop online at Tica London, a dedicated holiday shop with everything from swimwear to sandals and kaftans. The accessories and clothing offer a wide range and there's some good advice on finding swimwear to suit your body shape too.

• W: www.ticalondon.com

The insider's view from Globalista

Globalista lists out and recommends the best of the best, in one report, for a series of trips and places – from hotels and restaurants to shops and museums, and not just the obvious tourist attractions but also the hidden gems and insider recommendations on cities, ski resorts and regions throughout Europe and beyond.

Each guide is checked and assessed by residents in each destination. Come away from your holiday destination feeling as if you've got under the skin of that place, rather than simply settling for a tourist's overview.

• T: 020 7243 9066
• W: www.globalista.co.uk

If you like this section, see also O: Outdoor Pursuits for other activity ideas.

Just for fun

All work and no play makes Jill a dull girl. Ensure that you balance your hectic lifestyle with an equal dose of letting-your-hair-down time with this lot…

Club Boudoir

Every woman has the right to feel good about herself, and the team at Club Boudoir appreciate this more than most. The girls who perform as part of this leading burlesque cabaret know that feeling sexy isn't about how you look, it's about loving what you've got and knowing how to work it! OK, so this might be simplifying things a bit, but if you're sitting there thinking you're not sexy or could be more confident, then I suggest you try one of Club Boudoir's burlesque workshops. Whether you go on your own, as part of a group, or even with a hen party, you're guaranteed more fun than you can shake a tassle at.

Club Boudoir are based in the north-east, but travel around the UK and abroad performing at a host of public and private events.

• W: www.clubboudoir.co.uk

Time for Tease

In 2008 Time for Tease gave Kate Moss her birthday cake and a burlesque performance, and their Afternoon Tease teaches groups of women how to bump and grind for

J

Jet-Setting & 'Just For Fun'

themselves – a fabulous way to break the ice and get you all laughing. Afterwards, when you've worked up an appetite, Time For Tease will serve you a delightful afternoon tea. Burlesque, girly time and tea – how wonderful!

....

• T: 020 7831 1622 and 079 7113 0611
• W: www.timefortease.co.uk

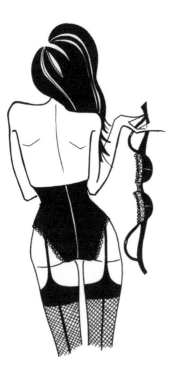

••••••••••••••••••••••••••••••••••

Discover new places with Fido on board: The Flying Dog Club

••••••••••••••••••••••••••••••••••

If your dog replaces diamonds as your best friend and you love to take him everywhere, you can now take your adoring four-legged friend on board a plane with you, giving him

the class he deserves!

The Flying Dog Club (FDC), founded by Canadian veterinarian Dr Peter Dobias, is an online gathering place where you can meet other like-minded people who believe that their dog is family, not luggage.

As the Flying Dog Club membership grows, you and other members will be able to collaborate and organize groups to charter a plane and fly to your favourite destination with your four-legged friend on board.

You no longer need to snorkel, play ball or explore alone. Now Fido can come with you to share all those memories. Genius!

....

• W: www.flyingdogclub.com
• E: contact@flyingdogclub.com

••••••••••••••••••••••••••••••••••

Drive a digger

••••••••••••••••••••••••••••••••••

Diggerland guarantees a fun-filled, exciting, action-packed day out for kids and adults of all ages. Children (and adults if they wish) have the opportunity to ride in, and drive, different types of construction machinery including dumper trucks, mini diggers and giant diggers (all under strict supervision). There are great opportunities to take photos, or learn about the workings of the machines from the fully trained instructors constantly on hand. You'd find it hard to compare this experience: it's not your average day out, but so much silly fun nonetheless!

....

• W: www.diggerland.com

••••••••••••••••••••••••••••••••••

Body casting

••••••••••••••••••••••••••••••••••

Brighton Body Casting is a company

that makes portrait sculptures of people cast directly from their bodies – from couples' hands entwined to whole bodies, boobs, bums, pregnant tummies, faces and kids' hands. The founder has frequently been on TV and in the news for such things as casting Trinny's and Susannah's bottoms and Lisa Roger's nether regions. There is something for everybody, from family portrait sculptures to sensual casts for couples and empowering body casts for women.

• **JAG open studio/gallery, Arch 283a, Madeira Drive, Brighton, East Sussex BN2 1PS**
• **T: 07961 338 045**
• **W: www.brightonbodycasting.com**

Flying high: the Gyrocopter

I loved the Gyrocopter experience! Deemed 'the motorbike of the sky', it looks like a small two-seater helicopter and flies slow enough and low enough for you to see what's happening in the world below – exhilarating! When the instructor told me I would be sitting in the front, I laughed out loud. 'Very funny,' I remarked sarcastically, climbing into the back. 'No, really!' said my instructor. He meant it.

We had a quick run through of the various mechanisms, the buttons I would be controlling, and pilot talk ('Check!'). Then came the reassurance that the Gyrocopter has dual controls which my instructor would be controlling, thus flying the machine from the back. Phew!

The whole flight was incredibly smooth, from take-off to landing, and

I felt limitless yet rested. We flew over York – such a beautiful place – so I lapped up the view below. As you fly at a certain height, you can see the detail of the roads and buildings below. It makes you look at the world in a new light.

For around two minutes, I actually flew the Gyrocopter myself! 'Just so you know, you're actually in complete control right now,' said my instructor, with both of his hands placed on my shoulders as I giggled nervously while trying not to nosedive.

But in all honesty, this experience was absolutely thrilling! I quickly felt rested and peaceful and enjoyed the ride. The instructor can take it slow or up the adrenalin-fuelled tricks if you like. Being a bit of a daredevil, I took the latter option, of course, and a few generous tilts and dips satisfied my enterprising side. Mostly, this will make you feel liberated and I finally understand the phrase about feeling 'as a free as a bird'.

The experience can be had nationwide, and I urge you to dare.

• **T: 0845 643 9476**
• **W: www.thegyrocopterexperience.co.uk**

Foot reading

Jane Sheehan is the UK's leading foot reader – she can read personality traits, emotions and feelings in the shape of the feet and toes. Jane does foot readings in person, or via the website using photographs, and even holds foot reading parties – a definite improvement on other 'party plan' get-togethers! Jane now travels the world teaching foot reading and doing talks at company events and product launches.

....

- **W: www.footreading.com**

Girls will be girls: Nunsmere Hall

If you're planning a hen do or just want some indulgent time with your friends, then visit Nunsmere Hall for a night of friends, fun, food and champagne.

You'll be provided with designer pyjamas; party food served in your award-winning bedroom; chilled champagne; a manicure and pedicure; and a full English breakfast the next day. In grounds boasting a 60-acre lake, the Hall makes executive life fade into the background and offers the ultimate girls' night in.

....

- **Nunsmere Hall, Tarporley Road, Oakmere, Northwich, Cheshire CW8 2ES**
- **W: www.primahotels.co.uk/nunsmere**

Be a karaoke queen with Lucky Voice

Lucky Voice believes in private karaoke. That means singing in front of friends, not strangers. You book a private karaoke room for just you and your closest friends, search the song list to create your own playlist, then use the touch screen in your booth to select those songs. There's even a 'thirsty' button to get drinks delivered to your room, if your warbling makes you parched (or you need a little Dutch courage)!

- **Available in London, Manchester and Cardiff**
- **W: www.luckyvoice.com**

PhotoFunia

Fancy being Marilyn Monroe, Superman or perhaps a carnival dancer? Upload your face and become them! This website is hilarious, easy and fun and will waste hours on a dull day at work.

....

- **W: www.photofunia.com**

No man needed with your Bookshelf Boyfriend

Visit bookshelfboyfriend.com for an invaluable website for modern independent women. It provides typically blokey information – on DIY, technology, motoring, sports, finance, etc. in girl-friendly, straightforward and non-patronizing articles, tips and how-to guides.

....

- **W: www.bookshelfboyfriend.com**

Keep fit *and* have fun!

I disagree with depriving myself and love to enjoy a glass of bubbly, afternoon tea or a cute cupcake. But I do realize that if I want all these treats *and* want to stay healthy, balance and moderation are key. Keeping fit and well is important; after all, your health is your wealth, so I test some of the best and most fun ways to get fit and keep fit…

Burlesque and pole dancing: Polestars

Polestars, the UK's largest alternative fitness school, offer fabulous burlesque classes, pole dancing lessons and can-can classes across the UK for fun and fitness. So ditch the gym and get yourself onto a sexy workout, which will not only tone up your body, but will leave you with bags of confidence, ready to take on the world.

Burlesque is particularly fun. This hugely popular performance art is designed to titillate, taunt and tease. I fancied myself as an aspiring Dita

Von Teese and absolutely loved the experience (as did my fella)!

• **For more information, contact Shing Mon Chung, Polestars, Unit 54, Eurolink Business Centre, 49 Effra Road, London SW2 1BZ**
• **T: 020 7274 4865 or 020 7274 4961**
• **W: www.polestars.net**

See also J: Just for Fun for burlesque workshops

Achieve something amazing with CARE Challenge

Why not get fit and support a good cause? CARE Challenge is an in-house events team for CARE International, with 14 years' experience of running mountain-based and multi-activity challenges for corporate teams and individuals. The money you fundraise is used towards fighting poverty in 70 countries, helping 48 million people each year.

One example is the UK mountain challenge: climb the highest mountains in England, Scotland and Wales in 24 hours! You'll begin in the Scottish Highlands on Saturday afternoon, where you and your team will take on the mighty Ben Nevis (1,334m). Then it's down to the Lake District for an early morning ascent of Scafell Pike (978m). The final mountain is Snowdon (1,085m) in North Wales, to be tackled on Sunday afternoon. You return to a celebratory meal, and expend any remaining reserves of energy at the post-event party!

You'll be supported throughout your fundraising, training and the event itself by the experienced CARE Challenge Team.

CARE Challenge allows you to take on a classic challenge, meet new people, experience some of the most spectacular scenery in the UK and, at the same time, help some of the poorest people in the world to overcome the challenges they face on a daily basis.

• **T: 020 7934 9334**
• **W: www.carechallenge.org.uk**

Get fit the virtual way with EA Sports Active

The EA Sports Active Personal Trainer is like having your very own personal trainer right in the comfort of your own home. The new interactive fitness product really makes you work up a sweat, and is guaranteed to improve your fitness levels. Like a personal trainer, it will motivate you to keep on moving, increase intensity levels and give you real-time feedback. It even features a '30 day challenge', which is a different 20-minute workout, five days a week, keeping you on track to reach your personal goals.

• **W: www.easportsactive.co.uk (N)**

Power Plates

I'm a fan of yoga and Pilates, but I do find some exercises too boring and I'm also short on time, as most of us are. Power Plates is the ideal solution. Twenty-five minutes, three times a week, is all Power Plates asks of you. Led by an instructor, you perform exercise moves on a vibrating machine which will work everything from your core to legs, bum and tum. Because of

K

Keep Fit

the vibrations, an easy 25 minutes on a Power Plate equates to 90 minutes of regular exercise. Easy peasy! Just watch out for the burn the day after…

• W: www.esporta.com (N)

Bikram Yoga

Practised in a steaming hot room, you will carry out a series of poses and because of the heat your joints will loosen, helping you to stretch more easily. You'll also literally sweat out toxins, so while you get toned and detox in one hit, you can forget vanity! Bikram yoga leaves no room for looking good, but one thing's for sure, if you push yourself and stick to it, you will look terrific afterwards.

• T: 020 7637 3095
• W: www.bikramyogasoho.co.uk

Yogahikes

Try a week of energetic physical and spiritual exercise consisting of four hours of yoga and two vigorous hikes – one compulsory and one optional – every day, a healthy diet, no caffeine, alcohol or cigarettes and complete silence during the morning. Does this sound like hell? It shouldn't – it's designed to lift you and help you find happiness within yourself. Does this sound deep? It should do – one week will provide you with much laughter, great food, new friendships and 'good karma'.

The retreat takes place in Val d'Ambra, the Golden Valley in Italy, north of Florence. Staying at Iesolana, a private 250-acre estate, participants

are secluded from the outside world by olive groves, forest and splendid grapevines. Getting fit has never sounded so beautiful.

• T: 07796 671 549
• W: www.yogahikes.com

X-Bike

The X-Bike is a high-tech exercise bike for modern women, complete with an iPod. You watch a video which guides you through a 30-minute workout and added resistance to the bike makes you assume correct form, which is why you benefit from a shorter workout time as your calorie burn is higher.

As long as you don't expect it to compare to the real thing, this is a short sharp workout ideal for lunch breaks that works you well and helps you escape to a fake outdoor cycle run for a wee while!

• X-Bike at Destination, 42–48 Great Portland Street, London W1
• T: 020 7636 4477
• W: www.x-biking.com

At home gym: Virtual Gym TV

VirtualGym TV is Europe's first online gym, offering a wide range of services and classes from aerobics, combat and Pilates to dance, tai chi and meditation/relaxation sessions.

Classes are strategically planned for time and target audience. For example, sessions in the morning are offered specifically as an early morning energizer. Sessions are broadcast across a range of ability standards, so you can choose what's suitable for you. You can

K

Keep Fit

also learn new skills with the 'starter' teaching sessions. All classes can be viewed using Windows Media Player, burnt to DVD and played back on a regular DVD player, or you can stream the video file directly to your standard television from your computer.

Will this eliminate cheesy 'celeb' fitness videos? We can only hope.

• W: www.virtualgym.tv

If it's Fit for a Princess, it's fit for me

Fit for a Princess is a fun, female-focused outdoor fitness business that specializes in Group Outdoor Workouts, Bootcamps, Running Clubs and Personal Training for women in a variety of London parks.

Janey Holliday is the founder and one of the UK's top female wellbeing experts. After having twins, Janey was back in shape in no time at all, proving that her way really does work.

Fit for a Princess Bootcamps are designed for women of all ages and abilities and are hugely popular – with up to 50 women training together at 6 a.m. all year round! The two-week intensive bootcamps maximize inch loss, shape change and fitness levels with fantastic results, using the split routine training method popular with Hollywood A-listers.

• T: 07711 260 336
• W: www.fitforaprincess.co.uk

Gyrotonic: look fabulous in high heels

Through simple yet superbly effective exercises, ex-dancer Sarah Toner will get you walking and standing more beautifully than you could possibly have imagined. You will feel and look 100% more confident in your stilettos (Sarah insists that you bring your most challenging shoes!), and it's not just about the way you wear your Manolos. Sarah's genuine concern for women's wellbeing makes for a therapeutic session, plenty of laughter and lots of story-swapping for the more vivacious. For those who prefer a more serene atmosphere, Sarah is sensitive to that too. You can book privately or as a group and both are equally as satisfying. Now you can wear those skyscrapers you pushed to the back of your wardrobe and don't have to worry about killing your feet in the process.

• W: www.sarahtoner.co.uk

See also F: Fashion for my tips on 'How to turn a wobble into a wiggle' – how to wear and walk in high heels.

The cheat's way: Sweatz Vest

Launched to help shift those extra stubborn pounds, the Sweatz Vest from Sweatz Sportz is a revolutionary new product to help weight loss. The patented, 100% toxin free, biodegradable vest is simply worn beneath your usual training clothing to help generate dynamic weight loss. The vest works by causing the body to sweat more, which uses up more calories. The water lost is replaced by drinking, but the calories used to create the sweat stay off. In addition, the sweating helps the body detoxify, eliminating chemicals stored in the fat cells and making weight loss easier.

• W: www.sweatzsportz.com

Diet with real food!

Hannah Sutter, founder of The Campaign for Natural Dieting, says that we should throw away the scales, pour meal replacements down the sink and forget calorie-counting. The secret to feeling great and looking fabulous in her view is real food! A diet based on protein, good fats (nuts and seeds) and some specific carbohydrates (leafy vegetables and low GI fruit) is the same diet that we have been evolved to eat over thousands of years. Not all of us have time to go out foraging for our food, so Hannah has created a home delivery service providing three nutritionally balanced meals and snacks, all designed to deliver a protein-rich source of real food that tastes great.

• W: www.golower.co.uk

10 top tips to keep you in fabulous tip-top condition by celebrity personal trainer, Lucy Wyndham-Read

Lucy is ex-army and specializes in women's fitness, having helped hundreds of women lose weight and keep it off. She is the founder of *www.lwrfitness.com*, which designs workouts for women to follow at home, with videos, fitness diaries, diets and lots of motivation. Lucy offers you her top ten tips on how to squeeze exercise into your busy daily routine, and explains how making small changes will make all the difference so you can look your best in no time at all…

1 Tone your arms in the supermarket. While doing your weekly shopping! Simply swap the trolley for two baskets. This will help to tone your arms and your shoulders, with the added bonus that you will only buy the items you really need, preventing you from loading up on high-calorie junk!

2 Brush and tone at the same time. Make this a rule of thumb now and every time you brush your teeth perform some squats at the same time. Not only will you have sparkling teeth, but you can also get a box-office butt. Simply stand with your feet slightly wider than hip-width distance apart and squat by bending your knees as if you are about to sit on a chair, hold for a second, then slowly push back up.

3 Take two. We've all heard of 'take the stairs instead of the lift', but go one better and take two stairs at a time. This will give you the same workout as you get from a lunge, so it will be toning your thighs as you're making a deeper and bigger movement by climbing two stairs at a time.

4 Invest in a pair of MBTs. (Special trainers that help to tone through your leg muscles and improve your posture while you're walking.) Head off to work with your killer heels in a bag and power-walk to the office. Not only will you be toning your legs, but that walk will melt away any excess body fat. You will arrive at your desk full of energy and glowing with self-righteousness, plus the pennies you'll save on travel can go towards a weekly manicure instead. Hurrah!

5 Fitness comes in all shapes and forms, so try to find something you enjoy. If you're a social diva, then find a local dancing class; if you like a challenge, find a local bootcamp, or if you just need to relax, then find a good Pilates class. Once you start to feel fitter, you won't want to stop.

6 Turn your front room into a gym. Simply use some blank card and on each piece write down an exercise, such as 'jog on the spot', or 'sit ups'. Choose between four and eight exercises, then place on the floor around the room. Play motivational music and go round each exercise station, using a stopwatch to perform each one for one minute, then move straight onto the next. This will get you toned and fighting fit.

7 Instantly look fabulous by standing with good posture. This will immediately make you look slimmer, taller and more confident, helping to realign all your muscles. Simply imagine that someone has just dropped an ice cube down your back: this automatically snaps you into shape.

8 Work out your abs while you walk. This is an easy way of sneaking in an ab workout on the go. While you're walking, pull in your belly button as tight as you can to your spine and hold for five seconds, release, then repeat.

9 If you can't live without a daily latte, just make sure you choose semi-skimmed or soya milk – and avoid all the little treats like the marshmallows or the caramel shot, as these are full of calories and can expand the waistline in no time at all!

10 Make the most of your lunch hour, and for 20 minutes do a quick power-walk. Get the girls from the office to join in, as this is a good way to catch up on office gossip and re-energize you for the afternoon, and you can burn up to 200 calories – so three times a week that's a total of 600.

• **W: www.lwrfitness.com**

'When the moon hits your eye like a big pizza pie, that's amore…' Whether loving yourself, one other or plenty of others, this section takes you from tips on how to unleash your inner sex goddess to ways of boosting your confidence and tried-and-tested dating agencies…

Love yourself

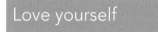

If the bombardment of air-brushed media images knocks your confidence and makes you feel as if you're competing with perfection (but let's face it, *no one* is perfect), then the following confidence-boosting tips by Polestars, the UK's largest alternative fitness school, will put you right.

It's important to feel good in your own skin and every individual has something special about them – so, with the help of the glamorous, curve-loving art that is burlesque, Polestars has created a few easy steps to help you 'fake it till you make it'! Ready that lipgloss and grab those heels…

'Fake it till you make it': A Polestars burlesque guide to faking confidence

Step 1: I am beautiful!

Lacking in confidence? Who needs to compliment you more than you do? No one person is perfect, nobody is flawless. Confidence is all about loving yourself and if you do, the world is your oyster. The art of burlesque teaches exactly this, embracing those curves and imperfections, cellulite and all. That's what makes you the woman you are, and what's sexier than that? So look at that person in the mirror and remind her exactly how great she is!

Step 2: From your head to your toes

We all know that age-old saying, 'If you look good, you'll feel good.' Well, trust us, ladies, it works. In order to look your best, there are a few things you need to do. And the best place to start is at the top – literally!

- **Hair**: Hair-styling is incredibly important in making a girl feel her best. How many good/bad-hair days have you had? Take time out to primp and preen those tresses. Take inspiration from some of burlesque's idols, like Dita Von Teese or Bette Page. Think glossy locks and lots of curls. For shorter-haired ladies, just add some fabulous encrusted hairpins. Remember that your hair is your crowning glory, so use it!

- **Make-up**: Forget what you've heard, diamonds aren't a girl's best friend; it's her make-up bag!

Whether day or night, our trusty sidekick is there for us, bursting with goodies to transform us into the sex kitten inside. Burlesque is all about feminine elegance, sophisticated style and, most importantly, glamour. It's all in the detail. Red lips are a must. Eyeliner is essential. However, don't be scared to try out something different. Individuality is beautiful.

- **Clothes**: Hiding under baggy clothes? Nothing eats at your confidence more than an ill-fitting wardrobe. Make a choice to look great. Embrace your curves, love those hips, and slip into something gorgeous. Take inspiration from Gypsy Rose Lee. Pencil skirts, corsets and high heels are in, while tracksuits and trainers are firmly out. It's not about being waif thin, but instead celebrating and embracing those womanly curves. Hourglass silhouettes are amazingly sexy.

- **Hands and feet**: We've got the hair, we've done the make-up, and we're in the clothes. Now we need to complete our look: the nails. They can be short, but they must be painted! Confidence is not about being perfect, but we're damn close.

Step 3: Walk tall

Confident people don't slouch; they don't drag their feet. You want to make a statement, you want to turn heads. Burlesque women revel in the attention, male or female. Use those high heels to perfect that womanly glide and sexy wiggle. Keep your head up, shoulders back and strut away!

L

Love

Step 4: Make eye contact

Eye contact is essential in exuding that all-important air of confidence. This powerful weapon is your constant interaction with the world around you. Whether going after that dream guy, the perfect job or just simply walking down the road, eye contact will keep all the attention on you. Burlesque is a perfect example of how to use and abuse this intoxicating art. A smouldering glance or suggestive wink is dangerously attractive when used properly, and boy, don't they know how to use it!

Step 5: Relax

After all this, we wouldn't be surprised if you're beginning to feel a bit stressed. Well, don't be. Enjoy what you have created. Remember to smile – and looking that good, what do you *not* have to smile about? Try to relax and just revel in your newly faked confidence! With the Polestars guide, those around won't know the difference and no doubt it will soon become *real* confidence. So take a deep breath and face your new adoring public, 'cos you look gorgeous!

• **For more information, contact Shing Mon Chung, Polestars, Unit 54, Eurolink Business Centre, 49 Effra Road, London SW2 1BZ**
• **T: 020 7274 4865 or 020 7274 4961**
• **W: www.polestars.net**

See also K: Keep Fit for burlesque classes and B: Beauty for some top make-up tips.

Top 10 ways to unleash your inner sex goddess from Olivia St Claire

Olivia St Claire is the author of the infamous **The Sex Devotional** and **203 Ways to Drive a Man Wild in Bed**, and she shares with us some top tips on how to love your own body – the secret, she says, to pleasing your partner: 'A sex goddess is a woman who knows the secrets of her own body – and reveals them to her lover as she chooses. The tastes, smells and textures that make you feel sensual are doorways to your libido. So to bring any guy to his knees, pleasure *yourself*.'

1 Smells go directly to the brain's arousal centre. Saturate a handkerchief with white ginger perfume, wear it next to your skin, then leave it beside his computer.

2 Oil your nipples and press them into his chest. Hard. Then slide them down his belly and circle his genitals.

3 The *Kama Sutra* says a woman's upper lip is directly connected to her clitoris. While receiving oral, bite your upper lip to make your orgasm – and his response – more powerful.

4 Sprinkle jasmine oil (for that sexy feeling) into your bathwater. Invite your man to join you and pour the scented water, with a cup, over his chest and genitals.

5 Place a fingertip on your G-spot, then set a vibrator on your hand. Just before orgasm, invite your

L

Love

145

man inside to feel your swollen and trembling vaginal walls.

6 Stockings and a garter belt make you feel like a dangerous diva. Slide one off and rub it on your man's package. Tie it around the base of his shaft and release it at the moment of climax.

7 Smooth ice over your nipples to make your skin come alive. Let him lick off the icy drippings.

8 Slice an orange in half and bring it to bed. Feed each other with one half and use the other to top his penis like a cap. Then twist and squeeze.

9 Lay a towel, warm from the dryer, between your upper torsos, while you slide against each other and join up all the remaining naked parts.

10 Ask him to lick your fingers while they massage your most private parts.

• **For more hot sex goddess tips, visit www.oliviastclaire.net**

Love another

Burlesque showgirl, Miss Tempest Rose is most accomplished in the ladylike pastimes of singing, ballet, needlepoint … and in the not-so-ladylike pastimes of soul-singing, tease, espionage and assassination, and is well aware of what the butler saw (she'll deal with him later)! Her performance credits include London's top cabaret venues, two

West End runs and appearances on Channel 4, ITV2, BBC3 and BBC Radio London. Described recently by *What's on Stage* **as having 'beautiful tones and murderous revelations', Tempest Rose may look like a lady, but she is not to be messed with! I get the gorgeous lady herself to offer advice on how to maintain ardour and zeal. You go, girl…**

Burlesque tips for impressing a new man or keeping the old one on his toes, by Tempest Rose

• **It's not just what you wear on the outside, but also underneath, that counts!** One thing burlesque is known for is beautiful and elegant lingerie. Throw away all your out-of-shape, grey-tinged, ill-fitting underwear and invest in some sexy matching lingerie. Knowing what you have underneath your clothes will instantly make you feel sexy and confident – even if the only person you let see it, at the end of the night, is you! If you are in a long-term relationship, wearing sexy underwear can help reignite passions and will also give your partner ideas for future gifts. You can't expect him to buy you Kiss Me Deadly if all you wear are sports bras and granny pants!

• **Tease, tease, tease!** At bedtime don't whip of all your clothes at once, jump under the covers and flick the light switch off! Take the time to remove each layer slowly: even if your partner has already seen you naked, the suspense will make them look at you in a new light. Trust me, it works!

• **Burlesque star Gypsy Rose Lee was famous for her brains and her quick wit, so take some time to improve your mind as well as your body**. Acting stupid may attract certain men, but they probably aren't the ones you want to be with. Plus keeping up on what's going on in the world may help you feel confident to jump into conversations with new people rather than fading into the background for fear of looking stupid.

• **Burlesque is all about loving what you have and making a feature of your best parts**. Each day, choose a different part of your body you like and dress accordingly to show it at its best – it could be your legs, your waist, your hands or eyes … you'll be surprised by how many of them there are.

• **Burlesque is about being ladylike**. I don't mean be a doormat! All burlesque performers are strong, confident women who aren't shy of voicing an opinion or two, but getting blind drunk, forgetting your pants, throwing up on the street and getting into fights are not going to nab you the man of your dreams – or many friends, for that matter.

• **The sexiness in burlesque is all in the tease and knowing that the performer is always in control**. Nothing is sexier than a woman who knows that what she has is special and is selective about who she shares

it with. Always be proud of yourself and what you've got and never do anything you don't want to do because you think it will make you feel wanted. It never does.

Miss Tempest Rose – burlesque performer and singer

• **W: www.tempestrose.com**
• **E: misstempestrose-enquiries@yahoo. co.uk**

Love plenty of others…? Best dating websites

As the internet plays an ever greater part in our social lives, with social networking sites helping us to keep in touch with our friends, it's inevitable that we also use it to help us run our love lives as well. Internet dating is no longer just for geeks, it's one of the modern ways to find someone special. There are specialist sites catering for all types of people and preferences, whether they are disabled, gay or lesbian or lovers of fine wine. There is even a site to help you find the perfect millionaire – hurrah!

Lavalife

Lavalife offers three categories: Dating, Relationship or Intimate, which means you can broadcast the level and type of relationship you want (and get the right one in return). There are loads of ways to communicate with other singles, including video webcam, Lavalife by

Love

L

phone and Lavalife mobile.

• W: www.lavalife.com

Ashley Madison

The Ashley Madison Agency is targeted towards people who feel 'monogamy becomes monotony', and are considering other options out there. I'm not certain of what they may or not be condoning here, but if you want to know who is out there, it is absolutely free to view member profiles and exchange photos.

• W: www.ashleymadison.com

Friend Finder

Friend Finder is a free service that is very easy to follow. You will be able to connect with lots of interesting people and browse the images and profiles with ease.

• W: www.friendfinder.com

Match.com

Match.com has enjoyed a lot of marketing and advertising and therefore growth over the last few years, so there are heaps of quality singles with photos and you can include up to ten images so you can see them from different angles and in different lights, so you don't have to wonder if they have posted their best ever photo (that they don't even closely resemble in the flesh).

• W: www.match.com

SugarDaddie

The SugarDaddie website is aimed at people who are either seeking a richer person to pamper them, or a richer person hunting for a lucky person to spend their millions on! It is very to-the-point, so the honesty in advertising what you're really looking for can cut to the chase and offer a short cut to happiness if this is for you. When you do a search, you specify 'golddiggers' or 'sugardaddies' or 'sugarmommies' – you can't get more obvious than that!

• W: www.sugardaddie.com

Gay.com

Meet other *gay.com* members who are looking for more than just a hook-up.

• W: www.gay.com

Easyflirt

If you're serious about meeting someone, this site helps build intimacy quickly with features such as the webcam chat. There are over 7 million, so you will be spoilt for choice.

• W: www.easyflirt.com

Dating Direct

Dating Direct is one of the biggest dating sites in the world. They also host regular member parties in various cities, so you get to meet others face to face.

• **W: www.datingdirect.com**

Millionairemate

At *Millionairemate.com* beauty and wealth are the key requirements! There are reams of wealthy singles and every one of them knows exactly what they want. If this sounds like you, then cut to the chase and find Mr Loaded.

• **W: www.MillionaireMate.com**

Love

Motoring

M & Motherhood

Motoring

Maria McCarthy is author of *The Girl's Car Handbook* and *The Girl's Guide to Losing Your L Plates* (published by Simon and Schuster), and she shares her fabulous advice with us. Finally we can up our know-how to avoid patronizing car mechanics and critical driving instructors ('What do you mean, I drive like a woman?')…

Driving instructors to avoid

The Gossip

His golf handicap, his divorce, his holiday … this driving instructor wants to talk about everything except your driving and will continue to ramble on, even when you're sweating over a manoeuvre and are in serious need of some help and advice. A certain amount of social chat can be fine and even relaxing. But if you feel he's not giving you enough attention, this needs to be dealt with. You're paying for his time, after all! Rather than putting up with it, explain that you find too much chatting distracting and you'd rather you both just concentrated on the driving. Hopefully that should sort the problem out. If not, it's time to look for another instructor.

The Critic

By their very nature, driving instructors have to give feedback – but it should be aimed at helping you to do better rather than bringing you down. This is a very personal thing and an instructor whose blunt approach is appreciated by one student could be found really scary by a less confident one. If you feel that your instructor's criticism is bringing you down, tell him you feel you could do with more encouragement. If he doesn't take your comments on board, then it's probably time to change.

The Short-Changer

As we all know, traffic can be unpredictable, so it's understandable if your instructor occasionally turns up late. However, this time should be made up to ensure you've got the full hour you've paid for – if not straight away, then at a later lesson. A few instructors can sometimes take advantage by 'just popping into' a shop or bank during your lesson time. Again, this shouldn't happen, but if it does the time should be made up. In some driving schools it's common practice for a student to take the previous student home during the first part of their lesson. However, this can be embarrassing and means you're often likely to be doing the route to their home rather than practising test routes. The whole lesson should be focused on improving your driving skills, not using you as a taxi service to ferry around other learners. This is a school to avoid.

The Lech

This is one to get rid of straight away! If you feel that your driving instructor is making over-personal remarks, trying to stare down your blouse or (shudder!) being unnecessarily tactile, then terminate your lessons and find someone

else. If you are upset by his behaviour, then you should report it to the Driving Standards Agency.

Overcoming driving test nerves

Some people feel completely calm at the prospect of taking their practical driving test and are confident they'll breeze through effortlessly. If that's you, then please feel free to skip this section, safe in the knowledge that the rest of us are teeth-grittingly envious of you.

If, on the other hand, the prospect makes you feel rather anxious, that's perfectly understandable. Exams are nerve-racking at the best of times, and driving tests can feel particularly harrowing. After all, with written exams, if you get something wrong you can always go back and cross it out, whereas if you reverse into a bollard on your practical test, then your fate is sealed. Knowing that someone is watching and judging your every move can feel pretty bizarre as well. It would be enough to make most people feel bumblingly self-conscious if they were just doing an everyday activity like folding laundry or eating beans on toast, let alone demonstrating a complex skill like driving.

Remember, nerves don't mean failure. Most people are nervous. If the only people who passed tests took them in a state of zen-like calm, there would be very few people on the roads!

A degree of nervous tension is actually a good thing – it releases adrenaline, helping you be extra-alert and on top of your game. But on the other hand, if you get too stressed out, that can lead you to make silly mistakes. Basically it's a balancing act, but there are plenty of techniques available to help you get it right.

The Girl's Guide to Losing Your L Plates covers a pick-and-mix selection of strategies you can use in the run-up to your test – ranging from scientifically proven mental and physical calming techniques to spells, crystals and wearing your lucky pants!

• W: www.mariamccarthy.co.uk

Car hire

If you don't want the expense of having your own car, or just require a car for a limited time, there are solutions.

Streetcar

With Streetcar you only pay for the miles you use, and you can fill up your Streetcar whenever you want with the fuel card provided. At the end of your trip the vehicle's computer will calculate how far you've been.

There is a registration fee that entitles you to your very own Streetcar smartcard, fully comprehensive insurance and 24/7/365 breakdown and recovery service. The fleet includes Volkswagen Golfs, Polo BlueMotions and Volkswagen Transporter vans.

• W: www.streetcar.co.uk

Limo Hire

From the elegant charm of vintage show cars from the 1930s to the glitz and glamour of a stretch limo, you can cruise downtown in style with Limo Hire. Available for hire in Exeter, Devon and the south-west, there are loads of styles to choose from.

• **7 Pollybrook, Town Lane, Woodbury, Exeter EX5 1NF**
• **T: 01395 232 432**
• **W: www.limohire.co.uk**

A choice of supercars: écurie25

écurie25 is London's ultimate supercar club. Membership gives you access to a vast stable of supercars, City and Knightsbridge bases, lifestyle concierge services and an exclusive calendar of member events.

Membership provides an economical and stress-free alternative to ownership. You'll be able to make use of a fleet of supercars, while benefiting from maintenance, servicing and insurance services.

The membership fee is yearly and you will be given a certain amount of credits that you can exchange for the use of a car. The credits are calculated by a combination of the daily credits (how often you use the cars) and the mileage credits (the distance you drive).

• **W: www.ecurie25.co.uk**

A dream drive on the open road

If cars have the same effect on you as the perfect pair of shoes, this has to offer the best range of vintage, veteran and modern classics. Examples of their modern classics include the Ferrari Enzo, Jaguar XK8R and Aston Martin DB9. Their fleet is designed to offer you a stylish mobile to drive on the open road in style, get away for the weekend and make that romantic getaway that bit more dream-like.

• **T: 0845 070 5142**
• **W: www.theopenroad.co.uk**

Luxury Car Hire

Available only in mainland UK, Luxury Car Hire offers you the opportunity to drive the most luxurious, exciting and coveted cars, providing a unique driving experience. Their cars combine luxury with style and performance and can be supplied for any occasion. They offer BMW, Mercedes and Jaguar along with many other performance and elite luxury cars in London, Manchester, Scotland and Oldham.

• **W: www.luxury-carhire.co.uk**

WhizzGo

I travel a lot with my job and rely on public transport. I say 'rely on' – perhaps I should have said 'battle with'. Then I came across WhizzGo pay-by-the-hour cars.

M

Motoring & Motherhood

WhizzGo members pay by the hour, therefore only paying for what they need. Cars can be hired for less than a fiver an hour, which includes insurance and fuel. Choose the low-emission Citröen C1 for an eco-chic ride.

• **W: www.whizzgo.co.uk**

Motherhood

If you're blessed with children (though during a 4 a.m. wake-up call, I know this may not seem the operative term), then this little lot will interest you and your bundle of joy…

Personal coaching … just for mums!

Being a mum is amazing, yet often unexpectedly changes your game plan. The Happy Mum™ work with you to put together a new master plan. They offer exclusive one-to-one coaching that allows you to take some time away from it all to breathe, talk, share your thoughts and feelings, and get your head together! Maybe you're a mum returning to work, a working mum, or just looking to get things into perspective. Claiming to be 'the manicure … for the mind', The Happy Mum™ are confident you will leave your session feeling polished, invigorated and pampered.

• **T: 07827 666 009 or 0161 777 6744**
• **W: www.thehappymum.co.uk**

The Ultimate Mummy Makeover

The UK's only Laser Gynaecology Centre in Harley Street, London, helps mothers regain their pre-pregnancy bodies. Bear with me on this one. Professor P. K. W. Dartey, founder of the UK Laser Gynaecology Centre, is working together with some of the best surgeons in the UK to offer a unique combination of surgery for mothers to cure urinary stress incontinence, repair lost vaginal muscle tone, lift sagging breasts, correct flabby stomachs and eliminate stretch marks. For some women no amount of exercise or natural beauty treatments can help them regain their pre-pregnancy bodies, and the Mummy Makeover offers a number of options. Each package is carefully designed to suit the individual. Support and care are given throughout the journey and not all operations would be performed at the same time. It's an option!

• **W: www.profdartey.com**

Cozypocket buggy gloves

Cozypocket is a glove (Mono) or pair of gloves (Duo), if you have a two-handled buggy, that stay permanently attached to your pushchair. Why? They keep your hands warm while leaving you free to remove them fast to drink coffee, wipe your child's nose, answer your phone, and generally multitask without the faffing around.

The Cozypocket fastens around

the pushchair handle with Velcro and adjusts to suit different hand sizes. Although not necessarily stylish and almost big enough to keep your teapot warm, you'll love these gloves if you feel stressed juggling a phone and a toddler on a cold day, or always end up losing your mitts.

• W: www.diddi.co.uk

Retro toys: Graham & Greene

From cute bear suits and monkey pyjama sets to nostalgic wooden toys and drum kits, Graham & Greene cater perfectly for stylish tots. The toys look so stylish you won't mind them cluttering up the living room when you have company – so you and your little'un are both happy.

Graham & Green have four shops in London and one in Reading – their first move outside the 'Big Smoke'.

• Unit 3 & 4, Capital Interchange Way, Brentford, London TW8 0EX
• T: 0845 130 66 22
• W: www.grahamandgreen.co.uk (N)

Cupcake Mum

Cupcake Mum is a members' club giving care and advice to mums, mums-to-be and their families. There is an on-site spa offering relaxing treatments, and the Cupcake Café offers delicious lunches. You can even take the Cupcake Mum experience away with you and have them organize your baby shower, afternoon tea and children's parties.

You don't necessarily have to be a member to reap all these lovely benefits: non-members can access the sleep pod, café, antenatal classes and spa treatments … and the all-important delivery of cupcakes.

Almost like a personal health care service, this company is giving first-time mothers the confidence and knowledge necessary to bring up a child. It is also bringing mothers together, and giving them the chance to relax and indulge in themselves, which is something they may not get to do very often.

• Cupcake, 10 Point Pleasant, Wandsworth Park, London SW18 1GG
• T: 020 8875 1065
• W: www.home.cupcakemum.com

Cheeky Funky childrenswear

Cheeky Funky is a clothing brand for 0–3 years offering babygrows, tees and hats in bright colours and exclusive funky designs. Creator Gemma Clifford wished to buy cool clothing for her little bundle of joy before its arrival, yet without knowing the sex, found it difficult to buy anything suitable. It transpired that many other expectant mothers felt the same, so Gemma invented a clothing brand that is playful, cheerful and stylish yet comfortable and practical. This brand certainly stands out and so will your very own cheeky funky in these fashionable togs!

• T: 01273 249751
• W: www.cheekyfunky.com (N)

Little Label

When shopping for yourself, you

always cater for your simple classic separates – those well-fitting jeans, a classic beige Mac, a simple white shirt, those as-flattering-as-possibly-can-be sweatpants. But what about your little ones? If they understood style completely (and I'm sure some of your little princesses probably do already), then I'm not convinced they'd opt for bears, bows and frills every time.

For simple separates in nine mix-and-match classic colours and 100% cotton, Little Label has got it spot on. The collection includes hipsters, underwear, V-necks and the cutest hoodies in sizes from 50cm (newborn) up to 128cm (8 years). Thoughtful touches include printing the label on the inside of the garment as opposed to stiching in a scratchy one around the neck, and since they're online, the shopping experience is hassle free. No queues, no sweaty changing rooms, no pushchair fights – just classic style for your tots. It's about time.

• W: www.littlelabel.co.uk

Positively preparing girls for puberty: PoGo

The arrival of a girl's first period can't be predicted, but mums can now ensure their daughter is prepared with the PoGo Pack™, a stylish all-in-one kit that contains everything a girl needs to understand and manage her periods with confidence. Contents include a range of pads specially selected to fit young girls, essential information about periods, a planner so girls can track their periods, disposal bags, tissues, a notebook and pen. It can be refilled with any brand of pad and is designed to last through her teens.

Ideal for holidays and sleepovers, there is also a discreet pull-out purse for girls to use at school. Girls can also visit PoGo's website for lots more resources and age-appropriate information. The PoGo Pack™ is a convenient solution for busy parents, taking the worry out of what to buy, and it's an easy way to introduce the subject of periods to girls, preparing them for this important time of change.

• **PoGo Limited, Fenwick House, 27 Kimberley Road, St Albans, Herts AL3 5PX**
• **T: 01727 762443**
• **W: www.pogopack.co.uk**

Children's parties: Myhotel Chelsea

Why not leave all the hard work of arranging and catering for your little one's birthday party to someone else? Myhotel Chelsea go all out in planning children's birthday parties – transforming the space into a magical wonderland, if that is what your child so desires! From imaginative décor to girls' world make-up sessions, clowns and magicians, Myhotel can arrange it. While you escape in the bar with a cocktail or afternoon tea, the team will look after the kids and supply a delicious menu of fairy cakes, jelly, finger sandwiches, juices and plenty of other treats.

• **Myhotel Chelsea, 35 Ixworth Place, London SW3 3QX**
• **T: 020 7225 7500**
• **W: www.myhotels.com**

Oliver Bonas

Oliver Bonas is one of my favourite stores, on and offline, for my cutesy dresses and kooky accessories, all at incredibly reasonable prices, but their online kids' section is also fantastic. There's a host of trendy clothing and accessory products and my favourite has to be the pale pink baby girl's bib with a photo print of a pearl necklace on the front. Who said babies can't be ladylike?

• W: www.oliverbonas.com

Find a doula

Doula (pronounced 'doola') is a Greek word meaning 'woman servant or caregiver'. Today, a doula offers emotional and practical support to a woman (or couple) before, during and after childbirth. Highly experienced, a doula provides support to mothers-to-be from day one of being pregnant, right into the early days of being a new mum, giving the type of support women crave and thus helping the whole family to relax and enjoy the experience as much as possible. If you visit the official website, you can contact doulas directly and it's a free resource. There are doulas with different levels of experience, qualifications and areas of expertise. From practical suggestions for your position of giving birth, to managing contractions and taking the pressure off those around you, your doula will be there for you. Perhaps 'angel' would be a more appropriate translation!

• W: www.doula.org.uk

Networking

Naughty pleasures

Every busy chick has to make time for her naughty pleasures, and this round-up should satisfy every one of your senses...

Amora

Amora takes you and your partner on a tour of desire and attraction, stimulating your senses via fun, games and education. There's a host of interactive and educational games, quizzes, facts and videos – where you can learn how to perform striptease or pick up some tips on the latest sexual positions. There's a bar boasting aphrodisiac cocktails, a boutique selling lots of sensual sex toys and fun ideas, plus a gallery of themed art from renowned artists. You'll find it tough not to be inspired. If you want to go a little deeper (sorry, I couldn't help it), Amora offers workshops and personal advice using their trained sex therapists.

• T: 020 7432 32 44
• W: www.amoralondon.com

The Mexican

You've tried the Brazilian landing strip. You've even survived a Hollywood, post-tequila slammer and aspirin (or is that just me?), so try a Mexican and dye your love fuzz! Yes, I actually said that. The treatment uses a gentle formulation made from organic ingredients: go for bright red, copper, dark brown or golden blonde. A post-dye, tidy-up wax is optional, complete with a full-on trim if required.

The treatment takes an hour and includes an eyelash and brow dye or a facial and shoulder massage while the dye takes effect. Once it does, it lasts six to eight weeks.

Home dye kits are also available for those who fancy coordinating their carpet and curtains at home, if you catch my drift…

- **Available at Scin, 27 Kensington Park Road, London W11 2EU**
- **T: 020 3220 0121**
- **W: www.scin.uk.com**

Buzzzzzz

For thousands of quality products from lubes to videos and sex toys for every pleasure spot on your body (and your partner's body), try the following websites:

- **W: www.bedtimeheaven.co.uk and www.lovehoney.co.uk**

Lelo's Gigi vibrator comes from a Swedish line of cleverly designed and aesthetically pleasing 'pleasure objects'. The Gigi is a dedicated pleasure object designed to hit the G spot with five pre-programmed pleasure modes and a virtually silent vibrator engine to deliver deep vibrations to stimulate your special spot of mystery! It is tiny and battery free, so there are no wires and no danger of running out of power at crucial moments – it just charges like a mobile phone. Ha!

- **W: www.lelo.com**

In the most decadent incarnation of the iconic **Little Something** vibrator, 'Eternity' brings luminous diamonds together with precious metals, making it nearly £2,000 worth of pleasure. At a modest 5.25 inches long, and 0.67 inches in diameter, this work of art and ultimate pleasure tool will impress on so many levels. Well, they do say that diamonds are a girl's best friend…

- **W: www.jimmyjane.com**

Silk seduction

The Silk Bow cushion by **And God Created Woman** has 4m of luxurious fabric wrapped around it like a parcel, finished with a generous bow on the front. Undo the bow and use as silk ties around your partner's wrists for a little light bondage, and if you undo the zip you'll find the secret inside pocket, ideal for storing a condom so you can reveal it mid-seduction (saves you rifling through your drawers and killing the mood at the crucial moment!).

Finishes come in fine Egyptian cotton (220 thread-count), 100% silk (smooth satin on one side and matt crepe on the other), or 100% silk super-luxe edition (heavyweight satin-backed crepe).

- **W: www.andgodcreatedwoman.co.uk**

N

Naughty Pleasures & Networking

Nua Lifestyle

Nua Lifestyle adopts the much-needed concept of creating a 'sophisticated and cultured' experience when shopping for adult toys and accessories that they term 'lifestyle products'.

Each shop is light and airy, with the door always open, removing any possible unnerving moments and making shopping for intimate goodies a relaxed and accessible experience. Check out their luxury selection of ceramic and gold vibrators and the satin accessories belt with detachable suspenders, blindfold, wrist ties and nipple tassels.

• **Stores are in Manchester, Sheffield and Brighton, and you can buy online**
• **W: www.nualifestyle.com**

Erotic salons: Coco de Mer

Coco de Mer's salons are based on a concept that dates back to the eighteenth century, where social gatherings in the 'grandes salons' of private residences were fuelled by dynamic hosting skills, intellectual debate, music and debauchery. Continuously striving to transform the way erotica is viewed, Coco de Mer has created 'The Salons' designed for both single people and couples. In warm and relaxing settings, salons take place at their boutique and offer a host of inspiration and learning.

In addition, Coco de Mer also offers Private Salons for individuals, couples or groups. These can be tailored to your needs and can be tutored by either Midori or Hannah.

• **23 Monmouth Street, Covent Garden, London WC2H 9DD**
• **To book, call Susie on 020 7836 8882**
• **W: www.coco-de-mer.com**

Chocolate

Like most girls, one of my naughty pleasures is, of course, chocolate, but I don't always enjoy the guilt that comes with demolishing a whole bar. The good news is that some of those treats you think are 'naughty' actually have some health benefits – like dark chocolate. Studies have shown that small amounts of dark chocolate can help decrease blood pressure, and the levels of flavonoids in dark chocolate are higher than in blueberries and green tea!

Another option for indulging without being unhealthy is to try **Skinny Candy** – keep your eye on the website for developments!

• **W: www.skinnycandy.com**

Networking

Women are doing it for themselves! Well, we are, aren't we? There are so many of us, more than ever before in senior roles, working for ourselves, taking a chance and climbing the ladder. Good on you, I say! Thankfully, there are heaps of cool communities and advice forums out there to aid our progression…

Is there More To Life Than Shoes?

More To Life Than Shoes helps women get out there and make their dreams happen, whoever they are and whatever they want to do. Say goodbye to lack of confidence, losing focus, dithering, self-doubt or just getting stuck before you've even started. Whatever you want to change about your life, whether you want to start a business, go on an adventure, find your dream job, learn something new or change your life completely, *www.MoreToLifeThanShoes.com* can help you make it real.

Interviews with gutsy women and articles on underground icons provide motivation and energy; the online coaching programme 'Shoeniversity' will help you work out what to do with your life and help you make it happen. There's practical support and advice from a panel of experts, plus there's plenty of encouragement in the site's social network. So, no more excuses, it's time to grab life by the balls!

- **T: 07855 766 1919**
- **W: www.moretolifethanshoes.com**

Snogging is the new networking, sister!

Sister Snog gives a fashionable and fun edge to business networking. For women only, members (endearingly termed 'sisters') meet up at sassy parties and lunches, breakfast mornings and posh dos to swap gossip and business cards. It's a very successful way to network, since sisters are paired up and the informal settings make for progressive chat. Membership is a one-off annual fee and you can try an event before you join to see if it's for you.

- **W: www.sistersnog.com**

Everywoman for herself

Everywoman, the network for female entrepreneurs, was set up to help women wanting to set up their own businesses, and it offers free advice with an online network of other businesswomen. It works with the support of the government, BERR in particular – the Department for Business, Enterprise and Regulatory Reform – and alongside partners such as NatWest. In addition, they hold awards to recognize outstanding women's achievements, some running with a view to increasing diversity within a sector. It is free to join and will update members regularly about topical issues and events.

- **T: 0871 7461800**
- **W: www.everywoman.com**

N

Naughty Pleasures & Networking

Online shopping

Online shopping is booming – many of us find it easier to shop online today (no queues, parking or fighting for the last item in your size)! Due to the boom, however, there is a saturation of online boutiques and blogs offering inspiration on what to buy, so I have tried and tested only the best. Each online boutique credited I've found to be user-friendly, inspirational in style and efficient in delivery. Happy shopping!

Shopcurious

Shopcurious is an online boutique that's crammed full of one-offs, limited editions, recycled clothing and vintage finds. A self-confessed 'backlash against the must-have consumer frenzy of the branded goods crazed brigade', Shopcurious is the ideal virtual destination for finding something truly individual, and if you buy a secondhand garment, you'd be giving it a new home, doing your eco-friendly bit too.

• W: www.shopcurious.com

Bored of the High Street

Bored of the High Street is an independent online retailer of high-end staple items mixed in with boutique styles and fashion favourites. Hudson Jeans, Juicy Couture, Seven for All Mankind, Bench, Motel and Paul Frank are just a few of the delights you will find here. If you've spotted a celebrity wearing something you fancy for yourself, you may well find it here with their dedicated 'celebrity' section, and though I think you do have to sift through some tack, I love the quirky slogan tees.

• W: www.boredofthehighstreet.com

All things Japanese: jlist

This site isn't great to look at, but the stuff they sell is bonkers – in a good way! I went crazy for the pink limited edition 'sparkling strawberry' flavour Kit-Kat (that I probably only truly like because it's pink), but in fact it's a huge hit in Japan with Kit-Kat being their best-selling chocolate. A very amusing, highly eccentric array of buys.

• W: www.jlist.com

You'll no longer be Missguided...

If you want to bag a bargain and remain totally on trend, Missguided adds new items every week so that you can track down the latest 'must-haves'. You'll soon know the difference between leggings, jeggings and preggings – phew!

• W: www.missguided.co.uk

Moonspark

Moonspark online offers the modern woman an online walk-in wardrobe of high-fashion clothing, handbags and accessories. Moonspark offers fabulous affordable items of a really high quality and stocks a wide range of niche brands such as Numph, Sugarhill Boutique, Traffic People, People's Market, Max C, Mischa Barton Bags, plus many more! Though I'm not keen on the name, affordable delivery and excellent customer service make up for it.

• W: www.moonsparkonline.co.uk

Shudoo

Shudoo.co.uk stocks some of the best designer and high-street footwear brands including Uggs, French Sole and Terry de Havilland. The news section is great for keeping you updated on all fashion- and footwear-related happenings.

• W: www.Shudoo.co.uk

Pandora

Pandora jewellery gives wearers the chance to create unique pieces which are exclusive to them. Each bracelet or necklace is created exclusively by the customer – beginning with a blank bracelet or chain which can then

O

be decorated with individual beads, gemstones, spacers and clips. There are more than 2.5 billion different combinations available, with new releases added to the range twice a year, so it is unlikely that any piece will ever be identically replicated.

• W: www.pandora-jewelry.com

Bedcrumb

Bedcrumb is a scrumptious sanctuary for exclusive accessories and gifts based on old-fashioned glamour and modern-day cheeky girlyness. Items include tea and coffee cosies (I love the 'Coffee, tea, me?' slogan cosie), vintage tea party sets, luxurious scarves, kooky pocket mirrors and quirky purses. Each features or is inspired by original illustrations of charmingly random ladies and gorgeous vintage finds and are completed with carefully sourced new and vintage fabrics, trims and accessories. Highly addictive!

• W: www.bedcrumb.co.uk

The Outnet

TheOutnet.com is an exclusive designer outlet where everyone is invited. Brought to you by the team behind the award-winning designer fashion website *net-a-porter.com*, the Outnet is a global shopping destination devoted to selling discounted designer womenswear and accessories.

• W: www.theoutnet.com

All Things Original

All Things Original is a superbly quirky UK-based website which brings together creative UK designers selling totally unique items handmade in the UK. There is a vast art and design selection with some very cool prints, vintage-style screen-printed purses and eco-shopper bags and some very romantic and unconventional jewellery. I browse this site for hours – it's all so beautiful. The only problem is, I end up with a huge shopping basket!

• W: www.allthingsoriginal.com

Etsy

Etsy is amazing. It is one huge global portal of buyers and sellers that come together to offer a vast collection of handmade and vintage items and supplies that help you go all crafty and create your own pieces of magic.

Expect to source clothing, accessories, artwork, homewares and one-off bits and bobs, from vintage wedding cake toppers and sterling silver rings embossed with your lover's fingerprint to handmade corsages, vintage tea dresses and kooky wall hangings.

The Gift Guides are great for narrowing your search and finding something truly special for a particular person or occasion. Pounce is a facility that directs you to new shops on Etsy or shops that have just sold their first item so you can literally 'pounce' on newly discovered gems, and Treasury offers other people's pick of the best for inspiration.

If you're a talented designer yourself, you can register for free then list your items. It costs '20 cents' to list an item for four months (prices subject to change). When your item sells, you'll pay a 3.5% transaction fee. A small price to pay to get discovered!

• W: www.etsy.com

Rosemary Twang

rosemarytwang.com is an exotic and luxurious website offering the modern Boho goddess a fine range of swimwear and beachwear all year long! Whether you're going to sun yourself on the white sands of St Tropez or bask in the glorious Caribbean sunshine, you're sure to find something fabulous to take along with you from Rosemary Twang! From kaftans to bikinis to leather sandals to hand-painted beach bags – there's something for every glamorous holidaymaker.

• W: www.rosemarytwang.com

Grab a bargain at Boohoo

Full to the brim of top trends at bargain prices, this is throwaway fashion at its best.

• W: www.boohoo.com

I Love Jeans

For diehard jeans lovers, I Love Jeans is your haven for denim loveliness, enabling you to shop by size, brand, cut and body shape.

There's a huge array of high street and designer labels and their affiliates pose a selection of top brands to choose from, including ethical label Del Forte and the very flattering Hudson Jeans, as well as some other hard-to-find up-and-coming brands. The Denim Dictionary is a helpful guide to all things denim to banish confusion on the many fits and washes out there. It is the wisdom of former stylist and founder Sam Remer that gives this site all its helpful hints and expert know-how. Shopping for your jeans has never been easier and, let's face it, it's not normally such a simple experience … the zip *will* go up – it's just a bit stiff…

• W: www.ilovejeans.com

20 Limited Editions

All pieces offered for sale on *20ltd.com* are limited editions available in limited numbers. Pieces referred to as 'limited' editions are either unique originals or those 'whose modifications are deemed sufficiently significant for them to be treated as a unique original'. Items referred to as 'special' editions are unique versions of an existing piece.

You'll find *the weird*, such as hand-polished gold hornets that intrigue and deter at once, *the wonderful*, like the gold and enamel jewellery worth in the region of £10,000, and *the wanted*, where the personally signed books by literary legends are certainly pieces of publishing history worth investing in.

• W: www.20ltd.com

Online Shopping & Outdoor Pursuits

O

Outdoor pursuits

There are so many activities and adventures at our fingertips today. From classes to improve your wellbeing and posture, to cause-related challenges, there is absolutely no reason to sit there on your designer-clad rear and do nothing!

Llama trekking

Situated in the heart of the Northamptonshire countryside, you will find 20 acres of native woodland with paths, rides, hay fields and … a herd of llamas and a few donkeys. Yes, really. The land is called Catanger, a Saxon word meaning 'where wild cats roam', so experience it by going llama trekking and enjoy the beautiful scenery, walking along bridleways, farm tracks and country lanes with your gorgeous llama. This sounded almost surreal to me, but it's actually an excellent way to de-stress and breathe in nature. Who'd have thought it!

- T: 01327 860808
- W: www.llamatrekking.co.uk

Wakeboarding

If you're new to wakeboarding, a wakeboard is a buoyant board (like a surf- or snowboard, but shorter in length) that is used to ride over water while being pulled along behind a motorboat.

WakeMK is one of the UK's newest cable wakeboard and water-ski centres. With 180 acres of landscaped parkland in Milton Keynes, it is said to be one of the best venues in the UK, and towards the end of the season they have free 'Fridays for Girls', so keep an eye out for details on their website.

- W: www.wakemk.com

Escape Surf School

You'll learn to surf in the UK's answer to surfer's paradise, Newquay, and as there's so much nightlife on offer, this makes a great hen do with a difference.

- W: www.escapesurfschool.co.uk

Airkix skydiving (indoor and outdoor)

Airkix presents the ultimate freefall experience and is the first UK wind tunnel, based at the Xscape Leisure and Entertainment Centre in Milton Keynes. The vertical wind tunnel enables people of all ages to feel the adrenalin of freefall, a.k.a body diving, in a controlled, safe environment. In the purpose-built tunnel you can perform a series of freefall manoeuvres in an airstream of up to 150mph. This suited me, as it completely satisfied my adrenalin junkie side without threatening my sensible side, as I felt safe and secure. Unlike other extreme sports, Airkix doesn't require any previous experience or sporting ability, which was welcome news. The finest (and often dishiest) instructors in the country make up the 'Aircrew' and are qualified by experts at the International Bodyflight Association in the USA, so you can rest assured you will be trained by specialists. This is so exhilarating, I'm wondering if they can fix me up with a regular go on Monday mornings – sure to get me going!

Airkix can also organize a Tandem Sky Dive or Accelerated Freefall, where you fly to around 12,000ft after training, flying both your body and parachute from a plane. The minimum age to skydive is 16 years (with parent consent); the maximum is 55 years for AFF Training and 70 years for Tandem Skydiving.

If you want to have the time of your life and raise money for a good cause, do a charity skydive. You can jump for your charity of choice, or Airkix will recommend one to you. You can parachute for free if you raise £295 or more in sponsorship (prices subject to change).

....

- T: 0845 331 6549
- W: www.airkix.com

....

Go Ape
....

Go Ape is a thrilling way to enjoy the great outdoors, have some high-wire fun and satisfy your sense of adventure. Before you set off on your Go Ape treetop journey you'll be fitted with a harness and given a safety briefing. The courses are split into five or six separate sections and linked together by natural footpaths. Each section begins with a rope ladder climb into the treetops, where an assortment of exciting obstacles and Tarzan swings lead to a thrilling zip slide back down to the forest floor. The zip slides were my favourite part of the day, something I'd wanted to try since I saw them on the action movies (or *Crystal Maze*)

as a kid.

Go Ape courses are set in some of the UK's most beautiful forest locations, so whatever the weather, you have the freedom to experience around three hours of adrenalin-fuelled fun and adventure with family, friends and colleagues (they offer team-building corporate trips). The only downside is that after the adrenalin rush of completing one obstacle, you may have to queue for the next one which almost saps your energy. Some queues were nearly 30 minutes long, so I'd advise going on a quieter day, and ensuring there are few large groups so you can hop around swiftly. A lot of fun for kids and big kids and the thrill of doing the course independently, and not with an instructor following you around, only adds to the experience.

If you go to the Rivington site, as I did, it can be thirsty work, so be sure to pop around the corner for a drink at the lovely Millstone Inn.

....

- T: 0845 643 2034
- W: www.goape.co.uk (N)

See P: Pubs and Bars for more on the Millstone Inn.

....

Air-Sphere
....

Air-Sphere is an extreme ride in Milton Keynes at the Xscape centre. Air-Sphereing® was created by merging the idea of rolling down a hill in a giant inflatable ball and using a vertical wind tunnel to fly people and objects – and yes, I tried it for you!

The specially made Air-Spheres are provided by SphereMania® and ensure a safe ride but guarantee a mix of unpredictability, adrenalin, intensity and plenty of fun! Sit face to face with your co-rider inside an 8ft inflatable ball as it's tossed and turned in 150mph winds – it's hilarious! A word of warning, though hold on tight and don't eat directly beforehand. It certainly jerks you around a bit. If you really want to experience the intensity, ask for the 'extreme' version. I dare you!

....

• **W: www.air-sphere.com (N)**

There may be some of you who like nothing more than to meet up with friends and grab a drink at the newest, trendiest cocktail bar in town, and while I tend to agree that this is a great way to spend an evening, remember that it isn't the only way. This section gives the low-down on an assortment of bars, great British pubs and cool hangouts...

Pubs

Albanach

Whisky is what this place is all about, with vintage malts aplenty, but it's not just for malt enthusiasts: real ales on hand pumps are available (I do get annoyed when they're not), and a typically Scottish food menu. The atmosphere offers a fairly cool vibe, but without any charade.

- **197 High Street, Edinburgh EH1 1PE**
- **T: 0131 220 5277**

The Chequers

The Chequers can be hard to find, since it's tucked away on a narrow cobbled alleyway, but it's worth finding for its ale selection alone. The roaring fire and cosy atmosphere make this little nook an ideal Sunday retreat.

- **131 High Street, Oxford OX1 4DH**
- **T: 01865 727 463**

The Original Oak

The Oak has a legendary beer garden where you can enjoy their long (and cheap) drinks list. Sit outside in the summer and enjoy – just look out for the students in fancy dress, a seemingly recurring theme in the area!

- **2 Otley Road, Leeds**
- **T: 0113 275 1322**

The Old Wellington

Reputed to be one of Manchester's oldest buildings, this was the one-time home of John Byrom. Before becoming a pub, it was used as a base for many businesses. Perhaps the Old Wellington's most poignant life event was the damage caused by a terrorist bomb in 1996. Since then, the building has been meticulously dismantled,

moved 100 metres, and put back together. Well, after all that effort, it would be rude not to visit.

- **4, Cathedral Gates, Manchester, Lancashire M3 1SW**
- **T: 0161 839 5179**

The Cow Pub & Restaurant

Most famous as one of the best places in London to enjoy a pint of the black stuff and a dozen oysters, Tom Conran's atmospheric Irish pub serves up well-thought-out, imaginative dishes that may seem a little pricey, but you do get a lot of grub for your money and there's a more accessible bar menu downstairs too.

- **The Cow Pub & Restaurant, 89 Westbourne Park Road, London W2 5QH**
- **T: 020 7221 0021**
- **W: www.thecowlondon.co.uk**

The Millstone Inn

The Millstone is situated next to Rivington reservoir in an area of outstanding beauty. This former public house has been transformed into a restaurant with that cosy pub feel. The wooden floors, strong Mediterranean colours and contemporary food menu make this establishment both modern and innovative, yet welcoming. The large gardens and gazebo are ideal for summer dining alfresco.

- **The Millstone Inn, Bolton Road, Anderton, Chorley, Nr Horwich, Lancashire PR6 9HU**
- **T: 01257 480205**

The Tunnel House

The Tunnel House is nestled between the Cotswold villages of Coates and Tarlton, and has a wonderfully welcoming atmosphere. Log fires make it cosy in the colder months and the garden is idyllic in the summer, with a children's play area (such a wonderful invention to have in a pub).

The barn here has a capacity for 80 standing and 50 seated, making it an ideal party venue – I love the mix of modern and traditional in this convivial setting.

• The Tunnel House Inn and Barn, Tarlton Road, Nr Cirencester, Gloucestershire GL7 6PW
• W: www.tunnelhouse.com

The Black Bull

Set on a cobbled high street, the Black Bull oozes tradition. Its walls date from around 300 years ago, so when I say this is a traditional pub, that would be completely accurate. There are two bars that serve a loyal crowd, as it remains the popular watering hole it has always been over the years.

• The Black Bull Pub, 40–42, High Street, Yarm, Cleveland TS15 9AE
• T: 01642 791251

The White Lion

In the heart of Covent Garden, this pub exudes an intimate charm with small booths that allow you to people-watch and soak in the buzzy ambience. It makes a good stop for a pre-theatre tipple, and in the summer everyone stands outside lapping up the amusements of the area.

• The White Lion Pub, 24 James Street, London WC2E 8NT
• T: 020 7240 1064

The FishBowl

The FishBowl in Brighton is a hit with the locals and tourists alike, with that famous seaside laid-back vibe. Bright blue and inviting from the outside, understated yet funky on the inside, FishBowl prides itself on its fish and chips using quality 8oz haddock fillets. You choose the batter and dip that you want. Choices include 'Traditional' served with homemade tartare sauce and fresh lemon wedges, 'Blackened Herb and Garlic', or 'Soy, Sesame and Spring Onion' served with wasabi mayonnaise. The crowd and atmosphere hot up on a weekend, making it an ideal venue to start and finish your night.

• 74 East Street, Brighton, East Sussex
• T: 01273 777505

Dry Dock

Dry Dock is actually an old barge in the middle of Leeds, though not based bang in the middle of the central buzz. An actual boat that has been converted into a bar inside, you'll find a bar, pool tables, affordable pub grub and an outdoor seating area on the 'upper deck'. The music is usually indie and it attracts

Pubs & Bars

P

many students in the area, but is suitable for every laid-back crooner.

• **Dry Dock, Woodhouse Lane, Leeds**
• **T: 0113 2031841**

Bars

If you do fancy a bar, you'll be happy with any one of these destinations:

Albert and Pearl

Albert and Pearl enjoys that laid-back, non-stuffy, intimate atmosphere that so few chic bars in London can muster. Believing that there's nothing finer in life than surrounding yourself with wonderful things (in their case, good food, fine wine and great company), there's something about this funky place that makes you smile. The mixed drinks and food, live DJs and beautiful young things are worth the visit.

• **181 Upper Street, Islington, London**
• **W: www.albertandpearl.com**

Electric Birdcage

Electric Birdcage is a dim sum parlour and late-night cocktail lounge in London's West End. Designed by Shaun Clarkson, the weird and wonderful interior design includes tables made from tree roots and iron birdcage chandeliers that hang from a hot pink ceiling. Dig into the fab cocktail list and try the champagne-based Electric Birdcage, which serves

eight – but not by yourself, you understand…

• **Electric Birdage, 11 Haymarket, London SW1Y 4BP**
• **T: 020 7839 2424**
• **W: electricbirdcage.com**

Popolo

Had *Sex and the City* been set in northern England (now there's a thought), then Popolo Bar, Lounge and Kitchen would undoubtedly have been a favourite haunt for Carrie and clan due to the mouth-watering, humongous cocktail menu. Available at both venues (Newcastle and Sheffield), the menu offers one of the widest selections you will find anywhere in the world and includes everything from the classic *mai tai* through to more unusual concoctions created by the bar staff themselves. Add this to the venue's unique combination of leather booths, exposed industrial pipework, cult film projections and moody red lighting, and you'll soon be feeling as if you've stepped straight off the street in England into a back-street bar in New York.

• **Popolo Newcastle, 82 Pilgrim Street, Newcastle upon Tyne**
• **T: 0191 232 8923**
• **Popolo Sheffield, Leopold Square, Sheffield S1 2JJ**
• **T: 0114 275 8405**
• **W: www.popolo.co.uk**

Late Lounge at InterContinental London Park Lane

InterContinental London Park Lane,

situated in the heart of Mayfair, has a very exclusive Late Lounge located in the hotel's lobby. Talk about making the most of the sleek space! London's DJ TK spins the tunes and what you have is the ultimate five-star private area in which to socialize seven nights a week until 3.00 a.m.

The Champagne Bar will keep you well stocked on bubbly, or you can choose a concoction from their extensive cocktail list, all served by your very own waitress.

Intimacy oozes from the velvet seating and enclosing drapes and if you work up an appetite boogying, Executive Chef Paul Bates has designed a dedicated late-night menu serving specialities such as 50g Iced Sevruga Caviar, Foie Gras canapés and Tiger prawns with a crayfish cocktail.

If it all gets too much, there are 60 elegant suites to choose from where you can catch some Zs after all that schmoozing.

• **One Hamilton Place, Park Lane, London W1J 7QY**
• **T: For reservations and private bookings, call 020 7409 3131**
• **W: www.InterContinental.com**

Do you like the idea of a bar that comes to you?

Mr Frothy is a former ice cream van turned mobile bar from the brains behind The Cross Keys, Further North and North Bar. Playing the Rocky theme tune as it approaches, this retro bar on wheels is available for hire all

Pubs & Bars

P

year round. This has to be the coolest
bar out there, and it comes to you!

• W: www.mrfrothy.co.uk

North Bar

I just mentioned North Bar – and
this is a must-visit! Though narrow
and modest in size, this welcoming
bar offers one of the most fantastic
selections of beers from around the
world that I've ever come across.
I'm not a beer connoisseur, but do
love to enjoy one, so I always ask the
friendly bar staff for their advice. Upon
establishing the flavour and types of
beer I most enjoy, they always come
up trumps in offering a beer to suit.
Modelled on the beer masters in
Belgium, their food menu is designed
to enhance your poison with plates of
cheese, meats and bread. No butter,
just mustard and those magically
delicious basic ingredients. You don't
half get a generous serving, too.
Delish.

• North Bar, 24 New Briggate, Leeds
LS1 6NU
• T: 0113 242 4540
• W: www.northbar.com

Quitting

If you're still trying to kick the smoking habit, you're not alone and there is great support out there...

Support

The Together Programme

The Together Programme is a totally free NHS programme where experts help you through each stage of the process, so you do it together. You get practical support, encouragement and advice, including regular mail packs, emails, supportive text messages and phone calls. You can choose which method of contact you prefer, so it isn't intrusive and easily fits into a busy schedule.

• **W: www.smokefree.nhs.uk**

Quit

Quit is a service that includes a free phone helpline for all sorts of people and ages.

- **Quit, 211 Old Street, London EC1V 9NR**
- **T: 020 7251 1551**
- **W: www.quit.org.uk**

Further information

The following websites might also help you:
- **W: www.givingupsmoking.co.uk**
- **W: www.sda.uk.net**
- **W: www.ash.org.uk**

Nicotine replacement therapy and other stop-smoking medicines

There is a range of different treatments available that can double your chances of going smoke free. In fact, if you use NHS support and a stop-smoking medicine to help manage your cravings, you are up to four times more likely to be successful!

Nicotine replacement therapy (NRT) is suitable for most people, but you should check with your doctor if you are pregnant, have a heart or circulatory condition, or if you take regular medication.

Nicotine gum and patches work best for regular smokers, as do nasal sprays that allow nicotine to absorb quickly into your bloodstream.

Zyban is a treatment which changes the way that your body responds to nicotine. You start taking Zyban one to two weeks before you intend to quit and treatment usually lasts for a couple of months, to help you through the withdrawal cravings.

Champix works by reducing your craving for a cigarette and by reducing the effects you feel if you

do have a cigarette. You set a date to stop smoking, and start taking tablets one or two weeks before this date. Treatment normally lasts for 12 weeks. Both Zyban and Champix are available on prescription, but are not suitable for pregnant women.

Alternative quit-smoking products

NicoBloc

NicoBloc is drug free and is an alternative to NRT, gums, patches and inhalers. A nicotine-free fluid is applied to the end of a cigarette filter immediately before smoking. The fluid works by moistening the cigarette filter, cooling the smoke down as it's drawn through. The tar and nicotine vapour molecules condense back into solid form, sticking to the filter material instead of being passed through to the smoker.

Designed as a gradual reduction method, the amount of nicotine that is inhaled is gradually reduced, allowing you to give up smoking in six weeks. One drop is applied in week one, two drops in week two and three drops from week three onwards. By this time up to 99% of tar and nicotine inhalation is blocked.

- **Available in independent pharmacies and online, with each pack including an instruction DVD, progress chart and a 15ml bottle which provides two weeks' supply for a typical 20-a-day smoker**
- **T: 01452 524 012**
- **W: www.nicobloc.co.uk**

Quitting

Q

Wrist Angel

Wrist Angel is a unique aromatherapy wristband designed to help smokers give up. If you feel a desire to smoke, you can instantly open your Wrist Angel band, inhale the natural aromatic soothing benefits of essential oil, and have an instant distraction and de-stress, until the craving has passed. Wrist Angel works because the sense of smell is the fastest route to our brains, and is proven to affect our emotions and thoughts. Aromas can give us a pleasant feeling and a good experience that can bring back lovely memories, reminding us of good things and even making us feel sensual and alive. Essential oils can have a variety of different effects on us and help provide the positivity, calmness and focus to deal with everyday problems. It uses specially blended 100% natural essential oils that are impregnated onto pads which come in sachets that are opened and placed inside the band compartment, and it's discreet so you don't have worry about looking like a berk!

• Available from Holland & Barrett (N) or online
• W: www.wristangel.co.uk

Nicolite and Katherine Jackson

Nicolite is manufactured by Chromogenex PLC, 'the UK's leading developer and manufacturer of laser and intense pulsed light (IPL) systems'. The Nicolite machine uses advanced technology with diode lasers to stimulate the body's energy points specifically linked to addiction. The result of this process in the body is what helps decrease the craving to smoke. At no time does this treatment put nicotine back into the body. The lasers from the Nicolite machine enable the process to work naturally.

This process also releases endorphins into the body, uplifting the patient's spirit and motivation level. This feel-good effect is what makes the first few days without smoking so much easier. Expert Katherine Jackson combines Nicolite sessions with the existing treatments offered in her Chelsea studio. The accuracy of the Nicolite machine combined with Katherine's many years of experience with alternative medicine produces a treatment programme not only proven to help reduce cigarette cravings, but also offering several other positive effects on patients' physical and mental health. Katherine Jackson is a fully qualified acupuncturist (including electrical acupuncture), and practitioner of Chinese medicine, shiatsu and reflexology with over 37 years of experience.

• W: www.katherinejackson.co.uk

See also B: Beauty for Katherine's other skills

Alternative Therapy: Hypnosis

Hypnotherapist, Colin Remmer is a Licentiate Member of the Hypnotherapy Society as well as a Member of The Society of NLP, a Master Practitioner of NLP as well as a Provisional Trainer of NLP with a whole stream of letters after his name equating to muchos experience! I picked his clever brain about hypnosis

Quitting

Q

and how it can help you to quit that bad habit...

'Hypnosis is nothing more than a natural state of mind where we alter our state. Where we become deeply engrossed in something, to the point where we experience or re-experience the feelings associated with those thoughts or memories.

'By becoming deeply engrossed in something, it shuts the critical part of the mind off and opens the unconscious mind to accept suggestions. By giving the appropriate suggestions, change can take place – it's that simple.

'All the therapist needs to know is the thought processes that a person is using to trigger the negative behaviour. By asking questions about the movies they run in their mind, the voice they talk to themselves with and the feelings they create within their body, the therapist can glean the information necessary to know where and how to make the necessary intervention.

'Most people have no conscious knowledge of what they are doing in order to trigger an old, unwanted behaviour, but a therapist is trained to read between the lines and listen for what is *missing* from the clients thoughts.

'Habit modification, such as stopping smoking can be carried out by finding the trigger that causes the client to reach for the cigarette and giving suggestions to do something else. By attaching negative feelings to the old habit and better feelings to the new behaviours, people will be much more inclined to carry them out. It's almost like coming to a fork in a road. Down one fork is the old road where the person smoked and was unhealthy, while the other road is the road down which the people see themselves looking and behaving in the new ways they want. They have a choice as to which road they take. *Making* someone stop smoking or trying to get them to stop eating certain foods is often inappropriate and unsuccessful as it creates 'resistance'. The person will often change for a short space of time, but will inevitably go back to their old habits.

'All behaviours have a positive intention, if not, we wouldn't carry them out and these positive intentions have to be taken into consideration.

'Hypnosis can be used for many things, changing habits, changing ways of thinking, creating new habits and thought patterns as well as improving the things you already do.

'The number of sessions can vary from client to client and problem to problem. Some problems can be resolved in one session, such as fears and phobias while others can take up to about five.'

....

- **E: c.remmer@sky.com**
- **T: 0113 267 6006 and 0793 255 2485**

Recycling & Relaxation

Recycling

Recycling is an excellent way of saving energy and conserving the environment, making it a big deal, but it's often too confusing when it comes to knowing where to start – until now, with your *Guide to Fabulousness...*

• •

Two for joy: Musicmagpie

• •

Musicmagpie is the UK's only website for turning your old CDs, DVDs or games into cash. If you're making space, you can make money from your old collections.

Musicmagpie is free. All you need to do is select your unloved discs (there are etiquette rules to follow – they won't accept any scratched or damaged CDs, for instance), then they will send you freepost labels so that you can mail your CDs, DVDs or games. Place them all in a suitable box or envelope, attaching the freepost label (which has a barcode that tells them who you are after registering online), post the packaged bag back and when they've received your goods, they'll check them over and issue a cheque to you.

• W: www.musicmagpie.co.uk

Freecycle your goods

Freecycling is the latest way to recycle goods for free (hence the name). The **Freecycle Network™** is made up of 4,678 groups with 6,429,857 members across the globe. It's a grassroots and entirely non-profit movement of people who are giving (and getting) stuff for free in their own towns and thus keeping good stuff out of landfills. Membership is free, and everything posted must be free, legal and appropriate for all ages. If you want to get rid of something or even find something else without spending a penny, this is the way to do it.

• W: www.freecycling.co.uk

Another way to turn your clutter into cash is by selling it for free on **Preloved**. All free ads include a photo and private ads are completely free, no listing fees, no selling fees and no catches.

• W: www.blog.preloved.co.uk

See also E: Eco-Living for eco-chic ideas and solutions.

Relaxation

Our ever-increasing hectic workloads, varied roles and busy social calendars entitle us to a little R&R, so rest up with my round-up of places and services that will each give you a well-deserved way to unwind...

Life Factory

The Life Factory offer expert advice and remedies on how to handle and alleviate stress, at work and in your personal life. They can send their massage team to conferences and offices, so you and your workforce can feel rejuvenated – more effective than a Kit-Kat at breaktime!

• W: www.lifefactory.co.uk

Ladies only spa: Waterfall

Waterfall Spa in Leeds is a ladies only spa with emphasis firmly placed on indulgence. This is my kind of spa, as there are no workouts, diets or detox. Instead, guests are treated to a gourmet restaurant, champagne and smoothie bar and an opulent boudoir for relaxing between treatments.

Successfully combining the feel-good factor of their treatments and the use of their own delicious product line, with dishes such as fresh fruit and marshmallows dipped in luscious Belgian chocolate, Waterfall Spa's unique offering gives you the spa experience to spoil yourself.

• Waterfall Spa, 3 Brewery Wharf, Dock Street, Leeds, Yorkshire LS10 1JF
• T: 0845 634 1399
• W: www.waterfallspa.co.uk

Elemis SpaPod

Elemis is one of my favourite skincare brands, quite simply because it works. They have over 1,200 leading spas and salons in 45 countries and I visited the Elemis SpaPod, a tiny treatment room dedicated to you, nestled behind closed doors at the Elemis Counter in Harvey Nichols, Leeds.

A skincare consultation identifies which of their five intensive Anti-Ageing Power Booster Facials is right for you. Without removing your clothes, you relax in an Intelligent Massage Chair, a state-of-the art chair that measures the length of the spine, takes your body weight, warms the body and delivers your customized body massage programme. Can you send me one for my home, please?

While your aches and pains are massaged away, the facial begins. My therapist advised the Skin Radiance facial. A unique mask, rich with amino acids, helps to regenerate skin cells, providing instant energy to the skin, applied after a gentle cleanse. As the mask works its magic, hot stones are stroked across your décolletage and neck – bliss!

I now have this treatment regularly. Not only does it help me relax while fitting into my schedule (it only takes 30 minutes), but my skin is so radiant afterwards. The first time I had this, I had a big event straight after and thought I'd have to rush to the loo to apply make-up so as not to scare the guests (not advised, I know), but my skin was glowing and there was truly no need. The whole experience is perfect for de-stressing and adding a vitamin boost to your complexion.

• UK and Ireland department stores that offer the treatments are: Harvey Nichols Birmingham, Dublin, Edinburgh, Knightsbridge, London, Leeds, Manchester; House of Fraser; Frasers, Glasgow; selected Debenhams, John Lewis and Selfridges stores nationwide
• T: 0845 279 5005 (customer enquiries)

State-of-the-art: One Spa

It is easy to see why One Spa is Europe's most advanced city spa, at The Sheraton Grand Hotel and Spa in Edinburgh. This high-tech haven offers a new concept with their 'One Spa Journeys'. These individually tailored programmes combine the use of the 19m sparkling infinity swimming pool, the rejuvenating Thermal Suite, iconic rooftop Hydropool and state-of-the-art gym, fitness and Kinesis studios with the latest ESPA treatments, nutritious spa cuisine and expertise from the Spa's wellness experts … phew!

With this clever combination, you will not only feel incredible, but the effects will be long-lasting. Packages are designed for a range of benefits, from pure relaxation to invigoration.

I opted for rejuvenation with an Espa Super Active Repairing and Restoring Facial. I'm serious when I say this is one of the best facials I've ever had, and I've had plenty. For a girl who finds it tough to switch off, I actually drifted to sleep at one point, and found the techniques used were advanced and the products superb. My guest commented that my skin looked radiant and as though I was 'wearing a good foundation', except that I wasn't. The rooftop hydropool which leads outdoors is the ultimate highlight to this high-tech, high-spec spa – with

R Relaxation & Recycling

views over the beautiful landscape of Edinburgh.

The hotel is quite a stark contrast to the spa, with its grandiose and traditional décor, but is nevertheless charming and the bold and beautiful Santini restaurant offers authentic Italian cuisine. Spa heaven and well worth a visit.

• **One Spa, 8 Conference Square, Edinburgh EH3 8AN**
• **T: 0131 221 7777**
• **W: www.onespa.com**

Ragdale Hall

Ragdale Hall is located in the rolling Leicestershire countryside. It combines state-of-the-art facilities with the charm of traditional Victorian architecture to create one of the most luxurious and relaxing health spas in the country.

They offer numerous packages, yet for truly indulgent relaxation the Twilight Taster Evening offers the choice of a Holistic Back and Scalp Therapy, a Prescription Facial or Exfoliation and Back Massage with Light Supper in the Verandah Bar.

• **Ragdale Hall Health Hydro and Thermal Spa, Ragdale Village, Melton Mowbray, Leicestershire LE14 3PB**
• **W: www.ragdalehall.co.uk**

Thai, Tea and Treatments: SenSpa

SenSpa at Careys Manor in the New Forest is Thai inspired, with its own organic product range. It boasts a large hydrotherapy area, the Zen Garden Restaurant, pool, jacuzzi, crystal sauna,

a herbal tea room and 16 treatment rooms. Definitely worth a visit!

• **T: 01590 263 551**
• **W: www.senspa.co.uk**

Shopping

A section dedicated to my favourite pastime, shopping – almost a religion for me that I practise daily. I adore independent boutiques and there's a full list of my favourites here. This guide is fractionally a backlash against the masses, and that's the reason why I choose to highlight some smaller, lesser-known brands that are due credit for their sheer talent and quality. Take your guide with you as you trawl the

shops to ensure that you visit the gems listed...

Boutiques

There are so many chainstores around that, personally speaking, I get bored with many of them, with their uniform, nationwide window displays, climbing prices and fad fashions. I don't enjoy looking the same as everyone else, so it's a shame when you hear about

Shopping

S

magical independent boutiques closing down due to poor trade. Don't get me wrong, I'm partial to the odd chainstore, especially with the likes of Topshop introducing original concessions and supporting new designers, but I really do feel we need to support the small businesses more. Here is my round-up of some of the most exquisite independent boutiques. You won't be disappointed!

Paper Scissor Stone

Paper Scissor Stone is an über-cool gallery-meets-boutique situated on New York Street in Leeds, slightly off the beaten track but still in the city centre (near Ego hair salon). Set up by clothing label Electronic Poet, graphic designer/illustrator Si Scott and art curator Jules Balchin, this one-of-a-kind concept store offers limited edition prints and original artwork along with quirky books, magazines, furniture, music and hard-to-find labels such as Ritten House from Australia.

To keep you in the loop of cool, you should know that Si Scott's hand-inked and penned artwork has been used by the likes of Orange, MTV, Nike, Guinness and Hugo Boss.

- **38 New York Street, Leeds LS2 7DF**
- **T: 0113 244 1398**
- **W: www.paper-scissor-stone.co.uk**

See also A: Art for curators and artists linked to this store.

Hox

Hox is a fashion label with old-

fashioned views on personal shopping, offering British-made clothes. The Hox collection is made up of linen dresses, hoodies, sequined evening dresses, skinny trousers, waistcoats and a range of jackets. Beautiful brocades, pure linens, comfortable cottons and vibrant velvets are just some of the fabrics sourced exclusively for Hox Boutique. You will not find them anywhere else on the high street. Hox is not about fads, fast fashion or seasonal trends. It's about classic cuts, timeless design and lifetime pieces. Hox can guarantee exclusivity as only small quantities are made of each garment. Once the fabric runs out, it's never repeated.

- **T: 0121 236 9632**
- **W: www.hoxboutique.com**

Beyond the Valley

Beyond the Valley® supports and promotes emerging new talent across the fashion, art and design industries, based in Central London. Their store and gallery provide new designers with a centrally located retail, gallery and studio space to launch new products into the market, stocking some 100 new designers. Products in-store include fashion, books, jewellery, design products and more, all produced in limited quantities and exclusive to Beyond the Valley, making them both fresh and sought-after. A side room offers exhibition space and is often home to some very cool launches – so get yourself on the mailing list!

- **Beyond the Valley, Store and Gallery, 2 Newburgh Street (off Carnaby Street), London W1F 7RD**

- T: 020 7437 7338
- W: www.beyondthevalley.com

The East End Thrift Store

What a find! Full of fantastic vintage pieces for both men and women, with most items under a tenner, this is one cult store that has fast become a favourite on most fashion-savvy people's shopping hit lists. When you can pick up a 1940s-style dress for less than you pay for an overpriced latte in London, you know you've found a gem. A joy to browse, but be warned, you'll leave with bagloads!

- Unit 1A Assembly Passage, London E1 4UT
- T: 020 7423 9700
- W: www.theeastendthriftstore.com

Bohemia

Bohemia is a treasure trove of the most gorgeous things the owners have discovered on their travels, with an array of global, original designers, independent labels and new finds. I adore the Moroccan travel bags, and the Sam Ubhi chainmail bags are just gorgeous, available in a delicious assortment of shimmering metallic colours. Sam Ubhi works predominantly in sterling silver mixed with precious and semi-precious stones, as well as her signature materials of bone, horn and shell – all materials used are eco-friendly.

My other favourites in this store include Totem, a Brazilian fashion label founded by Fred d'Orey. His love for travelling, music and surfing fuse with joyful Brazilian spirit, producing bold,

retro prints that are very flattering to wear.

'Big Baby' by No Tail is a range of fun acrylic jewellery, and Mor Australia is the luxury body and beauty brand that exudes intoxicatingly divine scents in every item.

Other ranges include French labels Bensimon and American Vintage, Vila Clothes and Odd Molly.

This covetable range of goodies makes it easy to see why Bohemia has won an array of awards, including the well-deserved Spring Fair Awards 2009 'Buying Team of the Year'.

- 31 Dundas Street, Edinburgh EH3 6QQ, and 17 Roseneath Street, Edinburgh EH9 1JH
- T: 0131 467 6660
- W: www.bohemiadesign.co.uk

Mee

Mee, in the heart of Bath, is a boutique that is as much a delight to experience as it is to purchase something from. From the Chinese peony painted on the floor to the antique chandeliers and furniture, Mee is sumptuously inviting.

From vintage birdcages to butterfly garlands and delicious chocolate treats, I was in shopping heaven! As well as the unique finds, you can get your mitts on designer goodies from the likes of Heidi Klein, Hudson Jeans, Angel Jackson and Christian Dior.

If you can't get to Bath, the good news is that you can buy the gorgeous titbits online too!

- Mee, 9A Bartlett Street, Bath BA1 2QZ
- T: 01225 442250
- W: www.meeboutique.com

Shopping

S

Leila

The founder claims that if you have ever thought, 'I wish there was a place that not only stocked my style, but also inspired me with new ideas,' then Leila is the store for you.

The first shop opened in 2001 and there are now three across London (Crouch End, Muswell Hill and Islington). One of the most impressive attributes of the store is the range of quality labels and unique finds at seriously affordable prices – the clothing and accessories are so fabulous I was certain I wouldn't be able to buy a thing before pay day and I was shocked (and delighted) when I looked at the price tags. I ended up buying half a new wardrobe and a few new additions to my home from their exquisite interiors section.

- **T: 020 8365 2122 (Muswell Hill store)**
- **W: www.leilalondon.com – browse the website for your nearest store (three stores in London; Crouch End, Muswell Hill and Islington)**

Comfort & Joy

Comfort & Joy is a great source of unusual, good-quality clothes at high-street prices. Most of the unique garments sold here are made by partners Ruth and Anthony Wilson, supplemented by items from other independent designers.

- **Comfort & Joy, 109 Essex Rd, London N1**
- **T: 020 7359 3898**

Hoxton Boutique

At this much-loved gallery-like shop done out in Studio 54 style complete with mirrorballs, you'll find an excellent selection of hard-to-get, desirable labels including Hussein Chalayan, Isabel Marant and Doctor Denim. The addition of a vintage section and accessory department has made this even more of a necessity.

- **Hoxton Boutique, 2 Hoxton St, London N1**
- **T: 020 7684 2083**
- **W: www.hoxtonboutique.co.uk**

Koh Samui

The shop is one of the few stockists of Lou Lou and Law – the collaboration between Ann-Louise Roswald and illustrator Natasha (sister of Jude) Law. The setting reminds me of a sumptuous girly boudoir with plenty of slinky designer labels and little treats on display.

- **Koh Samui, 65–67 Monmouth Street, London WC2**
- **T: 020 7240 4280**
- **W: www.kohsamui.co.uk**

Labour of Love

Designer-owner Francesca Forcolini brings together a beguiling blend of fashion in this fun-to-browse boutique.

Forcolini's own Labour of Love label achieves a classic style with a twist, with bustiers, sumptuous knitwear and silk-lined wool gabardine macs epitomizing the range.

They claim, 'The idea is simple: we

sell nice stuff. Not a champion of the big boys nor the one-man bands, if it's good enough, space is made.'

From shoes to clothing, jewellery to prints, bags to books – there is a flurry of fabulousness in this little store, and you can shop virtually too with their online store.

- **193 Upper Street, Islington, London N1 1RQ**
- **T: 020 7354 9333**
- **W: www.labour-of-love.co.uk**

Mungo & Maud

Husband-and-wife team Michael and Nicola Sacher founded this edgy concept in providing dog and cat stores that offer elegant, well-designed accessories for your pets to complement the contemporary home. Products range from hand-stitched leather collars and leads to wooden feeding bowls, cotton beds and Mungo & Maud's organic treats. Shopping for your pets has never been so chic.

- **W: www.mungoandmaud.com**

Liverpool ONE

Liverpool ONE houses more than 160 famous high-street stores and independent boutiques, along with cafés and restaurants perfect for relieving your weary feet after you've visited the vast array of brands on offer, with everything from All Saints to Zara.

- **W: www.liverpool-one.com**

Austique

Originally inspired by laid-back, girly boutiques in Australia, sisters Katie and Lindy Lopes have assembled a super-feminine collection of clothes, lingerie and accessories. The Austique philosophy has been that every girl should be beautifully and uniquely dressed, and they endeavour to find labels that are new, or little heard of, in the UK.

They also offer a bespoke service enabling you to personalize jewellery and lingerie. You'll be spoiled for choice with personalized, Carrie-Bradshaw-inspired gold name-plate necklaces, embroidered frothy knickers (names, proposals or personal messages are the most requested bespoke option here!) and design-your-own-motif Austique bikinis. Voted one of London's top ten shops by *vogue.com*.

- **Austique, 330 King's Road, London SW3**
- **T: 020 7376 3663**
- **W: www.austique.co.uk**

Kakao by K

Kakao (pronounced 'kah-kay-oh') means 'cocoa' in Danish, and Kakao by K is a women's fashion boutique situated in the heart of Edinburgh.

Cool Scandinavian designers combine with other international women's clothing labels, offering a blend of collections taking you from casual daywear to formal but elegant workwear and eveningwear. Plenty of eye-catching accessories are also on

Shopping

S

offer, including handbags, scarves and jewellery.

- **Kakao by K, 45 Thistle Street, Edinburgh EH2 1DY**
- **T: 0131 226 3584**
- **W: www.kakao.co.uk**

New ways to shop

Brighton Fashion Weekend

Brighton's annual Fashion Weekend is a celebration of creativity, style, diversity and imagination, founded on the ethos 'Be Who You Are'.

The weekend usually takes place each May and kicks off with the Brighton Frocks theatrical fashion catwalk show for independent designers. The weekend's shopping emporium also offers stalls from key designers and vintage suppliers, street performances, catwalk shows, creative workshops and a drinks lounge. Furthermore, you'll find open studios, workshops and fashion installations across the city all weekend. The event always finishes with a renowned closing party.

- **Contact Liz Bishop, Brighton Frocks Director**
- **T: 07917 103330**
- **E: liz@brightonfrocks.com**
- **W: www.brightonfrocks.com**

Swap shop: Swapaholix

Swapaholix is the brainchild of Jo and Lou, two women who have taken their passion for swapping the latest fashions out of the wardrobe and onto the web, in the firm belief that one girl's junk is another girl's treasure.

Their aim is to create an enormous internet wardrobe filled with designer outfits, fab labels and fashions to enable the dedicated shopper to convert to a swapper and exchange the unworn, unwanted or uncomfortable for the clothing of their dreams.

This is certainly a new way to shop, and there are copious amounts of other swap shops and 'swishing' events out there that enable you to get rid of old clothes and get new ones free of charge. The recycling element of this method ups the ethical bonus too.

- **W: www.swapaholix.co.uk**

Personal styling and shopping: Create Yourself

Create Yourself is a service that offers you your own (affordable) stylist who will advise you on the most flattering styles and colours of clothing to make the most of yourself. The stylist will weed out the clothes that are not right for you, create new outfits from what you already have and create a shopping list of key items that you need. Personal shopping trips and lifestyle management are also available to improve not only your wardrobe, but your confidence too.

- **T: 0845 257 9977**
- **W: www.createyourself.co.uk**

• Style Icon

Style icon, **Natalie Robinson** from

London is one of the leading fashion advisors, having shopped for and styled numerous celebrities including Kylie and Sophie Dahl.

If you want to look like a celeb for the day, treat yourself to Style Icon's 'Starlet' package. Natalie will spend the day in one store of your choice, providing you with lots of fashion tips and finding that perfect outfit. After that she will whisk you off to The Casting Suite, a top photographic studio based in Soho, for a one-hour photoshoot. You will be made to feel like a true star as well as a style icon: you will be photographed in your favourite purchases of the day, and you will have a make-up/hair makeover, with your hair styled professionally to suit your new wardrobe. Let's not forget the champagne which you will enjoy at the end of your shoot while choosing ten of your favourite pictures to place in your photo album.

Natalie Robinson is one of the country's leading stylists and shoppers and has featured in numerous magazines and newspapers, including the fashion bible *Look*, *New*, *handbag. com*, *MSN*, *Black Hair*, the *Daily Star*, *the Daily Mail*, etc. She has also consulted in the VIP area for London Fashion Week, as their resident club lounge stylist.

• T: 020 8820 0856
• W: www.style-icon.co.uk

Shopping

S

Tea

The formal tea party is said to have been created in the early nineteenth century by Anna Russell, the Duchess of Bedford. She began hosting tea parties to stave off her hunger before the late evening meal and today it has become rather fashionable amongst all types. Here is my pick of the best places to enjoy afternoon tea in style, along with where to buy your goodies, and my advice on how to host your own fabulous tea party.

Afternoon tea

W1J 9BR
• T: 020 7493 8181
• W: www.theritzlondon.com

The Ritz

Tea at The Ritz is an institution in itself. A member of the Tea Council's prestigious Tea Guild, The Ritz's delights are served in the spectacular Palm Court with a choice of several varieties of tea, traditional finely cut sandwiches, freshly baked scones, jam and clotted cream and a range of delicate pastries.

Befitting the elegant style of The Ritz, a formal dress code is in place which only adds to this grandiose experience. It's so spectacularly delicious that tables may need to be reserved at least 12 weeks in advance.

• **The Ritz London, 150 Piccadilly, London**

Prêt-à-Portea

The Berkeley London designer afternoon tea, Prêt-à-Portea, is inspired by the themes and colours of the fashion world. The menu is transformed every six months to follow the changing seasons in fashion, celebrated during London Fashion Week, and is available year round.

Served in the classically elegant Caramel Room of the hotel, daily from 1 p.m. to 6 p.m., you can choose from a selection of loose-leaf teas, herbal infusions and champagne to accompany a selection of miniature savoury skewers, taster spoons and elegant canapés.

Tea & Treatments

T

I tried the spring–summer 2009 collection and have never before eaten an Alexander McQueen 'Elvie' chocolate tote until now! This one was wrapped in mint-flavoured marzipan and filled with chocolate truffle – a tote that is truly ravishing in any form!

Served on vintage-style tiered cake stands and fine bone china, designed by Paul Smith for Thomas Goode, this feast is as delectably English as it is stylish and enjoyable. My gaggle of girlies sat next to a lady from Sydney, Australia, who, having read about Prêt-à-Portea, felt she had to jet across the world to try it! With that level of fondness on display, you must be tempted to try it!

• **The Berkeley, Wilton Place, Knightsbridge, London SW1X 7RL**
• **T: 020 7235 6000**
• **W: www.the-berkeley.co.uk**

'I drink Yorkshire Tea nowadays': Betty's & Taylor's

Betty's & Taylor's is a family-run company that opened its doors in 1919 and is dedicated to life's little pleasures – handmade cakes, mouth-watering chocolates, beautiful Café Tea Rooms, exclusive coffees and fine teas all set in stunning surroundings.

I'd heard of the infamous queues of people who wait up to one hour to be seated! Though not one to wait, I queued for a total of 40 minutes in order to find out if it was worth the wait or all hype.

I'm not certain the food or drinks were so spectacular that a long wait is justified, but you must experience the delicious treats once in your lifetime, made at their own Craft Bakery in

Harrogate … simply to be able to say you've been there, done that, drank the tea.

The Harrogate branch has recently expanded – and this should alleviate some of the waiting time and give us all more to choose from! There are six Betty's Café Tea Rooms to explore.

If you want the Betty's experience every day of the week (and to avoid queuing), you can enjoy the goods at home with the new online mail-order service

• **W: www.bettysandtaylors.co.uk, and (for the mail-order service) www.bettysbypost.com**

Bob Bob Ricard

Sitting in 'BBR' is like sitting in a 1950s diner or luxury train, in secluded booths and surrounded by the nostalgic charm and elegance of their lavish interior. Afternoon tea here makes for a very authentic experience. Served on tiered cake stands with matching china tea cups and saucers, you can expect an array of finger sandwiches, home-made mini cakes and the most delicious fresh scones and Devonshire clotted cream. Have the champagne afternoon tea for two and if you run dry, simply press the champagne button at your table to summon a trolley to top up your glass!

• **Bob Bob Ricard, 1 Upper James Street, Soho, London W1F 9DF**
• **T: 020 3145 1000**
• **W: www.bobbobricard.com**

See also D: Dining for more dining options.

Betty Blythe

Providing an old-fashioned shopping experience and a reason to make time for tea and cake, Betty Blythe sells a wide range of food from homemade cakes and sandwiches to specialist foodstuffs and tasty delicacies, as well as all the traditional favourites you might need to restock your larder.

Named after the 1920s Hollywood starlet, Betty Blythe's gorgeous, vintage décor offers the perfect spot for tea parties and baby showers. Also, by using the catering service, Betty Blythe can be enjoyed outside W14 to create a quintessentially English picnic.

• **Betty Blythe, 73 Blythe Road, Brook Green, London W14 0HP**
• **T: 020 7602 1177**
• **W: www.bettyblythe.co.uk**

See also D: Dining for the Betty Blythe advice on having the perfect picnic.

The Tea Cosy

The Tea Cosy is novel and sophisticated with a deliciously camp interior dedicated to the royal family and all things quintessentially English. Think kitsch English cottage meets hiding place of royal fanatic!

The menu includes a choice of tea packages, aptly named after members of the royal family. My favourite has to be The Queen Elizabeth Coronation High Tea, offering a selection of cut cakes, fruit scones, cream, jam, butter, fancy Welsh rarebit, hot crumpets, Lumpfish Black Caviar and cowslip cream cheese on toast, olives, a fruit basket, biscuit selection and your choice of tea. If that won't keep you going, I'm not sure what will!

Prices are incredibly reasonable and it's worth going just for the cream tea (one of the best I've tried), if not simply to admire the vibrant hubbub of the décor.

The adorable (and justified) tea room etiquette of The Tea Cosy completes the pleasurable and individual experience. Mobile phones are banned, as are dunking biscuits, blasphemy against the royal family, elbows on tables and clinking your spoon on the side of your cup. Ignore the etiquette and you could be asked to leave.

Be sure to visit on a Sunday in your Sunday best by 4 p.m., when guests are asked to stand 'as display of respect' for the National Anthem. Love it! This is one tea room you will never forget.

• **The Tea Cosy, 3 George Street, Kemptown, Brighton, East Sussex**
• **W: www.theteacosy.co.uk**

Liberty's

Liberty's intimate and friendly tea room, aptly named, erm, Tea, is situated on the ground floor right next to the delicious designer handbags, and this little hideaway appeals to a number of senses.

With over 40 fine, loose teas from around the world, a light lunch menu and a selection of handmade cakes, I was in heaven!

The décor was a little

Tea & Treatments

T

disappointing, with uncomfortably cool red plastic chairs and marble-topped tables. With no natural light, it looked harsh in comparison to the charm of Liberty's whimsical period finishing, but I just had to stay for the Liberty Champagne Afternoon Tea…

My friends and I were treated to a glass of chilled champagne with a selection of finger sandwiches, sliced cakes and fruit scones with organic strawberry jam and clotted cream, served with freshly brewed tea.

I must have consumed my daily calorie intake in one sitting, but who cares? This place is definitely worth a visit – great for solo dining, work or play (did that sound like an advert for a Mars Bar?).

For post-work drinkies, try Liberty's Oyster and Champagne Bar for seafood and bubbly and a stylish escape from the bustling West End!

• **Liberty Store, Regent Street, London W1B 5AH**
• **W: www.liberty.co.uk**

eteaket

eteaket Tea Boutique and Café is an elegant addition to the Edinburgh scene for discerning ladies who enjoy the good things in life. Unique loose-leaf teas have been expertly sourced from all over the world, tried and tested by the founder herself. From robust black tea to the light green teas and caffeine-free varieties, this chic little parlour has it all. I opted for the Afternoon Tea for One, offering a selection of hand-cut sandwiches, deluxe scones with the best clotted cream I have ever tasted, jam and a collection of mini-patisserie served on a tiered vintage cake stand. You can choose your sandwich filling from a tasty selection, and I chose the New York Deli with pastrami, Swiss cheese, gherkins and mustard. All tea is served in vintage mismatched china cups and saucers with a special tea-timer that tells you how long you need to leave it to brew for the best taste. All the teas, tea caddies and vintage cake stands are also available to buy in store and online.

• **eteaket Tea Boutique and Café, 41 Frederick Street, Edinburgh EH2 1EP**
• **T: 0131 226 2982**
• **W: www.eteaket.co.uk**

The Met's Afternoon De-Light

The Metropolitan Hotel in Park Lane, London, is most famous for its legendary cocktails and late-night parties with the stars, but its sophisticated Afternoon De-Light is an afternoon tea experience that is rather different from the rest. Still as indulgent as a traditional afternoon tea, but without all the calories, the Mets' Afternoon De-Light menu serves a selection of healthy sweet and savoury cupcakes, full scones and 'no-bread sandwiches' offering healthy alternatives, including flour substitutes and low-fat crème fraiche. Fresh fruit purees replace unrefined sugars, olive oil is used instead of butter and wherever possible, all produce is natural, organic and locally sourced – great if you love a treat but also love body con dresses, latex trousers, bikinis and skinny jeans!

• **W: www.metropolitan.london.como.bz**

The Lanesborough

The Lanesborough's **Footloose and Fancy Free Tea** is a wonderful girly treat. The hotel's Spa Studio offers you a pedicure and joins forces with their award-winning Afternoon Tea to present the perfect way of relieving your feet and satisfying your appetite after a hard day's shopping.

You will enjoy a 60-minute Pristine Pedicure that will ensure your feet are primped, preened and polished to perfection (using Leighton Denny's renowned range – one of my favourites), then you will be invited to take tea in Apsleys, the hotel's elegant restaurant.

London's original tea sommelier is on hand to guide you through the 56-strong tea menu, from their own signature blends to the rarer Darjeeling 'First Flush' – the champagne of teas. Delicate sandwiches and mouth-watering cakes, scones and pastries are also served, allowing you to sit back and enjoy the sound of the graceful piano. They also provide a gluten- and dairy-free tea if you make your preference known beforehand. Positively debonair.

- T: 020 7333 7700
- W: www.lanesborough.com

Where to buy your tea and accessories

Tea Palace

Tea Palace is a modern tea emporium that offers the widest selection of the finest quality teas and infusions, looking at tea as a global drink, not just a British tradition. They have over 160 varieties to purchase, from the finest Earl Grey, to the rarest hand-tied Chinese green tea, to herbal infusions made with Whole Organic Chamomile Flowers. Available to buy in their Covent Garden store and on online.

- **Tea Palace, 12 Covent Garden Market, Covent Garden, London WC2E 8RF**
- **W: www.teapalace.co.uk**

Tea Cosies from Poppy Treffry

Poppy Treffry is a small company in Cornwall that produces some delightful handmade tea cosies (amongst other goodies). You'll be looking to invite the vicar round to show off your cute table spread!

- **Studio Unit 3, Wesley Place, Newlyn, Cornwall TR18 5AZ**
- **T: 01736 369247**
- **W: www.poppytreffry.co.uk**

Funky tea shop: Leaf Tea

Leaf Tea Shop and Bar is the north-west's only music and arts tea shop, based in the same building as The Zutons, The Rascals and North West Talent. It makes a cool Liverpool hangout and collective haunt for trendy types.

- **W: www.thisisleaf.co.uk**

Tea & Treatments

T

195

Blends for Friends – the home of custom-made tea gifts

Founder of Blends for Friends, Alex Probyn can personally hand-blend the finest teas and herbs to create a highly personalized gift or addition to your collection. After years as a master tea taster, blending for one of the world's leading tea brands, Alex grew bored of the current offerings and began to blend individual teas and herbal infusions for his friends and family based on their personalities. Eventually the word spread enough to enable him to create a successful business from it.

Alex sourced teas from the finest estates around the world and now combines his many types of tea to suit you or the recipient of this sincerely novel gift.

To create your own blend, you simply fill in a form that asks you questions about the person you are blending for, whether that is you or another, the occasion (from 'just for me' to 'a wedding'), and traits of the recipient's personality and appearance. The rest is left to the expert, who will deliver a creation that should fit the bill.

The Tasting Events are also worth a try, where you'll taste 24 different types of teas and herbs and get the chance to create your own blend. They usually take place in London.

- **Blends For Friends Ltd, The Old Granary, Lower Austin Lodge Farm, Upper Austin Lodge Road, Eynsford, Dartford, Kent DA4 0HT**

- **T: 01322 868188**
- **E: alex@blendsforfriends.com**
- **W: www.blendsforfriends.com**

teapigs

teapigs are quite a small tea company who offer great quality whole-leaf tea without the pomp, bow ties and gold trim. They present their teas in biodegradable tea 'temples' (posh teabags) that give their special teas all the room they need to infuse properly.

They offer a range of 20 teas which include the very finest English Breakfast, Earl Grey, green teas, Oolong, white tea and a selection of herbal infusions including Rooibos (caffeine free).

Matcha is a super-power green tea and the teapigs version is fuelled with 137 times the antioxidants of standard green tea. Research suggests that it boosts your metabolism and gives your skin a healthy glow.

- **W: www.teapigs.co.uk (N)**

Teapots from Pheasant

Pheasant is a mail-order company presenting a tiny selection of home accessories and hand-picked goodies, all handmade and crafted in Yorkshire. The teapots are the best-selling and most irresistible products bound to get your tea party talking, with handmade designs mimicking pots of Marmite, Golden Syrup and Coleman's Mustard, and quirky designs such as a caravan or radio.

- **W: www.pheasantmailorder.co.uk**

Tea experiences

Tea leaf reading

Try a more refreshing alternative with Anne Brady, expert tea leaf reader, who hosts sessions at her house in Barbican, London. Just choose your tea (options including Earl Grey, Orange Pekoe and vanilla) and teacup. Once you've downed your cuppa, Brady tips the remaining leaves into a saucer and 'reads' the leftovers. She looks at their shapes and formations and translates them into themes of love, health, travel and family. If you're so engrossed that you forget it all, everything is recorded on a tape that you can take home.

• T: 07765 690 700

Blooming Great Tea Party for Marie Curie

Tea parties are now an essential in the social calendar, and what better excuse to eat cake than raising money for a truly fabulous cause? Marie Curie Cancer Care invites ladies to hold their own tea party to raise money for the charity each year. You can hold your party wherever you want – at home, work, school or in your local club. The party could be anything from tea with friends to an elegant high tea. All tea parties, however big or small, will help more Marie Curie Nurses to provide free care for terminally ill people in their own homes or one of the charity's hospices.

• **For your free Blooming Great Tea Party fundraising pack, contact Marie Curie Cancer Care**
• **T: 08700 340 040**
• **W: www.mariecurie.org.uk/teaparty (N)**

How to host your own fabulous tea party

Do tea parties conjure up images of blue-haired old dears with their pinkies in the air, or ladies who lunch all day long? Not so today; tea parties are in vogue again and they're for everyone. So brush down your tea dress, get the girls over and host your own fabulous tea party...

Tea parties are ideal for a lazy hostess, since the only thing you need to serve is the tea: the rest is laid out on the table and your guests help themselves, giving you more time to spend with your friends and relax.

Guest list and setting the tone

Setting the tone is down to you. Some tea parties can be very formal affairs, but personally I find they are a great excuse to catch up with the girls and gossip. I therefore take care with my guest list, ensuring a healthy mix of personalities and tastes but no complete strangers or clashes – a frosty atmosphere does not a fun tea party make.

Tea & Treatments

T

Once your guest list is finalized, send out your invitations. E-invites just will not do – keep it authentic and make your own, then post them or, better still, hand-deliver them. You can find some great craft ideas and bits'n'pieces from *www.hobbycraft.co.uk*. Don't forget to add a dress code. My choice would be 'vintage darlings'.

• **W: www.hobbycraft.co.uk**

Setting the table

If there is ever an occasion to bring out your best china, a tea party is it. Adorn your table with mismatched vintage china, silver and white linen for a truly bona fide, graceful appeal. I'm a huge fan of vintage china, as it reminds me of a time when we used to appreciate the finer little treasures we have in our lives, and there is a delectable English charm about holding a pre-loved cup and saucer in our manufactured world!

eBay has plenty of vintage china sets and separates to purchase at bargain prices, but *www.bedcrumb.co.uk* is my favourite for funky tea cosies, linen and vintage china. The vintage tea party sets include gorgeous individually sourced and deliberately mismatched china, handmade black cotton napkins and a great cupcake recipe, all packaged up in pink net and ribbons, with the luxury sets having their own feather-filled 'Dot' cushion. If you just want to host a one-off tea party, you can hire vintage china sets from *www.utterlysexycafe.co.uk*, catering from 10 to 110.

• **W: www.bedcrumb.co.uk**
• **W: www.utterlysexycafe.co.uk**

Food

Tea sandwiches are neither doorsteps nor foot-long baguettes, but delicate, easy-to-eat finger sandwiches. The idea is not to ruin your lovely tea dress or have a mouthful of dripping ingredients when asked a question (don't you just hate that?).

Traditional choices include white bread with cucumber filling, egg mayonnaise, and cream cheese and salmon, but today I suggest vamping it up a little and adding flavours that you may have tried on your travels. As long as you make it 'delicate', anything goes. My favourite is sundried tomato bread with pastrami, low-fat mayonnaise, gherkins (drained well), shredded iceberg lettuce and ripe tomatoes (put these in at the last minute to avoid mushy sarnies).

Don't overload them with butter, or they'll go soggy, and buy the best-quality fresh breads you can muster. Your local bakers are best, but buy the bread fresh on the day of your party and don't make the sandwiches too early or your beautiful creations will taste stale. The bread should be soft to touch and the ingredients should melt in your mouth.

Cakes and sweets are the fun part of the spread. Think cream-filled strawberries, shortbread, chocolate roll, cream puffs and scones, all served with a choice of clotted cream and jam – mmm! There are some fantastic recipe ideas from the Joy of Baking website. Do try a little baking, even if you just make a meringue and then pop to the shops for the rest (I won't tell anyone). Serve your cakes on tiered cake stands so your guests can pick what they would like and fill up their individual china plates with their own choices.

....

• W: www.joyofbaking.com/
EnglishTeaParty
• Get a genuine 1950s cake stand from Steptoes Antiques, at www.
steptoesantiques.co.uk

After you have invited the guests, set the table and prepared the food, next comes the star of the show…

••••••••••••••••••••••••••••••••••••••

How to brew and serve a 'proper' cup of tea

••••••••••••••••••••••••••••••••••••••

• Choose a ceramic teapot, as metal ones don't hold the heat as well and can affect the taste.

• Run the teapot under hot tap water before pouring in the boiling water so that it doesn't hit cold ceramic and cool quickly.

• Fill your kettle with fresh, cool water, preferably filtered, and bring to the boil.

• Add the tea leaves to the empty teapot, allowing one teaspoon of leaves per cup – so if you have five guests, add five teaspoons of leaves.

• Add the boiling water and let the tea brew for 3–6 minutes, depending on how strong you like it.

• You should provide a choice of milk, from whole to skimmed, cream and lemon to allow your guests to finish their own cup of tea to their taste.

• Serve the tea, but don't forget to use a strainer to catch the loose leaves or you will be straining it through your own teeth!

• Keep the teapot warm with a cute tea cosy and brew another if required.

Coffee

I remember when ordering a coffee didn't come with questions such as, 'Would that be a mocha or americano? Non-fat? What size? To

Fab Tip

If your guests like different teas, or prefer it at different strengths, why not serve them their very own mini teapot for one, personalized to their requirements? On the invitation, ask for their specific preferences when they RSVP so that you can prepare. Or you can take a tip from eteaket in Edinburgh and serve each pot of tea with its own tea-timer to indicate when it's brewed.

Tea & Treatments

T

go or stay in...?' Crikey. So for all you coffee lovers, I've asked coffee company Starbucks to give us a jargon-busting glossary of how to order your favourite tipple without the headache of remembering just what to say...

The Starbucks glossary: Beverage choice

Espresso

Coffee's purest, most intense form (a shot of espresso). Rich, caramelly sweet and delicious, freshly pulled shots of Starbucks Espresso Roast are at the heart of all Starbucks® espresso drinks. For a full-flavoured experience, enjoy a shot on its own.

Caffe Latte

A drink made with espresso and steamed milk (approx. quarter foamed milk). With perfectly steamed milk, rich espresso and a delicate topping of foamed milk, this is soothing and inviting anytime. Also available iced.

Cappuccino

A drink made with espresso and foamed milk (approx. half steamed milk and half foamed milk) – much frothier than the steamed milk in a Latte. A European coffeehouse staple, combining espresso with a small amount of steamed milk and a deep, luxurious layer of foam. Classic and complex, with stronger coffee flavour.

Americano

A coffee made with two shots of espresso and hot water. This European approach to American-style coffee combines espresso with steaming hot water. A great alternative for brewed coffee aficionados. Also available iced.

Mocha

A drink made with espresso, chocolate and steamed milk topped with whipped cream. A chocolately, indulgent treat. Espresso and intense, bittersweet chocolate syrup mixed with steamed milk – all topped by a cloud of whipped cream. The perfect bit of luxury. Also available iced.

Vanilla Frappuccino® Blended Crème

A deliciously creamy, classic combination of vanilla and milk, blended with ice, topped with whipped cream.

Tazo® Chai Tea Latte

A spicy drink of black tea infused with cardamom, cinnamon, black pepper and star anise, added to freshly steamed milk. Half Tazo black tea topped with steamed milk, and a little foamed milk.

The Starbucks glossary: Style of beverage

- **Decaf**: decaffeinated coffee.

- **Double**: adding an extra shot of espresso to a drink that ordinarily only has one.

- **Doubleshot**: 6.5 oz can with espresso and 'a touch' of cream; also comes in Doubleshot® Light (less fat and sugar).

- **Espresso**: highly concentrated, heavily caffeinated coffee; it comes in the form of a shot.

- **Frappuccino® Blended Coffee**: frozen drink made of coffee, milk and flavouring (many options), blended with ice, can be topped with whipped cream.

- **Frappuccino® Light Blended Coffee**: the same as regular, but with fewer calories, uses non-fat milk and sugar-free syrups if applicable.

- **Half-caf**: half caffeinated, half decaf.

. . . .

The Starbucks glossary: Beverage sizes
. . . .

- **Shot**: 1 oz, usually associated with espresso.

- **Tall**: the smallest size (seems counterintuitive, doesn't it?); hot espresso drinks come with 1 espresso shot: 12 fl oz.

- **Grande**: the middle-sized/medium drink at Starbucks; hot espresso drinks come with two espresso shots: 16 fl oz.

- **Venti**: the largest size; hot espresso drinks come with two espresso shots: 20 fl oz.

. . . .

The Starbucks glossary: Finishing touches
. . . .

- **Skinny**: made with non-fat milk; if

the drink has syrup, the syrup will be sugar-free.

- **Soy milk**: milk for those who either don't like or can't drink regular milk, made from soy beans, no lactose.

- **Triple**: adding a third espresso shot to a drink that normally has two.

Treatments

This section delivers reviews of some of the best treatments that really work and make a difference to you and your look, from reflexology to permanent make-up and lash extensions…

. . . .

Fabulous for restoring balance: Reflexology
. . . .

Reflexology works by encouraging the body to work naturally in restoring its own healthy balance. A traditional Oriental complementary therapy, stimulation and pressure is applied to the reflex points in the feet which, when massaged, release energy blockages throughout the whole body, restoring your balance and promoting healing.

I had reflexology with qualified practitioner Hilary Taylor, who used a range of massaging techniques for different areas of my foot, but for each person the application and effect of the therapy are unique. Hilary detected tiny deposits and imbalances in my feet, and by kneading these points released

Tea & Treatments

T

blockages, eased tension and encouraged circulation. She even picked up on the fact that I had a cold coming (sadly true) and made me feel a lot more rested.

In addition to easing stress, I believe reflexology is fantastic for maternity care and for treating infertility, which Hilary specializes in. She says, 'Anxiety and worry can create physical problems that prevent conception and reflexology encourages a deep relaxation which alleviates stress and tension so that conception may take place.' Research has shown that regular reflexology treatments during pregnancy can shorten the duration of labour too, with subjects often requiring less pain relief during the course of delivery.

• **Hilary Taylor MAR, Reflexology in Leeds**
• **T: 07854 411 053**
• **E: info@reflexologyinleeds.co.uk**
• **W: www.reflexologyinleeds.co.uk**
• **To find a practitioner like Hilary near you, visit the Association of Reflexologists at www.aor.org.uk or www.wahanda.com to find your nearest practising spa.**

Most fabulous for invigorating the body: Dry Flotation

If you like the idea of the tranquillity that flotation tanks can offer minus the closed space, try dry flotation. This complete exfoliation and skin-enhancing treatment will cleanse and invigorate the body, followed by a deeply relaxing float on a warm water-filled bed which superbly induces tranquillity and harmony in the mind and body. This is a perfect pre-holiday experience to get you glowing and help you to wind down after all that 'tying up' at work.

• **The Academy, Oakdale Place, Harrogate, North Yorkshire HG1 2LA**
• **W: www.theacademy.co.uk**

Most fabulous for fat-busting without the pain and all the gain: M.E.L.T.

M.E.L.T. stands for Medical – Energies – Lipo – Tightening. Dr Daniel Sister of BeautyWorksWest brings this to the UK for the first time, exclusive to him and his colleague Dr Cyrille Blum.

M.E.L.T. combines what used to be four different machines for the same treatment – Radio Frequency Monopolar, Infrared, Ultrasound and Magnetic. The fat is melted inside the fat cells, destroys the fat cells' membranes, increases the drainage and also tightens the skin. M.E.L.T. can be used on any area of the body and face and, depending on how much fat there is, would need an average of 3–4 sessions, but even after one session, results should be seen within two weeks.

There is no pain, no down time, no bandage-wearing, and the procedure requires no needles. It's almost similar to having an MRI scan in some ways. The procedure starts with the patient lying on a bed; a specific gel is applied to the skin where the treatment zone has been defined. The session lasts up to 45 minutes depending on the area. After wiping off the gel on completion of the session, the patient can resume normal daily activity.

....

• M.E.L.T. is available exclusively from **Dr Daniel Sister of BeautyWorksWest, Lambton Place, Westbourne Grove, Notting Hill, London W11 2SH**
• **T: 020 7221 2248**
• **W: www.Beautyworkswest.com**

....

Permanent make-up: Tracey Ager

....

I don't know about you, but I used to feel unsure about permanent make-up, attaching a negative stigma to it – there was something a little scary about the words 'permanent' and 'make-up' used in the same phrase. What if it goes wrong? Is it safe? But then I put myself in the firing line and tried it for myself, to give you the no-bullshit low-down…

Aesthetic therapist Tracey Ager is renowned for her expertise and dedication in all aspects of permanent make-up, medical tattooing and cosmetic camouflage. With over 25 years' experience, Tracey states, '"Permanent make-up" or "Micropigmentation" are the names given to this non-surgical procedure used to infuse a coloured pigment into the skin, creating or enhancing a natural cosmetic appearance. This procedure is a cosmetic tattoo and permanent in nature, therefore referred to as "permanent make-up". However, some people refer to this procedure as semi-permanent because the

colour may need to be refreshed from time to time, even though the procedure itself is permanent. Permanent make-up can create, enhance, define and accentuate eyebrows and lips, creating a natural effect and giving the impression of a younger, brighter appearance.'

So is she right? Did I feel naturally enhanced?

I decided to define my eyebrows and infill the gaps to lessen the need for applying eyebrow pencil every morning and, since the eyebrows frame the entire eye area, I felt this should make a positive improvement to my face.

Tracey talked me through a very thorough consultation, and had previously sent me a patch test kit and information forms. I signed those after agreeing that I was fully aware of what the procedure involved, and we chose the colour of the ink that would be applied. Then a numbing cream was applied to the area. I was made aware of possible symptoms, which for the eyebrow area includes minor swelling, mild tenderness, dry flaking skin and potential itchiness. This is because your skin has to go through three phases – healing, peeling and fading – just like a normal tattoo. I was feeling apprehensive at this stage, as I dreaded swollen flaky eyebrows (not a good look), but Tracey assured me it sounds a lot scarier than it actually is and thankfully, she was right.

Then came the treatment. I felt nervous about feeling pain or discomfort, but Tracey made me feel very relaxed and explained everything fully. Using a needle dipped in the chosen ink, she stroked on individual strands to my

Tea & Treatments

T

203

eyebrows, as you would yourself with a pencil. I was literally gobsmacked at how painless this was. I'm sure the numbing cream helped, but Tracey was very gentle and the touch was very light. It wasn't comfortable, but neither was it uncomfortable. There were certain areas that felt more tender than others and I did experience mild tenderness afterwards, but I was surprised and relieved at how easy the entire treatment was.

Once completed, my eyebrows were significantly more defined and, admittedly, darker than I would have liked, but Tracey told me before and after that the colour is more sharply defined for 10–14 days after application and as the healing process occurs the colour will soften and lighten, with the 'true colour' appearing after approximately four weeks.

After three days the colour had faded to a much more satisfying shade and after a couple of weeks I had my dream eyebrows. They look very naturally defined, the arch is more obvious and generally I think the look lifts my face and offers more definition to my whole eye area. The look is not made-up, just naturally enhanced, and any treatment that saves me time in the morning gets my vote.

Aftercare is simple and I was given an information sheet to take away as a reminder. I wouldn't advise having this treatment before a big event due to the potential flakiness, but if you want to enhance your beauty on a more permanent basis (not just until you wipe off your cosmetics at the end of the day), then try this – but make sure you choose a reputable therapist like Tracey Ager or Karen Betts (see entry below).

- **E: enquiries@tracey-ager.co.uk**
- **W: www.tracey-ager.co.uk**

Permanent make-up: Karen Betts

I also had permanent eyeliner applied by Karen Betts, who is the UK's leading practitioner and trainer for permanent make-up. She has appeared on *Channel M* and *10 Years Younger*, BBC's *Children In Need* and *Celebrity Scissor Hands*, *Extreme Makeover* and *This Morning*. She is flown all over the world for her skills in permanent make-up. Her clients are mainly very high profile, so it was only natural that I became a client too (I'm kidding)! Eyebrows and eyeliner are her most popular requests and with her track record I found it easy to put my faith in her.

A consultation decided the look and colour I wanted and Karen asked me to use an ordinary eyeliner pencil to draw on the shape and look I wanted to have on a permanent basis. Karen goes very in-depth and really gets rid of any doubts you may have. If clients ever feel too anxious or doubtful, she is unlikely to perform the treatment, but she's so excellent at identifying if this is right for you or not. Having had my eyebrows done with Tracey Ager, I felt more relaxed and Karen's knowledge and experience radiate from her.

After agreeing the look and having the area numbed with a special gel, Karen got to work. I opted for a natural line across my upper lashes with a gentle flick at the outer corner and subtle colour on the bottom lash line. It didn't hurt me at all, but felt more sensitive than my brow area. Karen performed the procedure with my eyes closed upon my request, as I have sensitive watery eyes. It was a lot more comfortable that way. I was able to check the look throughout the procedure so as to avoid any final 'surprises', and the end result was exactly what I asked for – naturally enhancing and suitable for a daytime look. This procedure has made my lashes look fuller and shaped my eyes without any over-obvious trickery!

I'd advise you to take a couple of days off work afterwards, as your eyes will go puffy from the pressure of the needle on such a delicate area. Karen advises that you apply the healing gel supplied every few hours. You can apply ice to the area to reduce any swelling, but I found that time healed the puffiness best. After one day, the puffiness had disappeared and I just looked 'tired'. After two days, I was back to normal.

The colour, as always with permanent make-up, was darker at first, but the true colour was realized after approximately four weeks. At that point Karen advises that you return for a retouch to improve the look if needed and to ensure that the procedure has gone perfectly well for you.

Karen is without doubt one of the best around.

- T: 0845 644 3994
- W: www.nouveaucontour.co.uk

Most fabulous for emergency beauty fixes around the clock: Doctor chez vous

BeautyWorksWest 'Doctor chez vous' is a 24/7 service with one of the best French doctors visiting patients direct to their door by motorbike. They can give you anything from Botox to Vi Peel, from Fillers to Weight Control Management, from jet lag control to travel medicine. Dr Cyrille Blum is the latest person to join the BeautyWorksWest family. If you're too busy to leave home or to quit your office, or even to come to London, then this exclusive service is the perfect luxury.

The BeautyWorksWest Spa will take the calls for the service during their opening hours and there's a permanent answering service for those clients wishing to book after hours.

- **BeautyWorksWest at Lambton Place, Westbourne Grove, Notting Hill, London W11 2SH**
- **T: 020 7221 2248**
- **W: www.Beautyworkswest.com**

Most fabulous for an overall eye makeover: Shavata Brow Studio

The undisputed Queen of Eyebrows, Shavata has brow studios nationwide. Simply shaping your brows can lift your features, give your face proportion and take years off you – and scary mono-brows have never been a good look, sorry!

The studios make the perfect place to get your brows into shape

Tea & Treatments

T

in a matter of minutes and really emphasize your eyes with a selection of treatments. You can choose from waxing or threading, lash and brow tinting and eyelash perming and extensions.

Shavata has over 20 years of experience in the beauty industry and all her technicians are trained to her exceptionally high standards. Celebrity clients who regularly visit her Brow Studios include Jade Jagger and Geri Halliwell.

• **Shavata Brow Studios are nationwide within Harrods, Harvey Nichols and House of Fraser branches, and even Terminal One, Heathrow**
• **W: www.shavata.co.uk (N)**

Most fabulous for taming brows in a hurry: Blink Brow Bars

Blink Brow Bars are also a great destination to perfect your brows and are most fabulous for offering last-minute availability. Their wondrous head and shoulder massages turn the less-than-relaxing procedure of eyebrow threading into a treatment you can actually wind down with, and their blend of ayurvedic eye soothing treatments, eyelash tints and eyelash extensions make them a chic pitstop for all your eye-related beauty needs. The eyelash extensions look best just applied to the outer corners as opposed to across the entire lash line due to their slightly synthetic appearance, but if you want eyebrow precision in a hurry, Blink Brow Bars are the new nail bars!

• **W: www.blinkbrowbar.com (N)**

Most fabulous 'Up North': Jo Pallan at Nicky Clarke, Leeds

For the lovely ladies in the north of England, you should make a stop at the home of eyebrow specialist Jo Pallan. Her rapidly growing beauty brand offers a range of beauty services at her Champagne Nail Bar, based on the ground floor of the gorgeous Nicky Clarke Salon in Leeds.

For my eyebrows, Jo used a gentle tint to darken my brows slightly, which added instant definition, followed by threading to define the shape further. Often threading can be a little painful or uncomfortable, but Jo Pallan is quick, highly skilled and now on my speed dial. Look out for her store roll-out.

• **W: www.nickyclarke.com (N)**

Most fabulous for perfectly defined brows: HD Brows

Though not a new concept, HD Brows is at the forefront of eyebrow shaping, combining the entire brow defining procedures to create the perfect look and shape for you. Taking its lead from threading, the multi-step procedure begins with assessing your face shape and hair colour to determine the most suitable design and tint, which is then expertly applied and will even coat any downy hair (the baby-fine, soft small hairs at the edges of your brows that are often lighter in colour). Your brows are then trimmed, waxed, threaded and plucked to perfection. A range of techniques is very effective as the hair differs in length, texture and growth pattern across the entire area of your eyebrow, making HD Brows the ultimate in brow perfection. It sounds lengthy and painful, but the whole process is efficient, completely bearable and so very worth it.

- **T: 0845 644 3994**
- **W: www.hdbrows.co.uk (N)**

Most fabulous for lifting and smoothing your butt: ESPA Stimulating Hip and Thigh Treatment at The Academy

This specialized ESPA treatment stimulates the circulatory and lymphatic systems, concentrating on the areas of the body prone to cellulite, fluid retention and uneven skin tone. Following a rigorous exfoliation with a special blend of seaweed, salt and oil, a deep, detoxifying massage using lymphatic drainage techniques takes place. Stimulating essential oils help purify and cleanse your body in addition to completely relaxing you, then relevant reflex zones and pressure points on your feet are activated to leave you feeling totally revitalized.

The massage was the most impressive part for me; I could almost feel it kneading away my dimples, as the techniques involve deep penetration, and it left me feeling invigorated. Though a series of treatments is recommended for more cellulite-prone skin, my skin looked and felt smooth after one treatment – so much so that my tight-fitting jeans were pulled out of storage!

- **The Academy, Oakdale Place, Harrogate, North Yorkshire HG1 2LA**
- **W: www.theacademy.co.uk**

Most fabulous for beautiful teeth: 76 Harley Street

76 Harley Street employ the latest computer imaging and laser technology to make the world's best cosmetic dental solutions locally available. The practice is led by Farid Monibi, a specialist prosthodontist whose fields of expertise are dental implantology and minimal intervention cosmetic and reconstructive dentistry.

This bespoke approach covers all specialities and dental operations including dental implants, specialist endodontistry, periodontistry and orthodontistry. The London Dental Veneers use the highest quality porcelain veneers, and there are two main types – handcrafted and laboratory-made veneers, ideal for perfect-looking (yet not scarily unnatural) teeth.

They also offer teeth whitening at the practice, or in kits that you can use at home. The UV light-activated ('laser') method lasts for around two hours and is ideal for those seeking an instantaneous result. First the gums are carefully covered for protection, then a whitening gel is applied to the teeth. A special 400nm spectrum light is then shone onto the gel to activate it. You will also receive moulded plastic applicator 'trays' to fit over your teeth so that you can use the gel at home to maintain the brightness of your teeth.

The home treatment offers you a kit comprising of applicator trays made to fit you, plus whitening gel. Following the instructions, it is easy to place the gel in the trays and then fit them over your teeth. The trays are normally worn for an hour or so each day for a period of 14 consecutive days, or until

Tea & Treatments

T

the desired shade has been achieved, so this option is best if you have the time and patience and wish for a more gradual change.

You'll be made to feel very welcome and it is very quickly apparent that you're in some of the best hands that Central London has to offer. 76 Harley Street should be your new dentistry haven.

- **76 Harley Street, London W1G 7HH**
- **T: 020 7631 3276**
- **E: info@76harleystreet.com**
- **W: www.76harleystreet.com**

Most fabulous for a deep cleanse: Colonic irrigation at Innercore Clinic

Colonic irrigation, also known as colon hydrotherapy, is a safe and painless procedure in which built-up waste is gently released from the colon by introducing warm filtered water. Egyptians used this method as an alternative to harsh purgatives or laxatives for colon-cleansing, and today it remains popular for the same reasons.

Specialized clinic Innercore isn't much to look at, but the expertise is what matters here. Practitioner Kirsty McEnroe RGN Dip HE is a qualified nurse with masses of experience who instantly puts you at ease. She not only begins with a thorough consultation addressing your lifestyle and diet, but also follows up with aftercare advice and provides her mobile phone number if you have any queries. This procedure ensures that every treatment is tailored for you and your needs, so you get the most out of it.

I thought it would be painful, embarrassing and/or disappointing. The thought of having a great pipe up my backside was hardly inviting, but I'm glad to say it was a far more dignified and easy-going treatment than I thought it would be.

I lay on my side on a treatment table, the tube was inserted, then the purified water was released. There are two tubes in the inserted nozzle: one is used to gently push the water in and the other carries it (and the contents of your colon) out, as the system automatically flushes it away. Though not at all painful, the feeling is a tad alien, but the benefits of colonic hydrotherapy are many – including stimulation of the liver which supports the immune system by decreasing toxic overload. This promotes a return to normal, regular bowel movements and the removal and cleaning of old hard waste material and harmful toxins from the colon. Sounds grim, but it's better to have it removed then, isn't it?

I noticed an immediate difference in my belly, which looked flatter, and I felt lighter and healthier on the inside. Just lie back and think of England! I realize it is normally a taboo subject, but seriously, you have to get past this and try it. I'm now signed up for seasonal sessions.

- **Innercore Clinics Ltd, Deanfield House, Asquith Avenue, Morley, Leeds LS27 9QS**
- **T: 0113 243 1255**
- **W: innercore.co.uk**

Most fabulous for clearing your head: Hopi Ear Candle at Innercore

Kirsty McEnroe of Innercore also carried out Hopi Ear Candling. The benefits include relieving earache, headaches, tinnitus and stress. Though Kirsty stresses that every client is different, results can also help promote lymphatic circulation and improve the immune system.

Each treatment can take approx 25–60 minutes and the entire experience is so relaxing, I nearly nodded off. You lie on your side and a candle is placed over the ear, held in place by the practitioner. The candle is then ignited and continuously monitored as it burns gently. You can hear a soft sizzling noise, like a smouldering log fire in your ear, which is incredibly relaxing.

Gradually any impurities are drained to the surface through a 'chimney effect', many of which are carried away through the candle. Slight suction within the ear pressures will be felt as the warm airs combine with the heat to soften ear wax and draw out the debris.

The best bit, if you're a little keen like me, is examining the debris at the end of the session as the candle is opened up. I personally found it very satisfying to see how effective the treatment had been and felt so uplifted and cleansed afterwards. I admit I wasn't convinced before, but seeing (and feeling) is believing!

....

• **Innercore Clinics Ltd, Deanfield House, Asquith Avenue, Morley, Leeds LS27 9QS**
• **T: 0113 243 1255**
• **W: innercore.co.uk**

• •

Most fabulous for a spiritual pick-me-up: Reiki Healing
• •

Sue Haynes is a highly regarded complementary therapist who treats

her clients from the tranquillity of her dedicated treatment room in her Leeds home. A professional therapist with five years' experience, she offers reflexology, Indian head massage and Reiki treatments. Reiki (pronounced 'ray-key') is one of the most ancient healing techniques known to man. It works on the principle that illness and disease (both physical and emotional) are the result of impairment to the natural flow of life energy. Reiki helps to reinstate the balance and flow of this energy through the body. During a Reiki treatment the therapist channels the life energy through her hands, into the receiver's body, thus enhancing the body's natural ability to heal itself. I personally think it helps (though it is not entirely necessary) if you are something of a spiritual person. I lay there visualizing, which enhanced the experience for me, and I felt relaxed, relieved (from what I'm not sure) and positive in mood. It did something for me, but if you like to see immediate results and enjoy mostly aesthetic outcomes, it may not be for you.

....

• **Sue Haynes, 7 Bentley Grove, Meanwood, Leeds LS6 4AT**
• **T: 0113 2698188**
• **W: www.leedshealing.co.uk**

• •

Most fabulous for a complete complexion boost: Ling Oxygen Plasma and Ultra-Sound Facial
• •

This amazing facial is designed by New York's hottest facialist Ling Chan, combining ancient techniques with state-of-the-art formulations for optimal skin health

T

and radiance. Apparently this is a firm favourite with Park Avenue Princesses and is now available to us UK beauties. The facial includes skin analysis, cleansing, exfoliation, steam-cleaning and extractions. You will then be treated to a Jade Massage, followed by the ultimate Oxygen Plasma and Ultra-Sound treatment and, to top it all off, an individualized herbal mask to heal any remaining imperfections. Don't plan to meet for drinks or attend a huge event straight after, however, as the extractions may leave your skin a little reddened in places, but this really is the ultimate facial, which produces exceptional results in 80 minutes.

• **BeautyWorksWest, Lambton Place, Westbourne Grove, Notting Hill, London W11 2SH**
• **T: 020 7221 2248**
• **W: www.Beautyworkswest.com**

Most fabulous for filling in the gaps: Juvederm Ultra

I'm not quite in need of it just yet, so I grabbed a volunteer to be put in the safe hands of Harrogate Aesthetics, a medical cosmetic clinic run by professional nurse practitioners Sharon Bennett and Anthea Whiteley.

I witnessed this patient being treated with Juvederm Ultra, the dermal filler from Allergan (the makers of Botox©). Juvederm Ultra is a biodegradable polysaccharide gel (hyaluronic acid) with the fantastic benefit of having some local anaesthetic added to it. To me and you, this means that the procedure,

whether it's for reshaping lips or gently lifting lines and wrinkles, can be completely pain-free.

It is very smooth so it gives a very soft, natural look and the results were instant. The patient had no bruising and little swelling, and said that it didn't hurt one bit. Believing that 'less is more', Sharon and Anthea are experts in achieving a natural, beautiful look. If you've always thought about it but had concerns, there's now no need to fear pain or swelling either!

Harrogate Aesthetics treat with a wide range of products, vitamin facial treatments, dermal injections and micro injections that are specifically tailored to the individual.

• **Harrogate Aesthetics, 13 East Parade, Harrogate HG1 5LF**
• **T: 01423 567567**
• **W: www.harrogateaesthetics.co.uk**

Best for maintaining youthful-looking hands: Cowshed Fruit Acid Manicure

Cowshed spas and stores are nationwide, with the original at Babington House voted as Tatler's International Spa of the Year 2009. All the Cowshed products contain a high ratio of 100% natural essential oils and are used for their therapeutic benefits that enhance mind and body wellbeing, making any treatment you choose a true pleasure. The ultimate in hand rejuvenation treatments, the Fruit Acid Manicure, includes a file and complete cuticle tidy and an application of a SkinCeuticals fruit acid peel which refines the texture of your hands leaving them extremely smooth. Next to your neck and décolletage, your hands are one of the first places to show age, so this treatment is great for anti-ageing. This is followed by a deep relaxing hand and arm massage and polish to finish (60 minutes).

W: www.cowshedonline.com (N) to find your nearest spa

How to get fabulous lashes

Let's face it, everyone's lashes look better with coatings of mascara. Whether spidery, long, short, sparse, mascara works wonders in lengthening those lashes to open up your peepers and increase your flutterability. The only issue I have is that we have to wipe away that gorgeousness every night and do it all over again the next day.

If only that length and thickness lasted, eh? Of course, I have found a solution…

Nouveau Lash Extensions

Nouveau Lashes are semi-permanent lash extensions that can last up to two months, depending on your lifestyle, maintenance care and growth of eyelashes.

Initially a cynic – 'Blimey, they have everything these days, even extensions for your lashes now, tsk!' – I was slightly dubious at first. Comparing them to false lashes, I thought they might feel too heavy as I couldn't remove them and wasn't sure if I'd end up with a look that was perhaps too dramatic for the daytime or, worse, openly fake.

I have to say, however, that they looked amazing – natural but lusciously long without being too obvious. They framed my eyes so well that I didn't feel the need to wear eye make-up and from simple added volume, I felt so much more

Tea & Treatments

T

confident to go *au naturel*.

The initial outlay for this treatment can be quite high, but maintenance is much less and comparable to the upkeep of a monthly manicure. If you have less than lustrous lashes, want extra batting power for a special occasion, or simply want to look your best, this is one treatment that should go on your fabulous list.

Nouveau Lashes have a unique colour range of three different natural hair shades – black, brown and light brown for a more realistic look. Eyelash tints are recommended to the fairest of us all pre-procedure. If you're brave/eccentric/stylish enough, they also come in fun colours of blue, green, purple and red for a wonderfully dramatic party look.

Name-dropping the celebrity wearers, Naomi Campbell, Victoria Beckham and Patsy Palmer are fans.

Two thicknesses are available, 'natural' and 'volume up'. 'Volume up' lashes are one and a half times thicker than natural lashes. Sizes are 6–15 mm and this is the option I chose. Elite trainer Jane asked me what sort of look I wanted to go for, so you won't end up with glamorous if what you require is casual.

As you lie down on a bed, cotton pads are placed beneath your lower lashes under your eye and you keep them closed for the duration of the treatment. Jane then uses tiny precision tweezers to bond the lash extensions to your own lashes with superb skill and accuracy. As a self-confessed perfectionist, Jane applied a few extra lashes with my eyes open, which is not always necessary and was the most challenging part of the treatment – the rest is a breeze. With a

pair of tweezers coming slowly towards your eye area, you naturally want to blink or close your eyes tight shut, but Jane is very efficient and the end result is astounding.

Jane warned me this could be addictive, as you will love the volume so much and get used to it! Oh dear, another addiction next to shoes, bags and frothy chai tea lattes…

Aftercare

The Nouveau Lashes 'Long-Life Coating' was recently launched for everyday use on Nouveau Lashes. It comes in a tube with an easy-to-use 'paint-on' brush to condition the lash extensions and make them last even longer.

For the first two hours after they're applied, do not allow water to contact the lashes and for two days after, do not steam the face or swim. Water-based mascara and remover are recommended (though you don't really need mascara, in my opinion!), and do not rub your eyes when washing your face.

I did find I'd often have to groom my eyelashes in the morning to keep them looking at their best, plus following the aftercare advice may make this treatment not the most practical, but for a special occasion or a definite boost, lash extensions are sure to give you the confidence and added loveliness that I felt. You'll soon be winking at all the boys!

• **For information on local salons providing this service, please call Nouveau Lashes at Nouveau Contour: 0845 644 3994**
• **W: www.nouveaulashes.co.uk (N)**

Rhonda Beattie

Rhonda Beattie is a beauty expert with 20 years of experience, having worked in London's Mayfair and Marylebone throughout her career. She also recommends lash extensions. With Rhonda, individual lashes are placed on your natural lashes to increase volume and lash density, and she even mixes black with blue and green lashes to bring out the colour of your eyes. She says lashes will last approximately 6–8 weeks, or longer if you top them up every 2–3 weeks. And she's right! These are definitely some of the very best lash extensions I've had. They seem softer and more comfortable than most and stay in place very well. Rhonda really knows her stuff and I highly recommend her.

• **Gielly Green, 42–44 George Street, London W1U 7ES**
• **T: 020 7034 3060**
• **W: www.giellygreen.co.uk**

Most fabulous for a quick fix: Blink & Go™

If you want long lashes in your lunch break, Blink & Go is the fastest eyelash extension treatment. In just 20 minutes your eyes can be transformed with thick, luscious lashes that last for two weeks.

The Blink & Go technique starts by using a framework with 10 individual lashes placed on top of your own lashes, building layers of more lashes for instant glam. Ideal if you're in a hurry and want to look extra-gorgeous for that special occasion or a first date.

• **Available in 600 salons nationwide, including Benito Bars and Urban Retreat at Harrods**
• **T: 0845 644 3994**
• **W: www.blinkandgo.co.uk (N)**

Straightening your lashes: LVL

We often think curling our lashes lengthens them, but LVL Lashes actually use the technique of straightening your own lashes to add the illusion of length. The whole process takes around 45 minutes and will last the life of your eyelashes (approx. 8–12 weeks).

The therapist will choose an LVL lashes Silicone Shield for the shape of your eyelid and secure it as close to the lid as possible to the lashes (just like when tinting your lashes). Then, using gel formulation, your lashes will be individually secured over this shield.

The LVL Lashes Lifting Balm with conditioning proteins coats every single lash carefully, and then your eyes are covered with pads, clingfilm and a warm towel. A volumizing fix is applied after 15 minutes and the eyes are covered with pads for a further 5 minutes.

The shield is then gently removed with a cotton bud and purified water, and finally a lubricating LVL Lashes Revitalizer is applied to encourage good condition and growth.

It sounds like a lengthy treatment, but the fine hairs of your eyelashes are delicate, so the care and attention is worth it and, best

Tea & Treatments

T

of all, they are your own lashes, just longer!

- **T: 0845 644 3994 ext 33**
- **W: www.lvl-lashes.co.uk (N)**

False eyelashes

If extensions don't appeal to you, or you just want a temporary look, then try falsies. False eyelashes have come on leaps and bounds in the last ten years, with major catwalks and salons across the globe realizing the importance of enhancing your eyes through plumper lashes. From feathers to glow-in-the-dark and couture limited edition varieties, there is a style to suit every mood.

Girls with Attitude is a fun brand with around 30 different false lash styles to suit your mood, all with playful names such as 'Vamp' and 'Sexy Kitten' (my two favourites) for full-on flutter allure. The glow-in-the-dark style will certainly light up the dance floor or make for an interesting cuddle in the dark!

- **W: www.asos.com**

Shu uemura has to be my favourite brand for falsies overall. You can follow my guide (below) on how to apply false eyelashes, but if you're still no good at applying them, visit your nearest shu uemura counter for the Tokyo Lash Bar where a qualified make-up artist or beauty therapist will apply them for you. As long as you buy the lashes from shu uemura (and there are 50 styles from natural to statement), this service is complimentary!

I adore the exclusive collections they create, turning fashion into fine

art. From gold leaf and fluffy tail lashes to translucent colours, kaleidoscopic wires and glittering diamanté-encrusted designs, shu uemura cater for my every mood and desire, taking me from subtle siren to show-stopping seductress whenever I wish.

- **T: Stockist enquiry line 020 7240 7635**
- **T: Mail order 020 7235 2375**

Applying false eyelashes

There are so many styles to choose from now. **Eyelure** produces two main types – full lashes which are a full set of lashes on a strip that you apply directly to your eye, and individual lashes which can be used to fill in sparse areas or dramatically open up the eye area. Full lashes are the easiest to apply, yet they're more dramatic, although there are some natural styles available. Individual lashes need a steady hand and patience as you apply them one by one. But both look fabulous and all it takes is practice, so follow my top tips to boost your flutterability…

1 Before you apply the lashes, apply your shadow and mascara and line your upper lash line with a black or dark brown liquid eyeliner which will help to conceal the lash band. It is difficult to apply make-up accurately afterwards.

2 Measure the lashes against your own lash line by simply placing the lashes on top of your own. If the ends stick in your eye a little, trim them down using nail scissors. Never trim from the inner corner, always trim from the outer edge to maintain the shape.

3 Once you have the correct length, apply the glue to your finger or a pair of tweezers, and lightly pull the lash band through the glue or dab on gently to individual lashes using your tweezers, ensuring you coat the very ends of the lash band, as this is the area most likely to become unstuck and give you away! Wait until the glue becomes a little tacky – about 20 seconds.

4 Apply the false lashes as close to your natural lash line as possible, starting at the outer edge then working inwards to your nose while pressing the lashes down for a few seconds on the outside of the eye. It's the same for individual lashes: apply them to the outside corners of the eye and work inwards. I often apply just a few individual lashes to the outer corners of my eyes for a really natural look that opens your peepers and lessens the need for mascara!

5 Don't worry about the glue: it will dry clear. Once dry, fill in any gaps with your liner and go flutter!

• **Eyelure eyelashes are available at leading chemists nationwide**

Enhance your own lashes: RevitaLash™

If you simply want your own lashes to look better, give Mother Nature a helping hand and boost your flutterability with RevitaLash™. This piece of magic is a revolutionary cosmetic eyelash conditioner developed by renowned American ophthalmologist Michael Brinkenhoff MD, who has been practising for more than 25 years. He developed the product for his wife, Gayle, who had been suffering from breast cancer and had lost most of her eyelashes. Revitalash™ achieved such impressive results that they agreed it should be shared with other women.

Celebrity fans include *Ugly Betty* actress Becki Newton (the character Amanda), Marcia Cross, Felicity Huffman, Debra Messing and Hayden Panettiere, and you can't deny they all have beautiful peepers.

To reap the benefits, all you need to do is apply it to the base of the eyelashes each evening (as though you were applying eyeliner) and then expect to see dramatic results after 6–8 weeks of use.

• **T: SkinBrands Limited, 020 8997 8541**
• **W: skinbrands.co.uk and www.hqhair.com**

Added extras

Most fabulous for dramatic cellulite busting: Tripollar Technology

The Regen Tripollar machine offers a way to tighten and smoothen skin, reduce cellulite and offer a safer alternative to going under the knife!

In a nutshell, Tripollar technology is a skin-tightening and body-contouring

Tea & Treatments

T

treatment uniquely using three electrodes to deliver focused radio frequency energy into the dermis. The energy efficiently targets the areas of loose skin, ultimately delivering first-time visible results. The effect of either the cellulite or the body-contouring treatment is a smoother, firmer and younger-looking skin in one 45-minute session.

I had the treatment on my not-so-smooth-since-drinking-too-much-coffee-and-getting-older rear and I am pleased to say I noticed the difference after just one session! My bootie felt tighter and looked more dimple-free – result!

• **Heather Irvine Clinic, 71 Rook Lane, Bradford BD4 9NA**
• **T: 01274 783333**
• **W: www.heatherirvine.com**

Most fabulous for turning your feet from scary to seductive: the Medi Pedi

The Deluxe Medi Pedi is the ultimate pedicure, as it combines medical techniques with cosmetic loveliness. Fruit enzymes are applied to your feet to soften hard skin and any stubborn areas including corns will be gently removed after that with expert tools. Nails are trimmed and cuticles tidied, and polish is applied if desired, followed by a thorough massage combining acupressure and lymphatic drainage (the best bit). Jackson uses her custom blend of organic extracts and oils to produce a very relaxing and painless treatment that leaves one's feet feeling beautiful and light.

• **W: www.katherineJackson.co.uk**

Useful Contacts

Some services exist purely to make your life easier, more convenient or simply more fabulous! I round up a new list of speed dial must-haves...

● ●

Pink Ladies

● ●

Pink Ladies is a members' club for women providing uniformed female drivers to drive the club's vehicles. All cars are bright pink Renault Kangoos (apart from 'Angel', their green wheelchair-accessible car), with pink leather interiors, each with its own personality and name. There's an Alison, Andrea, Leanna, Kerry, Trixie, Martha, Lily, Anne, Kathy, Dawn, Angel, Alison, Nigella, Paula and Cockney Rebel! Though not a taxi service, joining the club has many advantages in addition to getting home safely and in style.

Pink Ladies offer a safe and trusted way of getting home at night – and the pinkness is just a bonus!

● **T: 0845 124 7465**
● **W: www.pinkladiesmembers.co.uk**

Useful Chick Stuff

Useful Chick Stuff is exactly that – a site offering a range of products that every modern girl needs to avert any underwear *faux pas*. Their seamless lingerie helps avoid an embarrassingly unflattering VPL, and their 'Supportits' backless, strapless 'no-bra' is made of soft fabric that sticks and contours to your body, creating the ultimate bust line. It's an uplifting design that offers you the support of a bra except it's not a bra, so there are no straps, fastenings or giveaway lines – ideal for a backless, plunging dress.

• W: www.usefulchickstuff.com

Geek Squad

Geek Squad Support is 24/7 over-the-phone technology support and advice. Whether you're plagued by pop-ups, suffering in a world of web connection pain, fighting a printer that won't print, or stricken by a PC virus … whatever it is, a Geek Squad Agent is at the end of the line to release you from IT hell!

• W: www.geeksquad.co.uk

Dog Lost

If your pooch has gone walkies without you, register at Dog Lost and you can add a lost dog to their database and get assistance with your search from a national network of helpers.

• T: 0844 800 3220
• W: www.doglost.co.uk

Big Yellow

Big Yellow is a storage and moving solution haven. You can hire a storage unit by the week, month or year. If you have heavy goods, you can pull right up outside the unit to unload. No van? They can help you arrange van hire. No boxes to pack it all in? They have the equipment to sort you out. Ideal if you want to travel, are moving house, want extra space, or even when you just can't part with last season's garments but need to free up some wardrobe space for your new additions. Well, what goes around comes around!

• T: 0800 783 4949
• W: www.bigyellow.co.uk

Underwear

Save your greying pants for the bin and make sure you look amazing all the time! Besides, knowing you're wearing great underwear beneath your work suit or casual jeans and tee can make you feel fantastic and look fantastic too once the layers are removed. Aside from the glam factor, getting the right underwear to go underneath your clothing is like buying the correct canvas on which to paint. Buy a shoddy canvas and the picture is bound to turn out lumpy and cheap-looking. Get it right with this lot...

Pants to Poverty

Pants to Poverty are the essential

underwear brand for modern women. They are comfy, sexy, ethical, sustainable and 100% organic and pesticide-free, so contain none of the nasty chemicals that will go into other brands' knickers. Their range of flattering styles, including the classic boxer-cut fit with elasticated waistband, suit any figure and are convenient to wear under most garments.

With a flurry of bright colours and designer prints every season, Pants to Poverty will inject some life into your underwear drawer at an affordable price!

....

• T: 020 7739 7108
• W: www.asos.com or www. pantstopoverty.com

••••••••••••••••••••••••••••••••••••

Panty Postman
••••••••••••••••••••••••••••••••••••

Did you know that the life expectancy of a pair of panties is three months? Don't panic: with the Panty Postman you may never need to reach for those last-resort knickers again! This revolutionary service has knickers delivered to your door all year round. Choose from thongs or briefs, and three knickers in assorted colours will be delivered each quarter straight through your postbox. Crisis averted!

....

• W: www.cocoribbon.co.uk

••••••••••••••••••••••••••••••••••••

Elle Macpherson Intimates
••••••••••••••••••••••••••••••••••••

The gorgeous Elle Macpherson is not all about the beauty. Sorry ladies, but she has brains too and her Intimates collection proves it! As one of the most globally successful fashion lingerie brands, Elle creates a line that shows her passion for 'fit, function and fashionable design', as her stylish designs fit from an A cup right up to a G cup and include a maternity range! This approach reflects her personal ethos of creating luxurious but affordable garments for every day and for every woman. Her scrumptiously desirable range of lingerie includes lace, silk and other sensuous fabrics combined with playful colours and feminine yet racy styles. I feel extremely sexy yet feminine in my sets and they're so pretty, I don't mind having them peek out beneath a dress or top.

....

• Available at Liberty, Selfridges, Harvey Nichols and Fenwicks (N)
• W: www.ellemacphersonintimates.com

••••••••••••••••••••••••••••••••••••

The Modern Courtesan
••••••••••••••••••••••••••••••••••••

Conceived in New York and born in London, The Modern Courtesan offers one of the most decadently luxurious, fun yet sophisticated collections I've had the pleasure to wear. The fabrics are high quality and the va-va-voom appeal is also pretty top notch. Enjoy!

....

• T: 07894 906 879
• W: www.themoderncourtesan.com (N)

••••••••••••••••••••••••••••••••••••

Bordello
••••••••••••••••••••••••••••••••••••

Michele Scarr's East End-based lingerie store, Bordello, is a boudoir-meets-Aladdin's-Cave of elegant sauciness. Antique furniture, chandeliers and rich colours add a sense of indulgence and glamour – a theme that runs through to the seductive lingerie and hosiery in store. From push-up bras to negligees,

Useful Contacts & Underwear

U

Bordello is stocked with intimate treats from labels such as Myla, Made By Niki and Ell and Cee.

Men, expectant mothers and strumpets are all catered for here – so whatever the occasion, mood or preference, you'll discover some goodies to suit in this wonderful mélange of elegance and trash.

• **Bordello, 55 Great Eastern Street, London EC2A 3HP**
• **W: www.bordello-london.co.uk**

Sexy Panties and Naughty Knickers

Sexy Panties and Naughty Knickers was established in 2004 by Pom Lampson. Speaking about the brand, Lampson says, 'I'd like to think that as a label Sexy Panties and Naughty Knickers sits exactly in the middle of M&S and Agent Provocateur…' What you're left with is simple, comfortable underwear in soft, sensuous fabrics that fits well and is affordable. Bra sizes range from an A to an FF cup, so being busy need not mean compromising your style. It's about time.

• **W: www.sexypantiesandnaughty knickers.com (N)**

Baby Grand

Keep your luxury habit under wraps with the help of Baby Grand. The line of handmade lingerie and loungewear is inspired by 1940s and 1950s screen sirens, with a little post-war chic thrown in. Silk teddies and ruffled chiffon camisoles come in delicate ice cream shades, and there's an unusual collection of playsuits, too.

• **W: www.babygranduk.com**

Trinny and Susannah's Original Magic Knickers and Original Magic Tights

We all know about 'Bridget Jones knickers' and we all agree that we'd never, ever like to be seen by anyone else in them. I've found that with some designs, the tummy you're trying to flatten has to go somewhere and it's usually upwards – creating an unsightly spare tyre you didn't even realize you had! This doesn't exactly bode well for creating a smooth silhouette for your LBD.

Well, outspoken style gurus Trinny and Susannah have added more styles to their already popular shapewear collection. My favourites include the Magic Tummy Flattening Bikini Brief (far more attractive than most designs but with all the tummy-flattening, silhouette-smoothing magic) and the Fashion Net Tight (yes, shapewear meets hosiery). These are great beneath a dress in the winter, completely smoothing out any lumps and bumps and giving your hips, tummy and behind lift and support.

• **W: www.littlewoodsdirect.com**

Yummie Tummie™ Strappy T

An alternative is to wear a Yummie Tummie™ Strappy T, which is a modern body-contouring shaper. You wear it as a normal strappy top, but its extra benefits mean that your mid-section is slimmed and lumpy bits are smoothed out. The secret minimizing panel shapes the entire waistline from bust to hips and unlike some body-contouring items, the Yummy Tummie™ Strappy T is made with sleek yarn so it doesn't cling or make you sweaty. Though the straps are adjustable, the back is quite high, so it's not ideal underneath low-backed clothing, but it is chic enough to be worn alone and ideal underneath oversized vests and with your jeans.

• W: www.yummietummie.com

Freya

Freya has a whole range of gorgeous lingerie up to a J cup. There's a whole range of different styles for varying needs, from Freya Active which caters for larger-busted sports lovers, to Goddess which is designed to make you feel exactly that when you put on this fashionable and sumptuous collection. Elomi is one of my favourites in the range, offering styles in sizes 32 to 52C through to an H cup. As a bustier sort, I thank the lingerie lord for Freya – no more ill-fitting, granny-resembling over-the-shoulder boulder-holders for me, yay!

• W: www.freyalingerie.com (N)

Useful Contacts & Underwear

U

I've personally collected and sold vintage clothing and accessories for years after my love for vintage began with a pair of my grandmother's delicate cameo earrings and my mother's genuine 1960s sequin butterfly clasp belt and blue suede miniskirt! But since then, there has been an influx of vintage stores and brands in recent years. Many people get confused between what is vintage, just plain old or a bunch of cr*p.

Generally speaking, clothing produced before 1920 is considered to be antique, worthy of collecting or displaying in a museum, but not suitable for daily wear. Most clothing produced between 1920 and the late 1970s is considered vintage by most dealers, though some will take this to the mid-1980s. When something is considered 'retro', this is usually clothing from the 1960s and 1970s and sometimes to the mid-1980s, though boundaries do blur. Clothing produced after the mid-1980s is generally considered to be ... well ... just give it to charity.

Get your (genuine) retro and vintage fix with my list of the best...

Vintage vibes

Find your era at Ooh La La! Vintage

Ooh La La! Vintage offers fabulous trips and masterclasses that capture the exquisite charm and style of vintage years.

The masterclasses offer a fast-track introduction to vintage fashion, where you can learn about its history and social context since the 1900s to the present day and find which era suits you most. Of course, you get to try on lots of gorgeous clothing to boot, from their Customized Boutique, and you have the option to buy these lovely threads too.

Trips include personal shopping advice and tours to all the great vintage boutiques (in Paris or London), complete with afternoon tea and champagne and nibbles.

• T: 00 33 684 765 865
• W: www.oohlalavintage.com

Made-to-measure vintage threads: Madame Tra La La

Madame Tra La La is a made-to-order vintage-inspired collection. Way back when, women were teeny-tiny, so Madame Tra La La produces hand-finished vintage reproductions made to your size.

• W: www.madametralala.com

Vintage china

Gorgeous vintage and retro china is exquisitely boxed in delightful **Tea With Alice** boxes for the perfect gift or tea party, giving the perfect vintage touch to your home.

• W: www.teawithalice.com

Vintage pieces gathered from all over the world and truly unique finds are available at **Trinket Jewels**, an emporium of striking distinction.

• W: www.trinketjewels.co.uk

Weird and wonderful talking pieces for hire: A Most Curious Party

A Most Curious Party is one woman's collection of vintage objects and props that she has gathered and accumulated over time and now hires out for events, picnics, birthdays, weddings or photoshoots. They'll even do the styling for you and the website is an absolute delight as you view the gallery. Expect everything from vintage tea caddies to charming birdcages and 1940s-inspired bunting.

If you want to add a totally original look to your event or simply love the glamour of past decades, you will find that charming tea cup, that memorable table centrepiece and that weirdly wonderful finishing touch, right here. A must-see.

• W: www.amostcuriousparty.co.uk

Ruby, Ruby, Ruby, Ruby (ahhh-ha-ah ah ah)

The Ruby Emporium was created by vintage hair and make-up artist Ruby Rose. Ruby is one of the UK's leading experts in vintage hair and make-up techniques, with over 15 years' experience in the health and beauty industry. Ruby always wanted a shop that sold all the things her heart desired, full of all the things she couldn't live without, and with this in mind her Emporium of gems was created. Offering everything from feathers to frills, the shop is a real treat and Ruby also offers lessons in vintage make-up application and hairstyles.

- T: 07951 926 555
- W: www.rubyemporium.com

Vintage Fashion at Battersea

Anita's Vintage Fashion Fairs organize six fairs a year (held bi-monthly at Battersea Arts Centre, Lavender Hill, London SW11 5NT), totally devoted to vintage fashion, textiles and accessories dating from the 1800s to the 1970s.

Fairs typically comprise 65 stands, rich in colours, textures and variety, bringing to life a treasure trove of unique items – everything from vintage buttons, braids and trimmings to eighteenth-century costumes and couture from the 1930s to the 1960s.

Whether you're a professional buyer or simply someone looking for a special one-off piece to express your fashion style, you will find clothing and displays crammed with rare, time-travelled treasures – vintage Biba,

Vivienne Westwood, Zandra Rhodes, YSL and Chanel, to name but a few.

- **Anita's Vintage Fashion Fairs, 16 Garden Road, Sundridge Park, Bromley, Kent BR1 3LX**
- **T: 020 8325 5789 or 020 8290 1888**
- **W: www.vintagefashionfairs.com**

Absolute Vintage

With one of the largest secondhand shoe collections in Britain, you will be spoilt for choice at this colourful treasure trove of a store, based in Spitalfields, London. If you don't live in London, don't despair; their range of vintage accessories and clothing is also available to buy online.

- **15 Hanbury Street, Spitalfields, London E1 6QR**
- **T: 020 7247 3883**
- **W: www.absolutevintage.co.uk**

Tin Tin Collectables

Tin Tin Collectables are specialists in vintage costume and accessories from 1900 to 1940. Their top-quality clothing is hand-selected for condition and style. Fashion designers, film and television costume designers, museums and individual collectors are all frequent shoppers at this Edwardian Aladdin's Cave. Everything from simple lace trims and ostrich plumes to silk lamé robes and beaded flapper dresses are generally available.

- **Available online and at Alfies Antiques Market, 13–25 Church Street, London NW8 8DT**
- **W: www.tintincollectables.net**

Pips Trip

Pips Trip is an online boutique offering great quality retro/vintage ceramics and glass from the 1950s, 1960s and 1970s. Treat yourself or a friend to some original design, but without having to traipse around cold antique markets.

- T: 08451 650274
- www.pips-trip.co.uk

Planet Vintage

Laura Gaither, the owner of Planet Vintage Girl (UK), has been collecting twentieth-century objects for over 16 years. For Laura, collecting is really a part of an environmental philosophy – it's a beneficial act of landfill redirection. Collecting these objects saves them from being thrown away and creates an opportunity for another generation to appreciate them.

The public can purchase directly online or from one of her showrooms, located at the Failsworth Antique Centre, Failsworth (Sundays and by appointment), and at Insitu Manchester in Hulme. Also, look for stock on eBay auctions, under the eBay seller name 'vintagegirlantiques'.

- Planet Vintage Girl at Insitu, 252 Chester Road, Hulme M15 4EX
- T: 07989406858
- W: www.planetvintagegirl.com

Retro Boutique

Retro Boutique is a Pandora's Box full of eccentric but precious things. 1950s prom dresses, 1930s music boxes and 1980s jewels line up to distract you. The store is made up of several concessions, offering everything from the pre-loved to vintage and retro finds for your wardrobe and home. It's a bit of a labyrinth to walk around, but this makes it all the more appealing to hunt through and source a truly individual creation.

- 8–10 Headingley Lane, Leeds LS6
- T: 0113 278 2653

Tara Starlet

You'll find 'vintage-inspired' clothes with a pin-up girl, rockabilly style. They'll transform you into a silver-screen starlet from the golden era of Hollywood flicks, designed in London especially to give you that original starlet look.

- T: Joanne Scott, 020 8986 2089
- W: www.tarastarlet.com

Strawberry and Cream

'A veritable retail wonderland, hosting a range of exclusive brands from *Bagpuss* retro to decadent *Dynasty* glamour via chic, understated noughties übercool.' Many of the brands are exclusive to this online store and others are seen for the first time ever in the UK, so you are sure to find something that no one else will have, if you enjoy looking individual or being the first to wear a debut designer.

- T: 0845 254 5409
- W: www.strawberryandcream.com

Weddings

Planning a wedding can be one of the most stressful periods of your life, but the big day itself should be one of the most enjoyable and unforgettable. Getting married is also a great excuse to play princess for the day. With all eyes on you, it's both important and pleasurable to look your best. Go all out on your special day and create your dream wedding with this array of essential elements. Now there's no need to turn into Bridezilla: I've done all the sourcing for you…

The ring

Your dream engagement ring: Wint and Kidd

The Wint and Kidd 'brivka moment' allows your partner to choose the perfect diamond, which is presented in a black laquer box, and then, post-proposal, you can return together for a consultation over a

glass of champagne and have the perfect ring designed for you using that diamond.

....

• W: www.wintandkidd.com

• •

Heaven on a finger: Van Cleef and Arpels

• •

Every single diamond at Van Cleef and Arpels is inspected at every stage of production by a quality controller – 'the expert among experts' – with the most stunning bridal collections to take you from romantic engagement to illustrious wedding day. Founded in 1906, Van Cleef and Arpels continue to impress in the right circles, having been featured in the fashion shows of

Viktor & Rolf and Karl Lagerfeld. I think that says it all.

....

• **9 New Bond Street, London W1S 3SW**
• **T: 020 7493 0400**
• **W: www.vancleef-arpels.com**

• •

Accessible diamonds: Seventy Seven

• •

Diamonds bought via Seventy Seven Diamonds are more affordable than most with no huge mark-up. Pieces take inspiration from modern, classic and vintage designs, placing the diamond at the heart of every piece of jewellery, and they also create bespoke jewellery. To ensure peace of mind, each diamond is certified and available at the best value on the market. This is because Seventy Seven Diamonds cut out any middle men, so significant savings can be made on each piece.

• W: www.77diamonds.com

The venue

Jewels, pampering, organization and venue – in one hit at The Berkeley!

If you simply want an amazing day, as little hassle as possible and an excuse to look and feel amazing – even in the run-up to the wedding day – then look to luxury hotel The Berkeley with their *Berkeley Brides* package, in partnership with the ultra-chic, award-wining jeweller Lara Bohinc. The bride is invited with her bridesmaids to sip champagne and nibble on couture wedding dress biscuits in Lara's Sloane Street shop for a private bridal jewellery consultation and a presentation of the jewellery collections so the bride can choose a piece of signature jewellery that will be lent to her for the big day. This service is exclusive to brides who have chosen to hold their celebration at The Berkeley. Lara Bohinc's designs have adorned icons such as Sarah Jessica Parker, Kate Moss and Elle Macpherson.

The Berkeley is a wonderful wedding venue, with its elegant ballroom and über-cool Blue Bar, or even the rooftop pool for a celebration with a difference! The roof slides back so you can top up your tan (we all

hope for the sun) and the room boasts panoramic views of Hyde Park.

The Berkeley's Cloud Nine offers brides and grooms a complimentary nine-week membership to its health club and spa leading up to the wedding festivities. Get in shape with a personal training session, or simply relax and rejuvenate during your preparations. The dedicated spa team is on hand to arrange all pre-wedding necessities including manicures and pedicures, a professional make-up artist and hair appointments in the comforts of a private bridal suite.

• W: www.The-Berkeley.co.uk

Stunning Tents

If you want an outdoor venue but don't trust the weather, hire a specialist tent or marquee. Stunning Tents offer creations that can seat any number of guests from 6 to 2,000. 'The Giant Hat' is most ideal for your big day, providing an inspiring alternative to a marquee. Pitched like a tipi or like a giant witch's hat, this will create an unforgettable spectacle and a wonderful ambience.

• W: www.stunningtents.co.uk

Marrying abroad

Arranging a wedding independently can be hassle enough, but when you choose to do it abroad, there can be other complications that leave you screaming for help. A majority of tour operators now have wedding departments and specialized wedding brochures with varying packages available, though you often have to buy everything with them, from hotel to flights, which could work out quite pricey in comparison to shopping around yourself and liaising directly. Plus they don't often handle your matrimonial requirements.

Your best bet is to contact wedding coordinators in the country you wish to marry in, as they will have all the contacts you desire with suppliers, venues, caterers and entertainers, and will even be able to help you with the legalities of your ceremony. Always get written quotes from planners before signing any contracts! I'd also advise contacting the British Embassy in the country you wish to marry in, and they will provide some general information on marriage in that country.

You should also contact the local authorities of that country for more comprehensive advice, including the required documentation. Some countries require the bride and groom to reside in the country they wish to marry in for as much as 30 days prior to the ceremony, and you will need to prove that you have done this. Consider visas, vaccinations and travel insurance too.

There's a whole host of legal titbits on the Foreign and Commonwealth Office website to help you.

• W: www.fco.gov.uk

It may sound daunting, but it need not be with the right help and many wedding coordinators are English-speaking (if not English expatriates), and they charge very reasonable fees for their service. To form your own shortlist, look at the *Weddings*

Abroad Guide, which lists a selection of wedding planners in a number of different countries that have been personally recommended by couples who have used them.

• W: www.weddings-abroad-guide.com

Wedding list

Alternative wedding list service: The Bottom Drawer

The Bottom Drawer is the UK's leading alternative wedding gift list service. With The Bottom Drawer couples can use their gift list to collect contributions from their guests towards something they *really* want – not just another toaster, or his'n'hers towels that don't coordinate with your bathroom! Besides, today most couples have lived together for a number of years before they marry and have had plenty of time to collect their pots and pans, so go for the alternative.

Examples include a dream honeymoon, garden makeover, new kitchen, or maybe an original work of art. This is a much better use of the wedding list. Whatever gift a couple decides they would like, The Bottom Drawer can help them source it and create a gift list for it. So if a couple wanted a dream honeymoon, it could be broken into gifts of cocktails on arrival, romantic dinners in resort, pamper sessions, part of the flight cost, etc. A very efficient, modern way of getting what you want and giving people the option of paying towards that!

- **T: 0845 459 1705 or 0121 661 4417**
- **W: www.thebottomdrawer.co.uk**

The flowers

Blooming Gorgeous

Blooming Gorgeous Flowers are exactly that. They can create your dream floral arrangement from bouquets to table centrepieces and glamorous buttonholes. You'll first have a free consultation with an experienced floral designer to discuss your wedding arrangements, the types of flowers available, design, colour, shape and size, who will need flowers, where your venue is – and of course the colour and material of your dress will be taken into account too.

- **W: www.bloominggorgeousflowers.co.uk**

David Austin Roses

David Austin's garden roses have quickly become some of the most highly desired flowers in the world. Why? English cut roses gradually develop from tight buds into large, perfectly formed blooms that are truly spectacular with an incomparable natural charm, and they smell heavenly!

David Austin's luxury hand-tied bouquets are available for courier delivery all year round to UK mainland

addresses, but their exclusivity means you'll have to place your order in good time.

- **W: www.davidaustinroses.com**

Carrie Yeo crystal bouquets

If you don't want fresh posies and wish to opt for something different, go for a gorgeous crystal design bouquet. Carrie Yeo offers three different crystal bouquets, with each bouquet handmade in the UK using Swarovski crystals, freshwater pearls, Swarovski pearls and glass beads, finished with individual accessories to suit a beach theme or destination wedding, a classic wedding or a wedding rich in colour. One thing's for sure: they won't wilt and they'll become a stunning keepsake for the future.

- **W: www.carrieyeo.com**

Invitations and planning

Your own wedding website: Wedding Path

Every modern girl, when planning a wedding, now has her very own wedding website! Instead of reams of invitation paperwork, simply enclose a website address instead.

Wedding Path is a fabulous company that allows brides-to-be to build their very own wedding website, free of charge. As well as keeping couples up to date with the latest wedding industry gossip, features and newsletters, there's an amazing forum where the girls talk about pretty much everything from diets to disasters! You will get some great advice from other brides, but it's such a great way of communicating details to your guests. You can choose your own pages, from hen do details and photos to your gift list and venue details. It thinks of everything for you and it really is easy to do.

It's an excellent and eco-friendly way of managing RSVPs and menu choices – plus, for a small fee, you can buy extra services including a seating plan that collects all the details of your accepted invitations so you can play around with the names and plan your tables.

• W: www.weddingpath.co.uk

Paperless Post

Another way of sending paperless invites is by using Paperless Post. This is excellent for any event in your life. All you need to do is sign up for free and then you choose your preferred card design to customize your invitations. You are given 25 stamps, and after virtually posting your invitations you can track and manage your event too. More stamps can be earned by recommending the site to your friends, or you can simply purchase them.

• W: www.paperlesspost.com

Stylish invitations

If you do wish to opt for paper invites, Emily&Jo is a young and dynamic company, making headlines in the wedding industry. All the top wedding magazines in the country are happily writing about this duo and their vibrant wedding cards.

Emily&Jo combine beautiful patterns with classic, timeless typography and design. The quality of the product is exemplary and sets the perfect tone for a special wedding day. Their fresh, dynamic, on-trend portfolio fills a niche in the wedding stationery market that many modern-day brides crave.

• 40 Mount Ash Road, London SE26 6LY
• T: 020 82446338
• W: www.emilyandjo.co.uk

The dress

Temperley London

Temperley London's boutique provides a private environment in which to view their bridal collection, presented separately in the truly romantic adjoining Bridal Boutique. Temperley has to be one of my favourite designers and their bridal collections entice me to want to marry a number of times, just to wear all of their gowns … well, almost! Both made-to-order and off-the-peg bridal selections are available – all beautiful. Enjoy trying on your selections with a glass of champagne and the assistance of the knowledgeable personal shoppers.

• 2–10 Colville Mews, Lonsdale Road, London W11 2DA
• T: 020 7229 7957 ext 102
• W: www.temperleylondon.com

W

Weddings

Phillipa Lepley

Phillipa Lepley bravely established her namesake bridal business in 1988, in the midst of recession, working from a small South Kensington atelier. Her first bridal shop opened on London's Fulham Road in 1990. Since then, the Phillipa Lepley bridal couture business is one of the most desirable names on a bride's wishlist, known for the flattering fit and designs that are simple yet full of impact. Lace is one of the predominant themes, along with Swarovski detailing or a full-blown rose on the back.

• **Shop: 48 Fulham Road, Chelsea, London SW3 6HH**
• **T: 020 7590 9771**

• **Studio: 494 Fulham Road, Fulham, London SW6 5NH**
• **T: 020 7386 0927**
• **W: www.phillipalepley.com**

Finishing touches

Little touches: Little Cupcake Company

Ideal for weddings, The Little Cupcake Company bake delectable cupcakes, topped with sugar icing and 'his and hers' crystallized rose and violet petals. These cupcakes can be packaged specially to suit the occasion in

ibboned boxes or presented on a tier – a great idea as favours for your guests or even an alternative wedding cake.

- T: 0845 296 9188
- W: www.thelittlecupcakecompany.co.uk

Smart drinks

If you want a team of bartenders who are articulate, smart, knowledgeable mixologists with performing flair, then Bamboo will give you a troupe of good-looking experts to add extra oomph to your celebrations.

- W: www.eventmixology.com

Emergency dance lessons

If you've run out of time concentrating on every other aspect, but still want to do a Fred-and-Ginger on the dance floor for your first dance, you can have a last-minute emergency dance lesson. 'The Gold' offers you five 45-minute lessons individually tailored to you, and 'The Economy' offers three lessons.

- W: www.dancematrix.com/firstdance

Wedding favours that tell your fortune

Wedding Fortune Cookies are unique wedding favours. If you are looking for something which says a special thank you to your guests and adds style to your table decorations, then take a look at this range of unusual wedding favours. You can choose wedding fortune cookies personalized with your own words inside, or you can choose

cookies with a variety of themes – wedding day quotations, funny, romantic, traditional fortunes and children's jokes – all available in a wide choice of different coloured wrappers.

- W: www.weddingfortunecookies.co.uk

Top Table Hire

If you are planning a wedding in an empty venue or alfresco and wish to decorate it completely to your style, Top Table Hire gives you that option: you can choose from a range of linen, china, cutlery and even furniture for your wedding or private event. There are plenty of funky designs that allow you to put an original stamp on your big day.

- W: www.toptablehire.com

Imaginative menus from Blue Strawberry

The Blue Strawberry event team organize traditional and bespoke weddings for their clients all year round all over the UK. For brides who prefer to have a reception that encourages guests to mix and chat more intimately, they have a range of fine and unusual menus, from substantial canapés to bowl food and stalls.

With innovative food designs and party planning expertise, they take care of everything from venue to drinks list – taking a weight off your shoulders and keeping up with the times.

- OPB House, 26–28 Sidney Road, London SW9 0TS
- T: 020 7733 3151
- W: www.bluestrawberry.co.uk

The Modern Girl's Guide to Fabulousness

Weddings
W

233

The Utterly Sexy Café

The Utterly Sexy Café can offer a selection of menus for lunch, tea or dinner, including elegant canapés, mains and puddings, brought to your table by their courteous staff wearing 1950s aprons or served from a fabulously adorned and decorated buffet table. They can offer anything and everything from barbeques and outside cooking to a rather special afternoon tea, which can be the substantial 'Quintessential Teatime' menu, complementing their vintage china. You can also hire the vintage china without the catering or decorating service.

- T: 01747 870 812
- W: www.utterlysexycafe.co.uk

Release beautiful live butterflies at your wedding: Butterfly Celebration

Your wedding day should be full of never-to-be-forgotten moments, and a perfect way to create one is by releasing beautiful live Painted Lady butterflies outside to nature. For more than 40 years, Insect Lore has been raising butterflies for release to nature in celebration of life's truly remarkable moments. As the butterflies take flight, the sky above will fill with colour and motion, creating a magical event that you and your guests will remember for ever.

- T: Cindy Ryan, 0778 396 4136
- E: weddingbutterflies@gmail.com
- W: www.butterflycelebration.com

Accessories

Designer headpieces: Louis Mariette

Veils are a little old hat these days (excuse the pun), so have your own headpiece designed by Louis Mariette. A consultation with Louis himself, complete with a cocktail at his luxury Sloane Square atelier, will start off your celebrations when you will establish your needs as a bride and coordinate the bridesmaids with your look. Louis prides himself on his discerning eye for detail when considering every aspect of a bride's image, from headpiece down to shoes. He can also provide a team of hair, make-up and image stylists to suit your every need.

....

• **For a personal appointment call**
020 7730 3050
• **W: www.louismariette.co.uk/bridal.html**

• •

Wedding cushions: Oliver Laudus

• •

Olivier Laudus is an online bridal boutique for a range of accessories including tiaras, bridal jewellery, garters, guestbooks, bridal handbags and even sparkling Swarovski cake toppers. Faithful to the original concept of stylish design and beautiful beading, Olivier's personalized wedding cushions, which are presented in white boxes packed with luxury tissue paper, are ones to watch.

....

• **T: 020 8374 1239**
• **W: www.olivierlaudus.co.uk**

Boothnation, in a nutshell, is a photo booth, but not your average unflattering passport photo machine. Although designed to look and work in a reassuringly familiar way, the booths are in fact very sophisticated photographic studios kitted out with state-of-the-art lighting and high-end digital cameras.

The photo booths can be personalized to reflect the unique nature of your event. Graphics, backgrounds, even lighting can be tailor-made to suit your needs and it will present a relaxed and entertaining way to get people together and have fun. Whether capturing a whole bunch of people crammed in at once, the bride and her maids together, or that special moment with just you and your new hubbie, a booth will give you images no other wedding photography options could capture.

Your images are posted on Boothnation's website (with the option of a password-secure gallery), where they can be viewed and purchased by you and your guests, from all over the world.

....

• **Boothnation, 7 Ezra Street, London E2 7RH**
• **T: 020 7613 1560**
• **W: www.boothnation.com**

Photography

• •

Capture those moments: Boothnation

• •

Not exactly your usual photographer, but then if I just talked about ordinary stuff, it would bore you! Boothnation will capture your memories in a whole new way, created by the award-winning portrait photographer Seamus Ryan.

The cake

• •

Peggy Porschen

• •

When Elton John, Gwyneth Paltrow or Madonna throw parties, they order their patisserie from Peggy Porschen, 'The Queen of Cakes'. Her creations are almost too gorgeous to be cut, decorated with her now-famous handcrafted marzipan roses sprinkled with sparkling crystal powder.

Following an apprenticeship at Le Cordon Bleu London, a post as head of the patisserie in the famed Lanesborough Hotel and then as a successful caterer at Rhubarb Food Design and for the Konditor & Cook patisserie chain, Peggy Porschen finally went independent due to popular demand and the patissier's cake studio is now located in the London district of Battersea and is among the top addresses for people needing to order top-flight patisserie for festivities.

Peggy's legendary cakes have already thrilled Stella McCartney's wedding party, and it is the technique and attention to detail that particularly stuns. For instance, couples getting married are asked to bring along a piece of lace from the bride's dress, or an invitation card. When designing the cake, the team can then copy a pattern to the last detail. If you want reputable work of art to remember, this is your gal.

• W: www.peggyporschen.com/
Wedding.htm

Still need inspiration?

Whether you are looking to plan the traditional wedding of your dreams, or something that breaks away from the norm, **The National Wedding Show** is a must. It is the ultimate one-stop shopping experience for everything to do with the big day, with over 300 exhibitors: from over the moon to the honeymoon, from the venue to the menu, everything for weddings is there. The Designer and Boutique Areas house the UK's largest collection of wedding dresses under one roof – and why not finish the day with a chilled glass of champagne from the Celebrations Bar?

• **The National Wedding Show takes place four times a year nationwide. For further information and ticket sales, visit www. nationalweddingshow.co.uk**

OK, so I cheated a little in this section, but there are so few fabulous-worthy experiences starting with the letter X! You'll love this section of 'xtras' nevertheless, as it unveils a crowd of special things, from how to part-own a private jet to supporting key charities...

Xtra-fabulous...

What's Up My Street?

UpMyStreet is your essential guide to life in your area (or other areas, for that matter), whether you are looking for local news, checking out a town you are considering moving to, or just planning a night out! You can plan a house move, cut household bills, or just get more from your home and local area. Search for information on schools, policing and crime, leisure and fun, council tax, keeping fit, and much more. The 'Find My Nearest' search facility offers a virtual and speedy 'yellow pages' service, so you'll never be stuck while trying to source your local supplier/bar/yoga centre.

W: www.upmystreet.com

The chauffeur service that gets you and your car home safely: DriveMyCarHome

DriveMyCarHome.co.uk is a chauffeur service in Leicester where a fully insured chauffeur arrives on a unique foldable moped to meet you and drive you and your car home safely.

The moped is folded into a protective bag and placed in your car boot. Once home, the moped is unfolded and the chauffeur drives away, leaving your car in place and your mind at rest. This is a fantastic service if you want to enjoy having a drink or two without worrying about transport. Rates can often work out cheaper than a black cab and you don't have to worry about picking up your car the next day from wherever you left it. *Drink-driving is the ultimate no-no.* Don't risk it: use a service like this instead.

• W: www.drivemycarhome.co.uk

For the Dublin area, try the **Carhome** website.

• W: www.carhome.ie

From their Reading base, **Scooter Man** taxi-drive you and your car home throughout Berkshire, Surrey, Hampshire and Oxfordshire, as well as journeys into and out of London.

• W: www.scooterman.co.uk

The latest luxury trend: Fractional Life

If you want it all and want it now, but can't quite afford it, then fractional ownership and asset sharing gives you an ideal way to get the most out of your investment by purchasing only the shares or time you require from an asset. All other aspects are split – both the benefits and the costs – among a limited number of shareholders or members. Fractional ownership means you physically own a percentage of the asset until you decide to sell.

Quality time is becoming increasingly short in people's daily lives and a lot of us don't want the hassles of whole ownership of many luxuries these days. The Fractional Life website guides you through the whole process and categorizes everything based on your potential interests – including supercars, jets, yachts, property, residence clubs, condo-homes, vineyards, racehorses and even handbags!

• W: www.fractionallife.com

Whatruwearing? Never again be caught at an event wearing the same dress as someone else!

Whatruwearin? is a concept created to eradicate the very embarrassing situation of arriving at an event only to discover that another girl is wearing the same dress as you! It's free to register your event – you'll just need your email address, then you can inform your guests, who can simply log into your exclusive event area and register what they are wearing.

Users can search through registered outfits prior to shopping. They can also look at the directory to find ideas and suppliers. If you don't want to be caught wearing the same as someone else, but nor do you want to let everyone know what you are wearing, then you can keep that element of surprise and remain anonymous.

• **W: www.whatruwearing.co.uk**

Stylebible

Stylebible is the ultimate directory of fashion, beauty, boutique hotels, hip clubs and bars and restaurants. Becoming a member will give you the most up-to-date insider information on where to eat, sleep, drink, shop and be pampered – as well as access to beauty and fashion boutiques. Members also receive a variety of special perks, including hotel room upgrades, VIP entry to many private members' clubs, discounts on spa treatments and invites to exclusive events. From Amsterdam to New York, Stylebible has a reliable network of spies finding the hippest places to be, fashions to buy, places to eat and treatments to experience.

• **W: www.stylebible.com**

How to…

If you're unsure of how to tie a top knot, wear this season's fashion trends, hang a picture or even use a certain vibrator (!), there are sensible, professional and informative demonstrations online. The two best sites I have found are *www.wonderhowto.com* and *www.videojug.com* with thousands

of how-to videos for every area of your life, from dating to DIY.

• **W: www.wonderhowto.com**
• **W: www.videojug.com**

Oblong.org

Oblong.org makes use of the forgotten photo, making art out of the unruffled photograph. The quest is to Raise Photos™ by blowing images up to the size necessary to appreciate as outré art. Each photo is printed to a limited press of cotton canvas prints and is sold in store, online and in markets across the UK to raise money for the charity chosen by the donor of the photographs.

• **W: www.oblong.org and www.raisephotos.org**

Scooter Computer

Scooter Computer is a London-based at-home IT service. Technicians race around on their scooters to fix computers (both PCs and Macs) all over London, as well as dealing with printer problems, internet, email, viruses, etc. There's even a free downloadable guide on how to create your own home office space, with advice on finding the right broadband provider for you and backing up your work.

• **T: 020 7384 5949**
• **W: www.scootercomputer.co.uk**

X

Xtras

Sanitary wear: Moxie

I don't often get excited by sanitary wear, but Moxie has introduced a fashionable, vintage-style range of feminine hygiene products from Australia that are sure to make your periods a little prettier! Moxie, set up by Mia Klitsas, Jeff Gore and Natalie Koenen was the first line of sanitary products to offer 100% recyclable, crush-proof tins of tampons, pantyliners and pads.

The Daytime Pads and Sleepovers overnight pads deliver comfort, extra absorption and breathability, while the Scanty Panty Liners are perfect for everyday use, designed to keep you feeling fresh and confident throughout the day. The tampons are available in two different sizes, Regular and Super.

The products all come in gorgeous little tins inspired by the boudoir style of the 1930s, making them something you'd be proud to have on display on your bathroom shelf. Although Moxie doesn't promise to get rid of your stomach cramps or satisfy your chocolate cravings, they do make an otherwise glum experience a little more feminine and a lot more glam.

• W: www.superdrug.com (N)

Anything Left-Handed

Anything Left-Handed has been operating since 1968. Their website offers a full range of products and a lot of new ones are available online for worldwide delivery. As a lefty myself, the scissors are a godsend, but I'm hiding this discovery from my other half so he won't buy me a left-handed iron (my excuse is working so far!)

• T: 020 8770 3722
• W: www.anythingleft-handed.co.uk

There's nothing wrong with a few laughter lines. I try to avoid the unfriendly 'w' word (wrinkles ... shhh ...) and refer to them as 'character lines' instead. A few lines and blemishes are expected and an overly smooth, expressionless face is unnatural. However, for those fine lines that aren't so likeable, or to avoid them in the first place, there are some genius solutions to smoother, more radiant skin...

How to look fabulous, whatever your age!

••••••••••••••••••••••••••••••••••••

Lee Pycroft, internationally renowned make-up artist

••••••••••••••••••••••••••••••••••••

Lee's passion for make-up started in her late teens, when she became fascinated by the way in which colours and textures could change not only a woman's face but also, to a degree, her personality – how she would often start to exude more confidence and allure once her favourite make-up look had been completed. As she moved further into the world of sparkle and powder, she had the privilege of working on numerous magazines from weeklies to glossy monthlies, creating looks from high-fashion couture to accessible and wearable, but never, ever, mundane or routine.

The film world beckoned. Lee was invited to create looks for Hollywood starlets and genuine A-list stars. Lee states, 'From celluloid royalty to rock stars; from starlets to humble wannabes; the sheer transforming power of make-up is thrillingly undeniable.'

To date, clients have included Diane Krugar, Jessica Biel, Naomi Watts, Carla Gugino, Cate Blanchett, Gwyneth Paltrow, Sienna Miller, Julie Christie, Andie Macdowell, Elle Macpherson, Lauren Bacall, Leona Lewis, Reese Witherspoon, Kristin Davis, Kate Bosworth, Marcia Cross, Natascha McElhone and Gillian Anderson.

I asked Lee Pycroft to share her pearls of wisdom with us in regard to 'youthful looks' and looking your best across all ages, from your 20s to your 60s...

She said, 'The subject of ageing is an emotive one. We live in a culture that deifies youth and supports every anti-ageing potion that comes on the market claiming to help us repel the ravages of time from showing on our faces. The debate about what is "right" as to ageing as nature intended or using the advances in cosmetics and injectibles to halt the appearance of wrinkles is purely a personal one. It's down to the choice of the individual. The only important factor is what you decide is right for you. And whatever your decision, make-up can be your bag of 'feel-good tools' that can brighten smooth skin, help erase what you don't like and define what you do. You are the artist and the canvas is primed and waiting...'

20s

Skin

This is the time when prevention is the key to how the skin looks in the future. Cleansing, even if the night has got the better of you and jumping straight into bed seems like a great idea, is essential. Always devote a few minutes to removing your make-up along with debris and dead skin cells! Exfoliating the skin will increase cell turnover and create a more refined appearance. Wearing a sunscreen and using make-up that combines skincare ingredients and make-up will all contribute to the skin looking great as it ages. An SPF with UVA and UVB protection should be applied 30 minutes before going outside. If there is limited sun exposure, then a moisturizer with an SPF is a good option for gaining a touch of cover and protection.

It's a mystery to me when I see girls in their late teens to early 20s wearing foundation that is more noticeable than the quality of the skin. Make-up at this age isn't going to get much easier, so wearing a tinted moisturizer or blending a foundation with a brush so it's seamless will allow the skin to show through and result in a more appealing look. Anything goes, depending on the personality and lifestyle of the person wearing it. But if experimenting is your thing, then now is the time to do it … embellishing the skin's natural tones or adding a tawny glow will give a natural wash of colour. The important issue is texture. If the skin is oily, a powder will hold better than a cream. The same goes in a humid climate.

Eyes

Always invest in an eye cream that is suitable for your skin, as fine lines can be kept at bay and it will act as a great base for concealer. Try anything from bold liners in shades of black to jewel tones, shimmer shadows and anything experimental!

I love bushy but groomed brows. Don't be tempted to overpluck at this age as you will be entering a world of regret later on! Tweeze the smallest amount of hair, enough to shape the brow, and always invest in good tweezers. A gel through the brow will keep them groomed and polished-looking. Try Tweezerman tweezers: they make tools of outstanding quality and performance and give what is essentially a functional tool a groovy slick edge by creating fun, colourful tweezers.

Lips

Think fun and groovy! Vibrant tones in fuchsia, tangerine and cherry will give a flirtatious, playful look and are a great way of experimenting with colour. If full-on glossy coloured lips appeal, then now is the time to do it. If you're going for a loud mouth, it's advisable to keep the rest of the face

cleaner-looking so the lips are the focal point.

30s

Skin

If shadows and fines lines are creeping in now, a light-reflecting concealer mixed with an opaque one where you need it will help erase those first signs of ageing!

It's essential to moisturize the skin and a cream with light-reflecting particles can give an instant radiance to the skin. As we age, women have often said they feel that make-up applied to the skin can exaggerate lines. This is where a more specific application will help, rather than an application of foundation all over the face, and it can be a case of just finding the right product to suit your skin.

A wash of colour on the cheeks can be one of the greatest brighteners available! Pinky tones are fresh and create a natural flush of colour for the cheeks.

Eyes

Keep things simple and slick, like a glossy-looking black liner along the top lash line with precision-painted lashes. Liner can be best applied in several short strokes and an angled brush will help create the perfect line. Always use a gel liner as this avoids the problem with smudging that some liquids have. Make sure any redness on the lids is concealed first, so the whole effect is clean-looking. Painting the lashes to perfection can often involve using two mascaras, one for lengthening and one for volume. I love the plastic wands

Y

Youthful Looks

that separate and define, keeping the volume at the roots and the tips light and fluttering. Mac make a fab mascara brush that's great for making sure every tip of every lash is painted.

Lips

If strong lips are your thing, then changing to a more velvety texture will look more polished and refined than a loud gloss! If the lips need building up, apply the liner after the colour and sketch around the areas that need embellishment. Applying liner after lip colour will allow you to see what areas need adjustment. Consider applying the lipstick in a patting motion straight from the bullet or with the ring finger and press the colour into the lips. This gives a less painted and more natural line to the lips.

40s

Skin

The skin at this stage can be showing general signs of ageing, so using primers and products that help refine fine lines will help make-up stay on longer and give a flawless finish. Rather than wearing less make-up as the general consensus dictates, a more artful approach is the way forward and this could involve more make-up just applied in the right places. Broken veins, uneven skin tone and shadows can all be covered easily with the correct brushes and technique, so investing in a brush set is a good idea.

Cream blush will come into its own if the natural texture of the skin appears flatter. The essential rule is always to make sure the skin is

flawless underneath the blush that is applied, as any uneven skin tone will make the blush look murky. A touch of foundation on the cheeks before will erase redness and allow the blush to show its true colour.

Eyes

Although matt textures have a more sophisticated feel, a shadow with a satin finish is great for creating a translucent finish. A wash of satin/shimmer on the lids can create an eye-opening effect, as shine will brighten and enhance the eyes. The important things to remember is that as the face ages the radiance of the skin diminishes, but make-up can be a great tool for recreating that lost lustre, be it on the skin, eyes or lips.

Lips

Bold colours will look best if they have a more translucent finish, rather like a stain. This can be achieved by mixing a lip colour with a lip balm, which is a great way of using a favourite lip colour in a more natural way, or try one of the many lip stains on the market. Generally speaking, unless the lips are a great shape and naturally full, a more natural tone will be flattering.

50s

Skin

Now the skin will benefit most from a light reflecting foundation applied only where it is needed. This will allow the skin's natural texture to shine through, but will be enough to cover any areas of concern. The light-reflecting particles in the foundation will illuminate and refine the appearance of the skin.

Eyes

As the eyes age, it is important to pay attention to the brow area as an elevated brow can help open up the eye area. Try sketching brows in to lengthen and define them. Follow the outside line of the brow first and only fill in the middle of the brow when an accurate line has been established. If the brow hair is long or unruly, then brushing the hair in an upward direction and trimming the ends will give a more manicured look. A brow gel is essential in finishing the look.

Lips

If lip lines are becoming an issue, then lip primers and lipsticks that have staying power will help keep lip colour in place. Using a sheer textured lip pencil will give good definition to the lips and because the texture is smooth and glides on easily it can be used all over the lips too. Keep colours soft and in the neutral pink colour range, as those tones will have a soft, brightening effect on the face.

· ·

60s
· ·

Skin

Foundation would be the same as in the 50s, with the possibility of a touch more opaque concealer to cover any pigmentation. Creamy blushers are a must and luminizing powders will help keep any shine on the skin down without creating a powdery finish.

Eyes

Lashes often thin with age, so lining the lashes will give the perfect backdrop to them, making them appear thicker once the mascara is on. It will also define the eyes without looking as if there is much make-up on. Use a pencil, after any eye shadow is applied, and press it into the lashes in small stroking movements. Just line from where the lashes begin and end. If using eye shadow, stick to neutral tones that flatter the skin tone. When using mascara, apply the bulk of the product to the roots of the lashes. This can be done by using the tip of the wand to apply the mascara. Make sure the outer lashes are brushed in an upward direction, as this will give an elevation to the eyes. When eyelashes look groomed and styled, they give a heavenly eye-opening effect that looks both youthful and fresh.

Lips

Keep lips buffed and nourished-looking. A lip exfoliation can help to scuff off old skin, but it is best to prevent this from happening in the first place by using lip treatments. If hair is grey, then keep colours soft and diffused-looking: muted pinks and rosy shades will give the most flattering look to the lips, teeth and skin tone.

· ·

Products to try, as recommended by Lee Pycroft
· ·

- Chanel Pro Lumiere Foundation for a flawless finish that lasts.

- Rimmel London Renew and Lift Foundation for a foundation

> **Fab Tip**
>
> Don't forget to wash your make-up brushes! Many people forget or can't be bothered, but make-up particles and dirt will collect over time and what you're effectively doing is smearing them on your face – ugh! Keep them clean by washing carefully in a gentle shampoo, like Johnson's Baby Shampoo, and leave to dry naturally overnight.

that combines skincare and SPF ingredients; great for those on a budget.

- Clinique Air Brush Concealer, fantastic for under the eyes.

- Bobbi Brown Eye Brightener, a unique product that promises to lift and brighten dark areas of the face.

- Laura Mercier Illuminating Tinted Moisturizer, a must for a skin that needs instant lustre.

- Laura Mercier Secter Camouflage. This cult product is perfect for covering blemishes and can be used on the inner corners of the eyes over the top of a light-reflecting concealer.

- Sisley Nourishing Lip Balm will caress your lips into tip-top condition.

- Guerlain Luminizing Powder is perfect for reducing shine but keeping the skin looking moist.

- Guerlain Noir 2 Noir Mascara is a double-ended mascara that offers two different-sized wands for precision lashes.

- Rimmel London Sexy Curves – a great wand for grooming lashes and giving a light application of mascara.

- Mac Cream Blushers are the creamiest, lushest blushers around in an array of delectable shades.

- Mac Lip Pencils in Soar and Desire will build the lips of fair to medium skin tones and create an enviable pout.

- **All products available from leading chemists and department stores, subject to availability.**
- **T: Lee Pycroft 020 7896 3150**
- **W: www.My-Management.co.uk**

Plump up the volume: PureLogicol

PureLogicol Age-Defying Collagen Supplements boost the level of collagen in your skin, improving skin elasticity, reducing fine lines and wrinkles, promoting healthier joints and strengthening hair and nails. Madonna's even a fan of this product! After trying a series, my nails are longer and less brittle and the fine lines around my eyes are softer. You must try the lip plumper too. The breakthrough MVS LIPS™ nano-technology combines phospholipids, liquorice root and soybean extract which boost collagen, while the HA micro spheres, plant collagen and vitamin E hydrate, soothe and nourish. Your lips will visibly swell, in the most attractive manner, for a more youthful and kissable experience. The results are so impressive that trying this on before a crowd has become a bit of a party trick of mine, and now several friends and my dear mother are hooked!

What are you waiting for?

• W: www.purelogicol.com

Holistic Silk 'Anti-ageing' Silk Pillow Case

This fabulous silk pillowcase with a removable pure lavender insert is actually an excellent beauty product! The 'Anti–Ageing' pillowslip feels wonderful next to your skin, and unlike cotton, which is an absorbent fibre, silk does not absorb moisture or beauty creams from your face and hair while you sleep. This satin silk may also help prevent facial lines, wrinkles and 'bed head', as the super-smooth silk fibre glides rather than snags over your body, thus helping to prevent early morning skin creasing and long-term damage.

• W: www.holisiticsilk.co.uk

Grow young gracefully: STOP™

STOP™ is a sleek hand-held device using TriPollar™ radio frequency technology that stimulates dermal activity to tighten collagen fibres and increase new collagen production, reducing the appearance of fine lines and wrinkles. Clinical trials report an average reduction of 35% after six weeks and instant results of plumper and more radiant skin.

• Harvey Nichols (N)

Elemis Pro-Collagen Marine Cream

Elemis's no. 1-selling anti-ageing moisturizer, this lightweight cream has been clinically proven to reduce the appearance of wrinkles by up to 78% and the depth of wrinkles by up to 45%. It contains the marine algae Padina Pavonica which has the ability to mimic the skin's function for fast cell-renewal and encouraging production of collagen.

• Stockists: 01278 727830
• W: www.timetospa.co.uk

Heaven's Bee Venom Mask

Heaven's Bee Venom Mask is a kind of 'nature's Botox' which instantly lifts, firms and tightens the skin. Shea Butter, Rose and Lavender essential oils leave your skin feeling luxuriously soft and it smells delicious, but the wonder ingredients are Manuka honey, renowned for its soothing and healing properties, and the magic Bee Venom ingredient that works to control the facial muscles for immediate lifting, tightening and firming.

• T: 01952 461888
• W: www.heavenskincare.com (N)

Dr Bragi Age Management Marine Enzyme

Dr Bragi's Age Management Marine Enzyme is the signature product in a range developed to combat the signs of ageing. This is an oil-free but intensive moisturizer which stimulates circulation and cell renewal and even helps to fade wrinkles.

The unique anti-inflammatory formulation of Penzyme helps skin repair itself by encouraging the skin's defence and regeneration mechanisms, making it suitable for all skin types. Even the most sensitive skin, whether burnt, sun-damaged or menopausal, can benefit from the marine enzymes. It is even suitable for skin conditions like impetigo and is so pure that breastfeeding mothers can use it without any harm to their babies. Though pricey, it is a luxurious, fast-working and natural remedy.

• **W: www.victoriahealth.com and www.cultbeauty.co.uk**
• **Also available from the Bliss Spa, London**

Anne Sémonin

Famously dubbed 'the little pot of gold', Precious Serum from Anne Sémonin is a powerful night repair treatment that rejuvenates, regenerates and refreshes skin while you sleep.

A blend of essential oils including wheatgerm oil and St John's Wort flower oil combine to nourish skin and stimulate cellular activity in the epidermis, magically targeting hormonal imbalances, while also hydrating, softening and clarifying tired skin. If you're not a morning person, let this serum do all the hard work as you snooze, so all you have to do is wake to an improved complexion, grab your latte and go.

• **Available from all Anne Sémonin spas and beauty outlets, via mail order and online**
• **T: +33 0 1 47 05 09 50**
• **W: www.annesemonin.com**

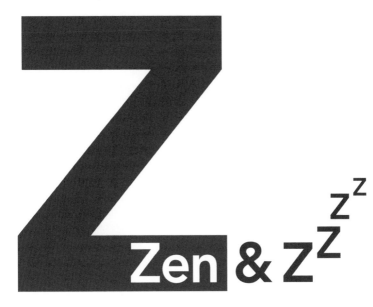

After all this fabulousness, catching a few Zs is essential. Getting enough beauty sleep is vital if you are to perform efficiently, revive your busy mind and reclaim your gorgeous looks. Here are some little blessings to help us switch off and drift into the Land of Nod...

Sleep well!

Omm...: FISU Meditation

Women in our modern times have to multitask, balancing jobs with children and running a home. For most, this can be demanding, tiring and stressful – we constantly feel under pressure and are always playing catch-up!

FISU Meditation is ideal to soothe away the stresses and strains of everyday life. When we are under stress, we lose objectivity so that the pressure we are under and the strains we have often seem heavier and more difficult than they actually are, making us feel that 'there aren't enough hours in the day'. After just a week of meditation, the objectivity and calmness experienced by the mind and central nervous system really

begin to show. Chant it out and gain perspective!

- **HQ, 58 Marlborough Road, London E4 9AL (27 UK centres)**
- **W: www.fisu.org**

Sleep tight: E Rejuvenation

E Rejuvenation could be your new refuge. Their forte is helping you to relax. If you have a stressful job and need to stay on top, tend to suffer from illnesses frequently, are often emotional, or just need a good night's sleep, you must visit.

Hopefully you don't suffer from all of the above, but if learning to relax and finding more energy sounds appealing, book a consultation to discuss your particular requirements. This may include a diagnosis with a Chinese doctor who can give you clear health-orientated goals or treatments with an acupuncturist or other specialist spa staff. An individualized wellness programme will then be designed specifically to help you

improve your quality of life.

They provide long-term solutions, so don't be looking for a quick-fix thrill. Instead address it as a lifestyle change in the right direction with a course of recommended treatments and tailored sessions. Saying that, results are impressively rapid. The Sleep Deprivation course includes five 60-minute sessions taken in one week, designed to rediscover deep, refreshing and satisfying sleep. Snore!

- **E Rejuvenation Centre, 132 Commercial Street, London E1 6NG**
- **W: www.erejuvenation.co.uk**

The Contour Memory Foam Leg Pillow

The Contour Memory Foam Leg Pillow aligns hips, legs and spine for all-night support and comfort, and relieves low back pain at night. The patented shape is made of solid memory foam that moulds to fit the exact shape of your legs, restoring lower body alignment. This small pillow will make a big difference in your lower back, hips and knees. Ideal for pregnancy too, if you cannot get comfortable.

• W: www.postapresent.co.uk

The best bed ... ever: Stearns & Foster

A Stearns & Foster bed is unlike any other bed – really!

They searched every corner of the globe for fine fabrics that would bring soothing softness and beauty to their beds. Natural fabrics such as elegant silk, rich cashmere or sumptuous suri alpaca are woven into Stearns & Foster® mattress layers, making for a luxurious, more breathable sleep surface.

Stearns & Foster are the iconic beds in the US, with the company originating back in 1846. They are reputed to be in all the best bedrooms from the White House to the Hamptons, from Texas to Hollywood, and now, at last, they have come to the UK – the first country outside America to be able to experience their deliciousness.

The voluptuous layers cushion the body, optimizing weight dispersal and relieving pressure points, while the technologically superior, individually wound posture coils provide essential push-back support for perfect spinal alignment. The additional patented Shock Absorber foundation spring system and Unirail protection system all combine together to provide unparalleled support and durability.

In a nutshell, it's simply one of the most comfortable beds you could ever sleep on.

• W: www.stearnsandfoster.com

Down time chic: Pyjama Room

If you often laze around in your greying joggers and oversized fleece, you've let yourself go! Harsh words, but lazing around does not give you a licence to dowdiness, so get thee to Pyjama Room, who believe that women should feel both elegant and effortlessly stylish during down time. The mix-and-match pieces, using luxury modal jersey (which feels like silk), will take you elegantly from after-work down time to sleep, off-duty days, casual entertaining at home, country weekends, lounging around villas and hotels and après ski. Everything is cut with the utmost attention to detail, so that each style is incredibly flattering. No excuses now!

• Pyjama Room, 21 Connaught Street, London W2 2AY
• T: 08456 800975
• W: www.pyjamaroom.com

Cosy Company

We spend a third of our lives asleep, so ensure your bed is the haven it needs to be with the finest-quality bedding and bed linen. The Cosy Company is a family-run British company that sells an exquisite collection of silk and cotton products. The beautiful hand-finished and luxuriously soft Italian bed linen is made from 300 thread count Egyptian cotton satin, and is currently available in three styles: Lily, Anna and Emma.

• The Cosy Company Ltd, 71 Broadwick Street, London W1F 9QY
• T: 0870 803 0190
• W: www.thecosycompany.com

Fab Tip

A slight drop in body temperature normally ensures a night's sleep, so by artificially creating a temperature drop, your body should fall into a lull more easily. Take a warm bath around two hours before you climb into bed to induce a temperature change and therefore encourage sleep. If you pop a few droplets of lavender aromatherapy oil into your bath too, the relaxation benefits will help you to wind down. Milk has sleep-enhancing properties, so enjoying a bedtime milky drink will also help you to drift off.

Patch-it!

These plaster-style patches are placed on the soles of the feet overnight, giving you the benefits of a mini spa in a patch – improving circulation using the principles of reflexology to help detoxify the body and help get rid of impurities. Amazing, really! An independent study found that Patch-it! improves the quality of sleep by 40%, including the time taken to get to sleep and the amount of hours spent asleep. I just love modern-day beauty remedies, and with this you don't have to move a muscle: just sleep and reap all the benefits.

• W: www.patch-it.info

Toxic Twins

The Toxic Twins, a.k.a Sinead and Lorna, are friends who developed a range of 'make-me-feel-good' or 'make-me-look-fab' fixes. Our body sometimes needs help in eliminating toxins circulating in the bloodstream, and The Toxic Twins' Dream On Sleep On It Detox Patches offer a solution with either a five-night or a one-night programme. Termed 'sap sheets', these patches are applied to the soles of both feet at night, helping to excrete excess toxins from the body, kick-start your metabolism and make you feel your usual fabulous self after a few days.

If you have been burning the candle at both ends, overindulging or experiencing restless sleep, then zap out the nasty toxins that make you feel less than wonderful with these little wonders.

• The Toxic Twins Ltd, 55 Ranelagh Village, Ranelagh, Dublin 6, Ireland
• T: 353 01 496 9711
• W: www.thetoxictwins.com (N)

Sound Asleep Pillow

This pillow has a speaker built inside it so you can listen to your chosen sounds to help you relax without disturbing your partner (so long as they're not a light sleeper), and the soft hollowfibre filling means you cannot feel the speaker inside. You can listen to audiobooks, or relaxation or self-help tracks, as you drift off, or even learn a foreign language as you rest. It requires a music source, such as your MP3 player or radio, as long as it has a 3.5 mm stereo plug to connect the pillow to. The pillow will not emit any sound until it is connected to your device. I prefer to listen to my chill-out albums, which helps me relax and gently doze off.

• **W: www.soundasleeppillow.co.uk**

PocketNap

A PocketNap is a downloadable audio relaxation MP3 of less than 20 minutes – with different sounds to suit your mood. When you take time out, even just for a short while, and give your mind and body a complete rest, your system naturally re-energizes and you feel much better. The idea is to close your eyes and experience the audio, which you can do sitting or lying down, and it works by using gentle imagery and specific language patterns to guide you into your own unique state of relaxation and renewal. They're specially designed to be short enough to fit into the busiest of schedules and skimpiest of lunch breaks. You can PocketNap to get going first thing in

the morning, to avoid brain drain, or to wind down at the end of a busy day.

PocketNaps are easily downloadable from the PocketShop and you can then transfer them to your choice of MP3 player, MP3 phone, burn to CD or listen straight from your Mac or PC.

• **W: www.PocketNap.com**

Chillow®

Sweltering summers or hormonal changes can keep a girl from her beauty sleep. The Chillow is a thin cushioned pad that works in harmony with the body's natural rhythms by taking heat away from the body and keeping you cool throughout the night, helping you to sleep naturally. It uses Soothsoft® technology with water to absorb and dissipate heat back into the air, producing a natural, cooling effect. You just add water once and then it is activated for as long as you need it, needing no pre-cooling or refrigeration – and it returns to room temperature during the day. I use mine to soothe and relieve headaches or throbbing ankles after too much wobbling on my stilettos!

• **T: 08700 117174**
• **W: www.chillow.co.uk**

N

Zen & Zzzzz

Bye for now Girls!!!

Bethanie xxx